UP WITH THE LARKS

Tessa Hainsworth worked as a marketing manager at The Body Shop. She now lives happily in Cornwall with her husband and two children.

UP WITH THE LARKS

STARTING AGAIN IN CORNWALL

Tessa Hainsworth

p

preface
publishing

This paperback edition published by Preface 2010

10 9 8 7

First published in Great Britain in 2009 by
Preface Publishing
20 Vauxhall Bridge Road
London SW1V 2SA

An imprint of The Random House Group Limited

www.randomhouse.co.uk
www.prefacepublishing.co.uk

Addresses for companies within The Random House Group Limited can be found at
www.randomhouse.co.uk

The Random House Group Limited Reg. No. 954009

A CIP catalogue record for this book is available from the British Library

ISBN 978 1 84809 161 0

Typeset by Palimpsest Book Production Limited,
Grangemouth, Stirlingshire

The Random House Group Limited supports The Forest Stewardship Council® (FSC®), the leading international forest-certification organisation. Our book   per. FSC is t   ing en

Prin

To the magical charms of Cornwall
which has seduced many a heart into staying . . .

To my dearest Richard, Tom and Georgie
with all my love and to my amazingly
supportive friends and family

and

To Nigel, Jules, Jacki, Adrian, Jeremy
and all their families

Acknowledgements

To the beginning of an amazing journey – I owe special thanks to Karen Hayes without whom this book would never have seen the light of day. Huge thanks also to my agent Jane Turnbull, to Brian Perman and to the great team at Preface Books.

Two books have been a valuable source of background information on Cornish history, legend and landscape: Lawrence O'Toole's *The Roseland* and Daphne du Maurier's *Vanishing Cornwall.*

The names of places and people featured in the book have been changed to protect their privacy.

Prologue

I'm having my lunch break on the estuary in Creek, a tiny Cornish village tucked away between a rolling hillside and the sea. The tide is out and I'm perched on an old sea wall nibbling on a homemade pasty given to me by one of my 'customers'.

It is winter now, a glorious December. It's nearly the Solstice and yet the low sun gives enough warmth for me to sit outside and bask in it. The seabirds are basking too, scuttling along the wet sand and chirping at each other as merry as spring. They hop and preen amongst the few old rowboats and the clumps of seaweed, looking at me now and again with inquiring eyes, for I'm the only person here in this secluded haven. The sky is as blue and cloudless as any summer day, and the water beyond the estuary is as green as shamrocks.

I finish my pasty and brush away the crumbs. The smell of sea, the lap of waves, the sound of gulls, lulls me into a half-doze, and I forget that I'm not on some idyllic holiday but actually at work. And I can't believe my luck. After all the upheavals, the false beginnings, the struggle not to give up, I'm exactly where I want to be. This time, it feels permanent.

Picking up my bag, I saunter over to my van parked by the sea wall.

It's the red van of the Royal Mail and yes, I'm the driver, the one who delivers the post.

I'm a postwoman for the Royal Mail in Cornwall and a year into the job, it still feels like a dream.

It's not even two years since I lived and worked in London – and abroad – in a high-powered exciting job with a lifestyle many people would die for. But the stresses of juggling family and work, of too much to do and not enough time to do it in, was taking its toll and tearing our family apart.

It had to change, and it did, finally. What none of us were prepared for were the near-disastrous consequences of that change.

I'm thinking about the past as I get into the postal van, of how I got from there – that glitzy glamorous life – to here: dressed in a Royal Mail uniform and on my way to deliver the post to the next tranquil seaside hamlet.

As I drive along the narrow curving lanes, catching glimpses of the December sun glinting on the sea beyond green fields and grazing sheep, feeling contentment and joy ooze out of my pores like rich Cornish clotted cream, I remember the beginning – the weirdness of that first day. That surreal feeling that I'd walked into another life, an alien life that I thought then would forever remain strange and alarming.

November

My first day as a postwoman for the Royal Mail and the first shock is the odour. Male sweat – the sorting room reeks of it – not rancid nor unclean, just ordinary bloke secretions, with all that testosterone crammed together in one room. I feel as though I'm in the wrong story, the one about warriors and adventures and manly prowess; a story that begins far too early, before dawn.

I turn to Susie, the postwoman who is showing me around the huge warehouse of the mail room. 'Are we the only women?' I ask, watching the riot of navy and red clad figures rushing about sorting the masses of post.

She shakes her head. 'No, but we're a minority. And let's face it, bird, in these uniforms, we don't look much different from the men. Hard to tell us apart, to be honest.'

I look down at my clothes: baggy dark blue trousers, far too big for me. Dr Martens boots, unflattering red shirt, shapeless navy fleece, all with the bright red Royal Mail insignia. Waterproof jacket as big as a tent, but necessary for the icy deluge lashing Truro on this early November morning. It isn't that warm in here either, which is probably just as well. The strong masculine air is overpowering enough now; goodness knows what it will be like on a hot summer's day.

I take a deep breath. It's like being locked up with the England rugby team after a tough first half.

'You OK?' Susie says. 'Anything wrong?'

'No, fine . . . It's just that . . .' I trail off. Susie gives me an odd look, half suspicious, half scornful. 'Not got cold feet, have you?'

She isn't talking about the weather, or about the cold floor, where about 50 to 70 men, and very few women, are gathering their post from the sorting boxes. It looks like something between a strange choreographed dance and complete confusion and chaos.

She is waiting for an answer.

My reply is flippant. 'Not just *cold* feet – *freezing*. I should have worn thicker socks with these boots.'

She gives me the look my pathetic attempt at humour deserves. I try to seem at ease. 'It's just . . . just a bit different, that's all. From my last job.'

I think of my work over the last twenty years, travelling all over the world for The Body Shop, an international cosmetics company, latterly as its UK Marketing Manager.

As I take another deep breath and inhale the earthy odour, that male smell mixed with cardboard, metal, paper, print and damp, I remember other rooms, just as busy where the scent was of the sweetest perfumes, lemongrass and lavender, mimosa and magnolia, fruity and flowery fragrances that permeated my clothes and stayed with me day and night. Delicate rose bath oils, moisturizers and night creams of myrrh and frankincense, shampoos and rinses of tea tree and aloe vera.

I look around at this warehouse which reminds me of an

aeroplane hangar. The huge rubber doors at the end are flapping like the wings of menacing ravens as the post deliverers come in to collect their stash and go back out with it loaded on huge trolleys.

My last place of work was a lush boutique office, designer decorated and scented with discreet but expensive aromatherapy oils.

Susie, normally an attractive healthy Cornish woman, looks stark and yellow at 4.30 in the morning under the rows and rows of overhead neon strip lighting and I'm sure I look just as bleak in the harsh glare. My colleagues at The Body Shop were all fashionably smart and stylish, trendy hair and bodies pampered with our products.

Susie is still looking at me, her face unreadable. 'I'm fine,' I repeat. 'It's just a bit different, that's all.'

She nods. I can almost see her thinking, *This one won't last a week*. But all she says is, 'OK, let's get to work.'

'Right,' I say, with more bravado than conviction in my voice.

She plunges into the scrum, nodding to me to join her in the noise and confusion.

'Let's get to work,' I echo, and follow her into my new job and my new life.

The journey that led me to that Royal Mail sorting office had begun the year before, during that slump that happens sometimes over the Christmas holidays when the kids are in bed, the fussing and feasting nearly over, and the parents, exhausted, overfed and over-indulged, collapse in a heap in front of the telly.

That's exactly what Ben and I were doing. It had been a hectic day, with our six-year-old son Will and four-and-a-half-year-old daughter Amy running riot with new toys and over-excitement. Now, however, they were in bed and we were settling down to watch a Jack Nicholson film, *As Good As It Gets*. I don't remember much of the movie now, but the title changed our lives.

Is this as good as it gets? I kept repeating to myself. To this day I haven't a clue what the film was about, but those few words in the title wouldn't leave me alone. Ben was half asleep, half snuggling me as we sprawled about on the sofa trying not to spill the glasses of Sancerre we were sipping. Gradually he began focusing on the movie, but instead of doing the same, I couldn't concentrate. The title kept repeating itself like a mantra.

Why? I wondered aloud. Ben, by now totally engrossed in the film, nudged me to shush but the noises in my head wouldn't keep quiet. *Why does that title bother me?*

There seemed to be no rational answer. Ben and I had everything, or so it seemed. We were in love and we had two gorgeous children. We also had a satisfactory working arrangement: I had the executive job which brought in the money, and Ben, a professional but out of work actor, was doing a brilliant job as house-husband, in charge of cooking and all the other aspects of keeping home and family together.

I'd just completed a successful Christmas Campaign for The Body Shop, with a massive budget. The twenty years I'd been in the job had been tremendously satisfying and adventurous, challenging and creative, too. In the past years I'd set up a £1.9 million visitors' centre for the firm; I'd met numerous stars and celebrities and even royalty, including Princess Diana and Prince Charles on separate occasions. I had been with Anita and Gordon Roddick, the founders of the company, since the earlier days and I loved being part of such an exciting and unique enterprise, for The Body Shop was at the forefront of the move towards more natural cosmetics.

It was exhilarating. I went all over the world organizing

conferences for as many as 500 delegates, many of whom were well-known, respected, inspiring, as our company was the first to advocate fair practices in cosmetic testing as well as introducing organic and ethical ingredients in the product. When the company set up franchises in America, I had the opportunity of living in New York City for nearly a year, creating their Communication Office linking new franchises in the USA and the UK. I had loved my job, passionately.

But ... but? What was the *but*? And why in my mind was I using the past tense when I listed the things I loved about my job?

I must have spoken aloud again, for Ben filled my wine glass, thinking I'd asked him for more. I murmured a thanks and snuggled up to him, determined to shut out the crazy voices in my head and concentrate on the film.

Is this really as good as it gets? The question wouldn't go away. Over the next few weeks it pecked at me like a great carnivorous bird, preying on my stressed mind, my unexercised, unhealthy, exhausted body.

My work had changed considerably since the earlier headier years. The company had expanded far beyond anyone's expectation, and in the past few years I'd found it more stressful than inspiring. Though I was often in London where most of my job was based, we lived in a faceless commuter neighbourhood on the outskirts of the city in a house that often seemed less a home than a hotel where I crashed out after meetings, conferences and business entertaining. When I wasn't travelling, I came home some nights well after the kids were in bed, shattered after the day's commuting. Getting to and from work was a nightmare of crowded trains that arrived late, tube lines closed, buses missed and taxis that never came. I hardly saw my kids, hardly saw Ben. I went from one extreme to the other, either revved up from the stresses of the job, or totally limp and exhausted.

'You've got to take it easier,' Ben said.

'I can't,' I snapped. 'I've got about six people after my job as it is.'

There was nothing to say to that, so we'd moved onto the children. 'By the way,' Ben said, 'the kids' school play is next week, remember?'

'Oh no, I nearly forgot.' I felt terrible.

'Amy needs a unicorn's horn, and Will wants to be a hedgehog. We've got to get the costumes together by Friday.'

It was Wednesday and I had to be in Brighton the next day. I was supposed to be entertaining people from Sydney the following week and would miss the play anyway. But when Ben reassured me that he'd already made the costumes and that I wasn't to worry, I felt even worse.

Ben comforted me. 'Never mind, love, it can't be helped. That's the way things are at the moment.'

He spoke quietly and I noticed the pensive look on his face. It reminded me that he too had had to accept the fact that life hadn't worked out as smoothly and perfectly as we'd hoped, when we both agreed to our working arrangement. I knew he missed the theatre, and acting. He was a good actor, and passionate about his profession, but had accepted that at this point in our lives, he couldn't pursue his career with the steely dedication required.

Though he didn't talk much about it these days, I knew that being a house-husband in the commuter belt of London wasn't the best substitute for the life he'd dreamed of.

Missing the school play was a kind of catalyst, I think, looking back on it now. I'd always missed not having enough time to be with the children, but now it worried me night and day. I had to leave for work early and some days came home so late I never saw them at all. After that first round of tears over the unicorn and hedgehog costumes, I realized that lately I had been doing a lot of crying, like the evening I got home to find Amy and Will distressed and disgruntled. They'd gone to school in their uniforms only to realize it was a special non-uniform day and all their mates were in jeans and trendy tops, while my two darlings were trussed up in their uniforms.

A small thing, perhaps – but not to them. Nor to me either, for I was the one who'd opened the note for the parents one morning on the way to work and forgotten to tell Ben or the children. I felt I'd failed them yet again.

Seeing their sad little faces, I once again felt the tears rolling down my face. It had been a bad day anyway; I'd had to fire a single mum against my will and I was crying for her too. Will and Amy, still feeling mortified at being the only children in school not in cool trendy clothes, decided to join me, and we were all bawling when Ben came in from the kitchen to say that dinner was ready.

'Oh God,' he said as he witnessed the sorry scene in front of him. 'Not again!'

'You're not very bloody sympathetic.'

'Tessa, I've been sympathizing with the kids ever since they got back from school in tears. Now let's all calm down and eat, OK?'

I wasn't hungry, and said so. He asked what was the point of cooking something special as he might as well have cooked fish fingers if only Will and Amy were going to eat.

We argued. Luckily the children had left the room by then – or unluckily I suppose, because we never argued around them. In fact we used to never argue at all. What was happening to us?

From that day, we seemed to go from bad to horrific. The children had a rash of illnesses, nothing serious but enough to keep them from school. Enough to keep Ben frazzled, and me tearful yet again because I couldn't be home with them. I couldn't concentrate at work for my focus was on home not the job. I came back tired and miserable, not much good to either Ben or the children.

And Ben was having a hard time too. We'd hoped that somehow we could share the work out, that I'd be able to ease my hours while he took on some acting roles, but it never worked out that way. My job entailed total commitment and long hours. Ben had just turned down, through necessity, a chance for a part in a short rep run from a director he knew. There was no way he could have taken it, but it left him restless and fidgety.

For weeks I brooded. The crying didn't stop, either – in the mornings, kissing Will and Amy a hurried good-bye, hoping I'd see them for that brief hour before they went to bed; in the evenings when I got home too late to see them awake. I cried even more when I left the country, spending long hours pacing the departure lounge in Heathrow or Gatwick wishing I were home with my family. This wasn't like me, these tears. *I can't do Supermum any more,* I thought, in the heaving throng on the train, the tube, in the London streets. I felt hemmed in and claustrophobic. I got angry at myself for being depressed and then I got depressed for being angry.

It had to stop.

One night after a particularly bad day for both of us – children ill with nasty coughs, Ben just getting over the flu, me struggling not to succumb to illness during a particularly sensitive turnover at work – we began to talk seriously of change. We were slumped in the living room, on edge because Amy's cough was particularly bad and we were afraid it was about to turn into rather nasty croup.

'Ben, I've had enough.' I leaned back against him on

the sofa, trying to relax but still listening intently to any sounds coming from the bedrooms.

'You're just tired.' He began to massage my shoulders in the way I loved, loosening the knots of tension.

'Not *just* tired. Totally exhausted. But that's not the problem. I'm not happy at work any more. I've been thinking loads about it.'

'I know you said the job's changed a lot.'

'Enormously. You know how the company's grown from the small cosy firm I started with to this huge multinational. I don't speak its language any more, Ben. Don't particularly want to.'

'Is it getting that bad?'

'Starting to. I'm fed up with London too, with the commuting, with everything.'

'Tessa, we chose this way of life, remember? You loved your job and wanted to keep it on.'

'I know. But the heart's gone out of marketing for me. It used to be creative and exciting. Now it's like looking in a rear view mirror.'

He dug his fingers deeper into my shoulders, trying to massage me out of what he saw as a temporary mood.

I was starting to unwind but I kept on talking. 'And the kids. I hardly see them. They're growing so fast – I want time with them. And with you too.'

He stopped kneading the tight muscles in my neck and flopped back against the cushions, closing his eyes. I could see the tension, the tiredness, in his face too. 'Oh Ben,' I wailed. '*Is* this as good as it gets? Don't you feel something is missing? Maybe we should be doing something else, something entirely different from this crazy life we're living.'

'It's the life we wanted, Tessa. There are problems, I know, but nothing's perfect.' Ben was sympathetic but firm. 'You're just having a bad patch. It'll pass.'

9

Before I could answer, we heard Amy begin to cry. Forgetting everything else, we both ran upstairs to her.

I brought up the possibility of change again and again, but we never got very far. The problem was, I didn't know then what the change should entail. Changing my job? Moving abroad? My sister lived in France so perhaps that was a possibility, but what would we do there?

And then we went on holiday.

Luckily, spring half-term was coming up and I had some time off from work. We decided to go to Cornwall, as we had so often in the past.

Though we'd stayed in various parts of the county before, we felt most at home on the South coast where we would holiday again this time. Cornwall, like Devon, is composed of many different landscapes, we had discovered as we went back year after year. There's the central backbone running up the middle with the unique and exotic landscape created by the old mining industry: around the Eden Project it looks like the craters of the moon; and all the way down to Cape Cornwall, amongst the heather and the little Methodist chapels, are fantastic old mine workings and industrial ruins.

And then there's West Penwith, the area below St Ives and around Lamorna, with the stone circles and wild moorland that some people think is the real Cornwall. Not for them the rugged North coast with its tremendous seas, surfs and trendiness; the Cornwall 'Posh Rock' and restaurants run by Jamie Oliver and Rick Stein cheek by jowl with caravan parks and Newquay. It is surfy heaven and a favourite venue for hen and stag nights.

Our favourite place for years now has been the South coast which is another Cornwall altogether. Here, there are gentle beaches sloping down to a usually tranquil sea, perfect for swimming or sailing. There are dozens of small green creeks meandering through lovely ancient forests that stretch to the water's edge. It's so unspoiled that you can imagine you're on a tributary of the Amazon, especially with the fertile soil and micro-climate that nurture the vast tree ferns and palms that grow nowhere else in England, only in the West Country.

Since the Bronze Age, this area has been a place of farming and fishing, and also the perfect area for smuggling, with its little inlets and creeks hidden by the lush foliage and woodlands. This was the area that inspired Daphne du Maurier to write books, like *Rebecca* and *Frenchman's Creek*.

It's an area that has always inspired me as well. I always returned from visits feeling calmer and yet energized, ready to tackle again the job of working mother back in London.

So as usual, we headed for the South of Cornwall, finding self-catering accommodation in a village called Poldowe, up the hill from the sea with a tiny harbour and beach. The village had one small post office and shop and to me it was perfect, like stepping back into the 19th century.

It was early spring, and though in London not even the daffodils had managed to emerge from their winter covering of grime, here it was almost summer. The camellias were exuberant: they seemed to be everywhere and so colourful that my eyes seemed permanently dazzled after the grey of winter. Even the primroses were out, blooming alongside the snowdrops that no doubt had appeared weeks earlier but refused to go, rather like a white cat curled on a favourite chair in a sunny room. South Cornwall was at its best that spring. It was as if, knowing our dissatisfaction, she was luring us to her.

The night we arrived at Poldowe, there was a thick fog. It enveloped the nearby harbour village of Morranport and crept up the hill to envelope the houses, the trees and the old church in the centre of a square. It was late when we got in so we unpacked the night clothes and the bag of provisions we'd brought, had a makeshift supper and piled into bed, relieved to be off the busy holiday roads and into our own cottage.

The next morning the sea mist still clung to the harbour and village like fine dewy cobwebs. I woke early and walked down along the footpath to the harbour then down the beach to the sea's edge with Jake our spaniel. My face and body were being moistened and moisturized by the clean, fresh sea-mist, better than by any of the potions and scented oils I dealt with.

I stood for ages at the edge of the sea, Jake jumping in and out of the waves like a lunatic dog from some kiddies' cartoon. The mist was beginning to lift, and sharp shafts of sunlight pierced the opaque whiteness like dozens of golden needles, darting on the smooth undulations of the sea and changing the colour from a dull grey to deep blue and turquoise.

I stood, mesmerized. My senses were being bombarded: the earthy smells of sea and stone and damp, the sounds of waves churning over the pebbly beach and of sea birds calling to each other overhead, and I could almost taste the salt in the air, it was so strong and pungent.

I was oblivious to Jake and his splashing, to his odd bark at the seagulls that landed too close. I watched those golden streaks on the sea, the mist snaking around as if it were playing hide and seek with the sun, and I knew, knew with all my heart, without a shadow of a doubt.

This is where we must go. This is where we belong, by the sea, in this place.

The knowledge, the certainty of my feelings made me suddenly wild and exhilarated. Jake, sensing my excitement, began barking and circling as I stood at the water's edge, daring me to go in. I didn't hesitate. I wanted now to *feel* the sea on my body, I wanted to actually taste the salt water on my lips. I wanted a baptism too, although I didn't form that thought till later. I wanted to immerse myself in my new certainty.

There was no one around as I tore off my clothes. I'd only worn jeans and underpants, hurriedly throwing on a pink sweatshirt without bothering with a bra. My jeans were boot-legged and wide enough to pull off with my trainers and socks still on, and I was in such a hurry to get into the water that I didn't bother to take them off, plunging stark naked into the icy sea whooping and shouting, Jake barking and splashing beside me. Together we created holy mayhem, both of us manic in our separate joy.

I didn't stay in long – it was freezing. The mist had gathered again as I staggered out, feeling like the first creature to crawl on dry land, looking around me at the awesome world I had not truly looked at before. I hadn't had the *time* to look before, or, if I *had* a rare moment to myself, the whirling voices in my head – planning, worrying – kept me from seeing anything.

So there I was, dancing about in my shoes and socks and nothing else but a goose-bumpy skin, still delirious with happiness. Then I looked down the beach and in the distance saw people walking along the sea's edge, coming quickly towards me. It was time I got dressed.

I came back to earth with a whoosh when I tried to get back into my clothes. Not only was I wet, they were too, for I'd left them too near the incoming tide. My flimsy, see-through red knickers had nearly washed out to sea, floating in a rock pool like an alien jelly-fish. I grabbed them and pulled them on, but there was no way my tight wet jeans would go on to my wet body, especially over the soaking shoes and socks that I hadn't had time to take off. I didn't come out of the house with a bra, but where was my sweatshirt? I couldn't find it anywhere.

Jake was barking again, trying to bully me into going back into the water to play. A sudden horrific thought went through my head. Jake had taken Amy's shoe once on the beach and carried it into the water; he was a dog who always had to have something in his mouth when he was larking around. Sure enough, there was my sweatshirt, a big pink blob, floating out to sea, too far away to retrieve.

What to do? The walkers were approaching fast, and I had to walk past them and through the waking village on my way home. So I improvised. So what if my creative skills were no longer needed at work, I said to myself, they're bloody well needed now.

As I walked past the post office shop on the harbour, a heavy-set man with grey hair wearing a postman's uniform was helping a lorry driver unload boxes of fishing tackle. 'Morning,' I glittered at them, smiling brightly and quickly moving on. 'Lovely morning for an early swim,' I called back, catching the looks of stunned disbelief on their faces.

I might have looked strange, but at least I wouldn't be arrested for indecent exposure, not quite anyway. Before I'd left the beach, I had taken the belt from my sopping jeans, tied it around my hips, and hung masses of green and brown hunks of seaweed from it so they hung down nearly to my knees. This hid enough of the sheer wet bikini panties to prevent my immediate disgrace.

As for the top half of me, I'd flung my jeans across my shoulders, so that one leg was draped modestly, if a bit drippingly, across each breast, tucking the flapping boot-legs into the belt around my hips. I was so pleased with my attire that I'd completed the outfit by placing dozens of shells in my hair, which by that time was so tangled and curly with salt that only a half dozen fell out as I made my way nonchalantly up the street and home to my still sleeping family.

I woke Ben with the news. 'We've got to move to Cornwall.' A few seashells fell onto his face and the duvet. I'd shed the wet jeans but the seaweed was still clinging to me. Somehow he wasn't surprised. Not by my appearance or by my announcement. I guess he knew me too well.

'Are you crazy or what?' Ben tried to sit up to see if I'd completely flipped, but I was rolling about with him on the bed trying to shed the seaweed. He was half shrieking at me to get off as I was soaking him and half laughing hysterically as I tickled him mischievously.

'I've had an epiphany. We're moving to Cornwall,' I said again.

'Don't be daft.'

'We've always loved it. The kids love it – it'll be a dream come true for them, living near the sea. We'll sell up, move here. To the South coast, our favourite place in the world.'

'It's completely impossible, you know that.'

'Nothing's impossible, Ben,' I muttered, stopping my tickling and beginning some kissing.

His voice got a bit huskier. 'And what about work, about jobs? What in God's name would we do in Cornwall?'

'Time enough to think of that later. For now, just hold on to that thought – we're moving to Cornwall! Forget about the rest. Now, are you going to start kissing me back or not?'

We moved to South Cornwall in the autumn, less than six months after that momentous epiphany by the sea.

Amy and Will were delighted from the start, but it took some convincing to get Ben on our side. Having put his acting career more or less on hold during the period when my work kept me away from home for so many long hours, his was the practical voice of reason in the midst of our wild fantasies.

'What will we do in Cornwall?' he continued to ask. 'You'll never get a high-powered job like you've got now.'

'I don't want one any more. You know that.'

'And what could I do? It's hard enough in the London theatre, where will I get an acting job in Cornwall?'

'But Ben, you'll have more time, as I'll have sole responsibility for Amy and Will. There are films and television — actors have to travel all over the world these days, so it shouldn't matter where you live. And you've said yourself that in some ways, regional theatre has more exciting opportunities for actors than the London theatre now.' I took his hand. 'Look, we'll find something. Both of us are willing to work, to do anything.'

He still wasn't convinced. 'It's not just work. What about our family and friends? How can you bear to leave them?'

But our families didn't live nearby anyway and as for our friends, I knew we'd probably see more of them in Cornwall, when they visited us for weekends and holidays, than we saw of them now in London.

We talked it over, until finally Ben succumbed to the idea and we made the decision to move. Once he'd decided, Ben was as enthusiastic as I was and, like me, eager to get on and start our new life.

We made plans. We would sell our house and use the proceeds to buy another one in Cornwall as well as starting our own business. The idea we finally hit on was a paint-your-own-pottery business. There were several of these in our area in London and they were immensely popular; our own children and their friends loved to go to them and we'd heard that it was a lucrative business. It was something we could do from home too, converting a shed or a garage into premises.

Before we moved, we prepared, determined to do this right. We read everything we could about starting a small business and being self-employed. We drew up our own business plan, wrote letters asking for advice, talked to others and wrote out charts and projected goals. We were so well-prepared for our new Cornish life that the reality of it, when it hit, was doubly hard to come to terms with.

At first, everything went swimmingly. I didn't even have to quit my job – by a wonderful quirk of luck, I was made redundant before I handed in my notice. Pretending to be grief-stricken at the news that a restructuring meant my job would have to go, I phoned Ben at once to celebrate. The redundancy pay would help cover the cost of the move and even some unemployed time as our new business took off.

And then our house sold, quicker than we'd expected. Now all we had to do was find one in Cornwall, to make into our new home. How smoothly it was all going, we thought smugly. How simple it all was, once we'd thought it through and made our decision. And how wrong we were. How terribly, horribly wrong.

To begin with, finding a house in Cornwall was mind-blowingly difficult. It seemed everyone had suddenly fallen in love with the place and wanted a second home there, which made house prices go ballistic. It was happening everywhere else too, but in Cornwall it seemed even crazier.

As houses on the market were snapped up within twenty-four hours, before we had a chance to even look at them, we heard dire tales. Buyers were throwing up to £70,000 over the asking prices at properties. We heard that 5,000 folk a month were moving into Cornwall and we nearly got side-swept away in the rush.

We soon learned that it's a lot different living in a place than holidaying. Many of the lovely seaside villages we'd adored on holiday were empty ghost towns in winter with most of the properties owned as holiday homes. There were other villages inhabited mainly by the retired who had sold their properties Up Country (the Cornish label for just about every place across the Tamar River) to follow their dreams of living by the sea.

Some of these second-home and retirement villages seemed to have no heart: no school, a pub empty except in summer, no shop, no post office. Others were 'drive-through' villages which seemed to have nothing but the road leading in and out, with not even a pub or a newsagent, only a cluster of houses to call themselves a village.

We wanted more. We had two children who needed more, as did we and we were determined to find it. They were out there, those perfect Cornish towns and villages but properties there were scarce, pricey and didn't often come on to the market.

We spent a fortune driving up and down every weekend between South Cornwall and London, looking at houses. We viewed eighty in all and were gazumped twice. The final contracts were signed on our old house which meant we had to move out and spend more money on rented accommodation. We wanted to do this in Cornwall but the kids were still in school and, since we didn't know where in the county we'd end up, we thought it best to leave them where they were until we could move permanently.

'We've got to start thinking outside the box,' I said to Ben one night, just before yet another weekend of house hunting. 'Talk to people in the community who might have inside knowledge of properties for sale. It's the only way we'll ever get a house.'

The next day we raced down to Cornwall again, this time to look at a property in Treverny, one of the villages that had all the things we wanted and was charming as well. The place we viewed was far too small, despite the estate agent trying to convince us that a cramped, dark, walk-in cupboard would make an excellent bedroom for one of the children.

Disappointed, Ben and I decided to wander around the village as it was a hot summer's day and Treverny is an idyllic spot. In the middle of the tree-lined tiny main street there is an ancient church and adjacent to that, a shaded park, complete with babbling brook and a tranquil pond. Benches are scattered here and there under willow and beech trees along the stream.

Ben wanted to see inside the church and I needed to get a cold drink from the shop so we split up and agreed to meet by the brook in half an hour. Will and Amy were staying with friends for the weekend, which meant I had time on my own to savour the village. It was just what we wanted, but the only house for sale, according to the estate agent, was the one we'd looked at.

I walked down a tiny lane alongside the village green and saw a window cleaner hard at work at one of the houses. It was a hot sunny day full of flowers and birdsong, and it was summer, so he wasn't surprised that an 'emmett' (the Cornish word for tourist) from Up Country should begin waxing lyrical about the area. 'Wonderful day, isn't it?' I called. He was working on the ground floor windows so I didn't have to shout up to him.

He turned to look at me. I was wearing red shorts and a sleeveless white shirt. My long blonde hair was curling madly around my head and face in the heat and humidity. I tossed it back, giving him my biggest smile.

Maybe he thought I fancied him, for he nodded an affirmative and left his work to chat with me. He was young and good-looking, with those great dark Cornish eyes and hair. His voice was laconic and his words to the point. 'Tourist?' he was too polite to call me an emmett to my face.

He perched on the garden wall in front of the house, indicating he was quite happy to sit with this stranger. I joined him, wondering if the owner – his employer – was watching through the net curtains.

I turned on the charm, doing my best bubbly bit. 'Visiting

for now, but not for long I hope. Still living Up Country but coming down every weekend to house hunt.' He nodded appreciatively. I didn't know if it was my skilful use of the Cornish 'Up Country' or my newly tanned and waxed legs that prompted his appreciation.

He listened while I rambled on for a bit about the charms of the county, the seaside, the village and the weather. When I got to the weather he baulked. 'You don't go movin' here 'cause of the weather, y'know. T'is wet most of the time,' he squinted against the sun to peer at the windows still not cleaned, and shifted uneasily. I sensed the guilt at not using every moment of sunshine was starting to get to him, so I made my move quickly.

'We've had so much trouble finding a house down here.' I lowered my eyes and added a note of tragedy to my voice. *Ben eat your heart out*, I thought. 'I wonder if you might know of something? You work and live here, you must know if anything might be coming up for sale soon.'

He turned back from gazing at the windows to gazing at me again. 'Well matter of fact, I do. House for sale right here in the village. Just about to go to the estate agent's.'

My excitement showed in my face. 'Fantastic.'

'Good sturdy house. Decent garden, big an'all.'

'Fantastic,' I was repeating myself but I didn't care. I'd already moved Ben, Will, Amy and Jake and was already planning colour schemes and garden plants.

'Yep. Good house. Was me mum's for years. She died a couple weeks back, suddenly like.'

'How many bedrooms?'

He looked at me with horror and I realized what I'd said. I'd been away with the fairies, frolicking around our beautiful garden in this lovely Cornish village, with my sweet children and my gorgeous husband. I'd heard his words but hadn't taken them in, so wrapped up was I in my own dreams and schemes.

I felt dreadful. Mortified, embarrassed and guilt-stricken. 'Oh God, I didn't mean – oh I'm sorry, I'm so sorry. About your mother. Poor her. Poor you. Oh what you must think of me, so inconsiderate, so unfeeling.' I went on in this fashion for a few more sentences, feeling terrible and desperately trying to make amends.

Finally I dithered to an end. He was backing away from me but opening his mouth like a fish gasping for water, no doubt to utter some ancient Cornish curse on my soul.

'Three,' he said.

'Pardon?'

'Three bedrooms. There was a fourth, but Ma used it for her best parlour.'

We didn't buy that house, though we did look at it. It wasn't quite right for us, but very shortly afterwards, through word of mouth, we found another house in the same stunning village of Treverny.

My first week with Royal Mail is a blur. Kindly folk in the post office show me the ropes, get me acquainted with the rules, regulations and various quirks of a vast government body. They're kind, but there's a wariness in their attitude towards me, a kind of aloofness. Like Susie, they don't think I'll be around long.

Susie has shown me around: the main sorting office in Truro and the two small post offices where I'll be based, in St Geraint and Morranport, two harbour villages. I've also been shown the various routes that I will cover, a sixty-mile round by van and seven miles by foot. I'm doing relief work, covering for Susie and an older postman called Reg. I've had a go on my own but only with an experienced Royal Mail helper shadowing and backing me up.

But now all that is over and today I am a proper postperson, completely on my own.

I plunge gamely into the controlled chaos in the mail room, sort my letters and parcels, load them onto my trolley in proper order and even manage a light-hearted raunchy joke or two with the others as we gather our post.

Feeling smug and well pleased with myself, I push open the two massive rubber doors with my trolley and trundle outside into the darkness and the rain. And that's when the panic hits. There is a huge car park chock-a-block with Royal Mail vans, all looking exactly alike to me. I realize I haven't a clue which one is mine. I was so excited to find a space that I had not even noticed where I'd parked.

There are at least fifty red vans, parked in rows. Fifty, a hundred, thousands even, I think in despair, all the red postal vans in the world, sitting in the huge car park, all taunting me with their sameness.

There is no one to help me out. I'm alone in this vast universe of identical red vans, lashed by what's beginning to feel like a cyclone, wondering if I'll have to try my keys in every single one before I find my own. If it weren't so cold and wet I'd sit down by my trolley and cry.

Instead, I plunge into the midst of them and set about trying to discover which van is mine. My tent of a coat is blowing like the sails of a yacht in this endless Cornish wind and rain. I look like Jack wearing the giant's coat, the sleeves reaching way below my hands and the whole thing nearly encasing my legs. Though it's cold outside, I'm sweating inside because I have not yet learned what all the other posties know, that the nylon lining inside has got to be removed precisely for this reason. I can see that getting the temperature right inside this jacket is an art I haven't yet mastered. If you open it too wide to keep from perspiring you end up shivering as an icy

22

breeze creeps inside, followed by the gales and rain. But it's only November and I have all winter to figure it out.

Finally after walking up and down the parked vehicles for what seems like hours, trying my key in nearly every van, despairing of ever finding the right one, I'm saved! There ahead of me, perched in the front window of one of the vans, is a black and white cat, staring out at the rain as if each drop was a tiny mouse ripe for the catching. For a moment I think I'm hallucinating, then with a rush of relief I recognize the van. It's not mine, nor Postman Pat's, but Susie's who is covering for someone else today. And now I remember that I'd parked mine right next to hers when I arrived this morning. The cat, who comes with Susie now and again on her rounds – the only real cat I've ever met who likes to ride in a car – eyes me without much interest. I grin maniacally at it, tap the window lightly in friendly if slightly hysterical greeting, and at last leap into my own sweet red van.

At home, Ben and the children will still be fast asleep. Truro is deserted as I drive down its windy streets, passing the old brewery and taking a short cut out of the town. On the hill leaving the city, I can see the cathedral, still lit up and shining like a vision through the misty rain. It is so awesome, so breath-taking, that I slow and then stop when I see no one is either behind or in front of me.

I stay like this for a full five minutes, taking in the spires and the towers, the gauzy light shining through the pale rain, and for a moment my mind and heart are still. No head noise, no noise at all. Just me, *still* for once, not rushing, not frantic, not stressed.

It is cold in the van, the rain starts to pick up outside and I have a long delivery route to complete, much of it in the dark, in a rural isolated area. My eyes are sticky with lack of sleep and I can feel water dripping from where it has collected in my rolled-up sleeves onto my trousers. Time to move on, I say to myself. I need this job and the money I'll be bringing in.

So far, moving to Cornwall has not been the idyllic move we'd hoped it would be and even now, if I lose this job, we might still have to give up and move back to London. Today I am doing Susie's route, on my own for the first time. I've got a list of quirky requests and instructions a mile long. It's a van run today not a walking one, in some isolated rural hamlets and farmhouses. I drive to the sea's edge to drop off the bag of mail for the Morranport post office on the harbour. Another postman, Reg, is there already, preparing for his round. 'Wish me luck, Reg,' I say brightly. 'I'm on my own today.'

He nods in his usual taciturn way, his equivalent to a good luck wish I suppose. Reg is getting on, as he keeps telling us. He's slow as well as laconic, slow physically that is. I feel like a hare on speed next to his tortoise-like crawl.

He is quite a contrast to Nell, who runs the Morranport post office and shop. She's either about to be eighty, or just past it, depending on whom you talk to. She's got the energy of four twenty-year-olds and puts us all to shame.

'You be fine, Tessa,' Nell calls out from behind the counter. 'Good luck, maid.'

I stand to attention, click my Dr Martens heels and salute smartly. Nell laughs and even Reg manages what could possibly pass as a tiny smile. I jump into the van and am off and away. My nervousness is gone and I feel fearless. I am the Royal Mail, getting through come thick or thin.

I manage the first few farmhouses despite the dark morning, the potholed dirt tracks that lead up to the houses and the many farm gates I have to open and close. Relieved that I have found them all without getting lost, I set off for another rural spot, the house of a woman named Eleanor Gibland. I feel I know her, though I've never met her. Susie has been delivering post to her for nearly eighteen years and they have become close. Although they rarely see each other much outside of Eleanor's house, they talk for ages on days when Susie is not in a tearing hurry. Sometimes they sit in the tiny front garden and chat; other, colder or wetter days, Susie accepts a cup of tea in Eleanor's pristine kitchen. They have become good friends in an odd sort of way.

I'm feeling almost euphoric now. I've managed to get through the prep and the sorting with no more mishaps than losing the van temporarily. I've negotiated a few tricky isolated homesteads and now the rest should be easy. The rain has stopped and in the lightening sky with only patchy cloud, I can see the faint outline of a rainbow arching over the sea and the cliffs. Before I get to Eleanor's house, I pull the van to the side of the road to marvel.

The sea is a heaving hulking mass of churning foam. The rainbow is coming right up out of the water and curving over harbour and beach. I turn my head and see it has made a perfect half circle, ending, it seems, at Eleanor's place. I wonder if I'm imagining it, this bit of pale colour in the early morning sky. Opening the window to see more clearly, a blast of icy wind hits me in the face like a wet glove. I shut the window quickly. I'll have enough walking my rounds in this kind of weather, no need to get carried away.

Besides, there's a rainbow to follow. Isn't there supposed to be a pot of gold at the end of it? I haven't thought of pots of gold since childhood. Cornwall, with its legends and myths, charms and magic, has got to me already. If owls are bearers of bad news and hares can turn into witches if you're not careful, then why not a pot of gold at the end of a rainbow? And look, the rainbow seems to be ending right at my next delivery point!

The drive up to Eleanor's neat cottage is flanked by woodland, trees shorn of leaves, glistening with raindrops and draped with pockets of mist which are pierced with shafts of light from the rising sun. The colours of the rainbow are stronger now as it cuts through the woods and seems to end at the edge of a tiny creek which flows past the top of the small front garden. The house looks quiet and there are no lights on anywhere. I know Eleanor is an early riser as Susie has told me she is often dressed and ready for her elevenses at 8 a.m., and it's way past that now. She must be having a lie-in, I decide seeing no one about.

I can't resist. I stop the van, jump out and rush over to the creek's edge. The earth here is damp and marshy. I love these little streams and rivers of South Cornwall, the tiny waterfalls and wetlands. They seem to be everywhere: running behind gardens, alongside tiny rural roads and appearing as if by magic in the least expected places. When the Cornish call something 'a moor-y spot', they mean something damp or swampy.

This is definitely a moor-y piece of ground and my sturdy postie boots are squelching as I walk. If anyone sees me I'll feel a fool, mooching around someone's little stream in the middle of winter. I don't believe in fairies or pots of gold at the end of rainbows but Cornwall is such an enchanted place, so different from anywhere else I've been and so full of folklore. After being here a time you can't help feeling that there's something in these stories about elves and fairies, about ghosts and spirits. The sea, the mist, the rocky shoreline and the inlets, hills and foggy moorland, all contribute to the feeling of mystery, of things unsaid and unknown. Besides, the rainbow feels like an omen after the last few weeks when everything seemed to be falling apart. So, knowing I'm being ridiculous, I try to pinpoint the rainbow's end. This is where it looked like it was ending, this squidgy hummock of grassy marsh where I'm standing, with the creek gurgling over the tops of my boots. Luckily they are waterproof. I can see it, just eluding me every time I try to reach out and touch it. The early November light seems brighter, or is it a false dawn, or even the remnants of moonlight? The early winter sun through a low black cloud casts a sudden eerie light on a cluster of rocks half in, half out of the shallow creek, lending it a shiny, yellow glow. *My pot of gold*, I think, squatting down to take a closer look. I feel crazy with excitement. It's like finding a hundred four-leaf clovers, all at once.

A booming voice scares the wits out of me. 'What in the name of God do you think you are doing down there? And who are you, anyway? Where's Susie?'

I am too embarrassed to answer for a second or two. Before I can recover my wits she snaps, 'Whoever you are, will you please get out of my creek?'

I scramble out of the water, where I'd fallen on my knees with the surprise of her voice. It must be Eleanor Gibland, dressed in the kind of housedress women wore in the fifties, slip-on gardening shoes and holding a pale blue umbrella over her head even though the rain has stopped.

'I'm Tessa, the relief postwoman. We haven't met. The day I came here with Susie, you weren't in.'

She stares at me disdainfully. She is a woman of indeterminate age, with permed grey hair surrounding a circle of a face and a short round body. Susie had told me that Eleanor is a Cornish woman but had been sent away to the Home Counties as a young girl to become a nanny, returning twenty years ago when her mother died to take over her house.

'You have only answered one of my questions. Do you have a surname or were you born without one? If so, why?'

I tell her my full name and she repeats, 'Where is Susie? And what were you doing paddling about in my creek?' She gives me a steely stare, as if I were a very naughty child.

I lie. I have no choice. How can I tell this formidable woman

27

the truth, that I was chasing a rainbow? 'I lost something. It blew out of the van and I had to retrieve it.' I give her my best, friendliest smile. 'Susie's day off today.'

'I hope it wasn't the Royal Mail property that you lost. That would be unforgivable.' She gives me another of her looks. 'And I hope you are telling me the truth. I would be very cross indeed if I thought you were fishing in my creek. It is private property as you must be well aware.'

I hang my head in what I hope looks like a chastised manner. 'No, m'am,' I say humbly. 'I certainly wasn't fishing. I wouldn't dream of it.'

This at least is true. I hand over her post from the van. She takes it without a word, looks at it suspiciously, then back at me again.

This short squat woman is making me feel like a five-year-old. It's starting to rain again but I don't feel able to go without her permission. Perhaps she is going to rap me on the knuckles for fooling about in her creek. I wait to be dismissed. Glancing away from her while she makes up her mind what to do about me, I see a robin sitting on a nearby gate post. It's looking at me with great interest, as if it too is wondering what to do with a recalcitrant postwoman.

After a long pause Eleanor says, with a long-suffering sigh, 'You'd better come in for a cup of tea. You'll catch a chill, else.'

It is a command not an offer, as is the cup of tea she puts in front of me. She commands me, like a brusque nanny, to drink it while it's hot. I'm wet and cold enough to do so gratefully, looking around at her kitchen as I do so. It is as it should be: a place for everything, and everything in its place. Eleanor, whom I address as Miss Gibland of course, makes tea with loose English Breakfast leaves in a round brown teapot and doesn't ask if I take milk, just pours it into the cup first from a blue-and-white striped jug. As we drink our tea she asks me several pointed questions, such as my marital state, my background and my origins of birth. She wants to make quite sure that Susie's relief postie is of the right sort. I answer without going into too much detail. I am trying hard to be friendly and pleasant, though it's starting to be something of a struggle. Though she's drowning me in tea, she hasn't once smiled.

When I finish my tea she says abruptly, 'Will Susie be back tomorrow?'

I assure her that she will. 'Oh thank goodness for that,' she exclaims, smiling for the first time. It's definitely not a smile for me, though. She's already standing up, snatching my empty cup away.

I leave with a mega sense of failure. The fact that she's known Susie for eighteen years does nothing to stem the tide of inadequacy drowning my modest ambition to be a really good postwoman. *I'm just not cut out for this*, I think sadly as I plod back into the rain. Eighteen years, Susie's been a postwoman. At this point I doubt if I'll stick eighteen days.

As I climb back into my van and set off, I start musing about where I was all those years ago. I didn't even know Ben then, I think as I drive on to the little hamlet down the road. It's hard to remember how it was before I met him. The way we met, though, is unforgettable. Not because it was romantic, but just too bizarre to forget.

I was in London, on a diploma aromatherapy course. Working for a cosmetics firm, having learned about the benefits of various plants and oils not just for cosmetic purposes but also for therapeutic ones, I wanted to learn how to use them for healing and massage.

I'd read the blurb about the course, stating that on the first day there would be background lectures, theory, history and so on. This was fine by me and I came dressed accordingly, wearing a new, casual white tracksuit.

When I got there I felt relieved that I'd worn something fairly flattering. The white of the outfit set off the tan I'd acquired on a recent work related week in Florida. I'd worn my hair down, as we wouldn't be doing practical work, and it tumbled around my shoulders, even blonder than usual because of the sun streaks. There were mostly women on the course, already waiting when I arrived, and a handful of men.

One man caught my eye immediately. Dishy but with an open, intelligent, good-humoured face that I instantly liked. As if he knew I was looking at him, he turned to me and smiled.

I by-passed the others and sat in the chair next to his. 'Hi, I'm Tessa.'

'Ben.'

We eyed each other appraisingly. This was going to be a good course, I thought.

All went well until the lunch break, when our tutor announced that we should choose a partner to do some practical work in the afternoon. Ben turned to me. 'Can we work together?'

I panicked. There was nothing I'd like more but there was a huge problem. I had nothing on under my track suit bottoms. Because they were white and fitted snugly, there was a visible panty line if I wore them, so I did without. How was I to know that we were required to shed our outer garments in the afternoon session, so that we could start working with the aromatherapy oils?

'What's the matter?' Ben looked confused. 'Would you rather work with someone else?'

'No. Uh, no, no, not at all.'

I couldn't explain, not then. He went on, 'Then should we grab a sandwich? We've got a half hour before the practical and there's a café on the corner.'

'No!' I realized I was shouting and toned down my voice. 'I mean, no thanks. I've got a few things to do during the break.' I was thinking fast.

I ran outside. The course was being held in one of those residential parts of London where there wasn't a shop for miles, not the kind that sold women's lingerie anyway, but an ex-boyfriend of mine, Tony, lived only a street away. While I got his number on my mobile, I crossed the fingers of my other hand and prayed that Tony was home. He was.

I explained the problem. Tony, knowing me well, somehow wasn't surprised. 'How can I help, though? You want to borrow a pair of my boxers? They'll be a bit big.' Tony is huge, broad and muscular.

'Not yours. I was thinking of Caro's.' She was his girlfriend and though they didn't live together, I knew she was at his place often.

At last Tony got back to me. 'I found a good stash. You're in luck.' I ran most of the way. Tony was waiting at the door, a pair of white bikini briefs edged with pale blue lace dangling from his little finger.

I got back just as the group was beginning the practice session. Half the class was lying on the special treatment beds, clad in panties and bra, and the other half were being given oils to work with and directions by the tutor.

Ben was waiting for me. I mumbled an apology for being late. 'Should you go first or should I?' he asked.

I didn't mind. I was now chastely covered where it mattered, and would not be disgraced in front of the whole class.

We smiled at each other. I knew that it wouldn't be long before we'd be getting to know each other much, much better, and that I'd be telling him the whole story of my ex-boyfriend's girlfriend's knickers.

* * *

Firmly back in the present, I stop at the hamlet down from Eleanor Gibland's cottage. It is a cluster of six granite and slate houses on a slope overlooking the sea and I park the van where Susie had parked when she was showing me the route, in a rough lay-by at the edge of the narrow track up to the houses. Then I grab my satchel ready to set out, but first I have to sort out the dog biscuits, as this is deep canine country. Susie had given me a list of each dog's requirements. The first two houses have either sheepdogs or mutts that will eat anything, the third one with a yellow door has a cat and no dog, but the last three are tricky. There is the border terrier that will only eat the green biscuits and an odd poodle/bearded collie cross that likes only the bone-shaped yellow ones. As for that last house at the edge of the cluster, there is a black German shepherd dog that will eat anything you throw into the enclosed garden, including posties if you're not careful.

'But not to worry, m'bird,' Susie had said, nodding her sage head. 'He's locked in the garden and the postbox be outside so he can't get to you.'

It starts well enough. The first two houses are silent and closed, the owners either still in bed or not at home. The dogs inside bark but no one comes to look so I put the post inside the front porch of one as I'd been shown and drop the letters for the other into a plastic box with a lid and a rock on top, just outside the door. I put a dog biscuit inside each one, too, so as not to disappoint the dogs. The house with the yellow door and the cat looks empty but there is a proper letterbox in the door and I slot the post in there.

The owner of the border terrier is a sweet, simple sort of woman who wishes me the luck of the Irish in my new job. She doesn't sound at all Irish, and I'm sure I don't either, but I'll accept any luck thrust on me and thank her profusely. We grin happily at each other. Her dog Lily is happy too, sitting down without being told for her green biscuit. I am so impressed I give her two.

'Now that 'twas kind of you, maid, but we mustn't do that. Only one. Lily would get fat, now wouldn't you, me darling,' she chuckles over the dog who is eyeing me hopefully, knowing a sucker when she sees one.

The bearded collie/poodle cross is a bouncy dog that comes bounding out when its owners come to the door: a roly-poly man with his roly-poly wife peering over his shoulder. I'd met them before, with Susie, so we greet each other like old friends and I give their dog his yellow bone-shaped biscuit. Only one this time, though. I've learned my lesson.

The man says, 'Oh poor Blackie.'

His wife tuts behind him, 'Susie always gives him at least two.' Their initial friendliness is turning to disapproval.

'Oh, right. Of course. Here, Blackie, here's another one. Good dog – hey, gentle! OK, good boy.'

'Girl,' comes the chorus from Tweedledee and Tweedledum.

The last house is the one with the German shepherd. By now the fog and rain have cleared and the sky is black and blue with racing storm clouds over the sea. The light is exquisite, one minute a mustard yellow dawn colour, the next dark and shadowy as the clouds clump together. I am feeling jaunty and pleased with myself. Maybe I can do this job after all.

The dog must be inside the house as there is no sign of him in the garden. I don't hear him either and assume he is out with his owner whom I haven't met yet. I put the post in the letterbox outside the gate and am turning to go when there is an almighty racket, barking and howls like a wild beastie, along with more human but petrified shouts and screams.

'Batman, stop! Come back, stop! Here boy, here!'

Batman? I think wildly as I stand frozen to the garden wall. Then there is a roar and a growl as a huge monster of a dog jumps onto my chest and pins me back against the wall, his massive jaw at my throat. I nearly faint with terror.

'Batman, get off! Leave, stop!' The woman, who is as tiny as her dog is huge, is pulling on the beast which refuses to budge. I can smell his rancid breath in my face. I am scared witless.

'Batman!' she screams one last time as he's about to devour me. 'Ham!!'

The dog wilts. Like a pussycat, he daintily disengages his huge paws from my shoulders and meekly sits down at his owner's feet. 'Sorry, be right back, don't go away,' she murmurs as I try to stop hyperventilating. 'I must be givin' 'im his ham now or he won't believe me next time.'

To my horror she scuttles away into the house, leaving me alone with the beast. But he doesn't even glance at me, he's too busy salivating in the direction the woman disappeared.

She comes back with a thick slice of ham as round as a dinner plate. I've collapsed on a large stone in her garden, trying to recover the movement and strength in my limbs that fear has drained away. We both eye the dog as he gulps down the food. When he finishes he lies at her feet and goes to sleep, meek as a lamb.

I'm still in a state so I say, testily, 'I could have had a heart attack there, the way he leapt up at me ready to tear my tongue out.'

'I don't understand,' she says. 'He's never done that before.'

It is the first time I have heard those words but I seem to intuit that it won't be the last. Not just from this woman and this particular dog, but from the owners of countless other yappy, tiny creatures and huge, hulking hounds who think baiting – or eating – the post man or woman is the greatest thrill life has to offer.

Now the woman begins to apologize as I take deep breaths

with one eye still on the dog. Then I take a good look at her. She's not young and she's the tiniest woman I've ever seen. She looks as if a gentle sea breeze would knock her over. What is a woman like this doing with a dog like that? The dog opens an eye and growls, as if he knows what I'm thinking.

The woman knows too, for she says, 'He be my great-grandson's. Eee 'ad him since a pup. Batman stays down-along with me most times, when the lad's over t'Newquay surfing. A great one for the surf, that boy.'

Great-grandson? She might be frail, but she only looks late middle-aged. Maybe they breed young in this rural doggie hamlet, or else there's a fountain of youth tucked somewhere behind one of the creeks.

I give her the biscuit that I'd been clutching in my hand before the attack. 'Here, you can give it to – did you say his name is Batman?'

She looks up at me. Her smile is bigger than the rest of her put together. 'Our lad 'twas only a young sprog when he got the pup. He named it. Sounds a bit daft, I know.'

I'm not so sure. Isn't the original Batman a bit of a tear-away, leaping about giving criminals their due? Maybe this one can't distinguish between criminals and the Royal Mail. He knows his food, though. The biscuit is snapped up and she's lucky a finger didn't go with it.

We say goodbye amicably after she apologizes again for not having Batman locked up in the garden, for she knows he can be 'a bit of a handful'.

'Oh, that's fine, no problem,' I wave merrily as I run back to the van, listening to Batman's renewed barks and howls as he wakes from his slumber and realizes I've dashed away before he can dismember me.

The day continues to be traumatic. As well as the dog, there's a feral cat hiding behind a monstrous spider plant in the front porch of one of the houses I deliver to. 'Just stick any letters under one of the plants; the porch door is never locked,' Susie had told me. She must have forgotten about the cat, or maybe the creature only likes Susie – like Eleanor Gibland, I think ruefully. Maybe cats, dogs and humans all know instinctively I'm just not a proper post person, I muse as I scrabble for a tissue to wipe the blood from my hand. The overfed tabby leapt on me as I lay the post under the plant, scratching my hand badly.

After the cat, I start to relax. I've been attacked by both domestic animals and the chances are low that lightning will strike twice. Besides, I hear no barking as I park the van at the next farmhouse and walk up a gravelly path to the front door. Some sparrows are hopping about at the edge of a puddle but there's no other sign of life.

And then I hear it. It's the weirdest noise, like the gargling of a strange beast. Gurgle, gurgle . . . gobble, gobble . . .

'Help!' I yelp as a mass of feathers, flapping wings and strange gurgling noises flies towards me.

There are more shouts, human ones this time, and the feathered *thing* gets driven back. I've been driven back too, against my van where I'm panting heavily, trying to get my heart beating normally again.

'Yo, m'lover, you be alright, maid? 'Tis only Reginald. Ee be gettin' a bit frisky now and agin, gettin' out'a his pen and all.'

It turns out Reginald is a turkey, being fattened up for the family for Christmas. 'You're . . . you're going to eat Reginald?' I ask, a bit nonplussed that they're going to eat a creature they've named.

'Aye, maid. That un's Reginald the Seventh. Been keepin' our own turkeys fer seven years now. Tastier than any old job-lot bought at the butchers.'

There is only one more trauma, a minor one compared to the others, when the van stalls as I'm driving up a steep incline on a concrete road to a farmhouse and starts to roll backwards. I manage to get it going again and chug slowly up the hill, getting halfway before it stalls again and back down I go.

I try a third time, revving the accelerator and trying to ignore the smell of burnt clutch. Finally at the top, the sight of a tall, skinny man standing at the farm gate staring at me like some raggedy scarecrow causes me to forget to put the handbrake on and as soon as I jump out to give him his post, the van starts to roll backwards again.

'Goin' agin,' he observes.

'I can see that,' I say tightly as I jump back in to put on the brake.

I hand him what look like a couple of bills and a sheaf of adverts. He takes them and grunts. I wave goodbye, striving for a cheery expression. After all, Christmas is next month.

His farewell words follow me down the hill, 'You best get a vehicle that goes forward d'reckly and not back where it came from.' I hear him guffawing at his little joke all the way down to the main road.

The van coughs and splutters on a few more hills but manages to get back to the post office in St Geraint where I leave it at the Royal Mail parking space behind the boat yard. Then I take my bag and anything I couldn't deliver such as registered post where no one was in to sign for it or parcels that didn't fit through a letterbox and there was no dry place to put them, back to the post office.

St Geraint is quite a bit larger than Morranport with its one post office, two pubs and one shop. This is a large village, with several pubs, a couple of hotels and a decent size grocery store. It has at least a half dozen boutique speciality shops selling anything from local crafts to designer clothes, as well as a bank, a chemist and an excellent butcher. There's a Spar shop like none I've ever seen before, selling a vast selection of speciality teas, pasta, different kinds of imported rice as well as a deli section with no less than eight types of olives. All the stores face the seafront and in the centre is an exquisitely beautiful harbour with more million pound yachts per square inch than anywhere else in England.

The post office, though, has nothing luxurious about it. It's tiny and cramped. There are four people in it now and it feels crowded. The shop sells cold drinks, sweets, newspapers, a bit of stationery, and not much else. At the back is the post office counter, where I squeeze in behind the woman already there.

'So, how was your first day?' asks Margaret after she finishes selling stamps to a customer and listening to tales of his lumbago. She's being friendly but I can still hear the smirk in her voice. Is it obvious to everyone what a townie and how unsuitable I am for this job?

I'm a bit wary of Margaret as she seems so frighteningly competent in a pleasant but no-nonsense way.

'Not too bad a day,' I say, fingers crossed behind my back. 'A few cat scratches and Batman, of course.'

She nods, 'Susie warn you about him?'

'Yes, but never mentioned his name. Or the fact that he sometimes escapes from the garden and lies in wait, eager to maim and destroy any postwoman who happens by.'

Margaret shrugs, not even bothering to look up. 'You never know,' she says cryptically. 'You just never ever know.'

I dump my stuff, say goodbye and turn to go, wondering if I can crawl into bed for a good sleep when I get home. I'm cold, wet and slightly traumatized by mad dogs, vicious cats and potentially dangerous vans.

'Oh by the way, Tessa, I've got a message for you,'

Margaret calls me back. 'Customer dropped by just half hour ago and asked me to tell you something.'

'Oh? Who? And what was it?'

'Mrs Grey in the cottages outside Trehallow. You know, the hamlet with Batman and all the dogs. Mrs Grey is the one with the cat. The nice ginger one that is, not the other.'

'Oh, you know about the other? Look at my hand!'

But Margaret is not going to waste good pity on the battle scars of a wimpy new postwoman. 'The house with the yellow door. That's Mrs Grey.'

'I know the one. She wasn't around when I called so I posted her stuff through the letterbox.'

'So she said.'

'Was something wrong?'

'She said to tell that posh postie that the next time she delivers to her, to make sure she comes in the kitchen door and puts the post on top of the fridge, as she's got another kitten now and it's been housetrained to pee on newspapers.'

'But – I don't deliver the newspaper.'

'Doesn't matter. The cat pees on anything that's paper apparently and her letter was soaked when she got home. She was particularly distressed as it was from her sister in Canada.'

Margaret allows herself a grin. It's amazingly like a smirk, 'So remember that, Posh Postie.'

She is still chuckling as I leave the shop. I know without a doubt that the nickname will be in all the sorting offices of the South Cornwall Royal Mail by next morning.

December

It is approaching Christmas with only two weeks to go and I am staggering under the weight of cards, parcels and masses of advertisements. I still hardly know my customers. As a relief postwoman I'm on a different round every day and it's confusing. I can't seem to get the hang of remembering all the hidden lanes, quirky houses and weird letterboxes. I've left post in plastic envelopes under stones, under tyres in garages, under logs in a woodpile, on top of cars and under cars, in makeshift boxes, bags and even a tree house. These are all at the customers' requests – at their insistence, in fact. I can't believe how few houses there are on my rounds that have proper letter slots in their doors or mailboxes outside.

To add to the difficulties, Cornwall has been hit by massive storms and winds, whipping up the sea and toppling trees not prepared to go with the flow and bend. With some folk there's an entirely different set of rules for delivering post when it's wet. The post under the woodpile is to be transferred to a shelf in the shed; the plastic envelope under the stone is, when raining, to be covered with the blue plastic bucket found in the nearest barn. None of this is written down but passed on from old postie to new, like ancient folklore and Cornish myths.

The weather is not exactly conducive to standing outside the front door and chatting to your local post person. Not that anyone seems inclined to chat with me even on the rare days when the weather is decent. Even Eleanor Gibland hasn't asked me in again, nodding only a gruff greeting if she's around when I arrive and saying, sniffingly, 'And where is Susie today? Another day off?'

I'm known now to all and sundry as the Posh Postie, thanks to Mrs Grey with the cat and the newspaper. I'm not sure how to take this, whether it's complimentary or derogatory, and I'm afraid to ask Susie directly. I tried hinting about it, once, and Susie just said, 'You be different, me bird, can't help that. Not a local like me or the other folk in the post office. You can't help looking and talking oddly.'

She gazed at me sorrowfully, not without sympathy, thinking of my disadvantaged life being born and bred Up Country. I could tell she was sure the odds were against my staying on, not just in the new job but also in my new life.

Ben and I have spent months wondering the same thing, as every day brings us new problems. Cornwall is not turning out to be the dream move we'd expected. We have been in our new house in the idyllic village of Treverny now since the beginning of September. Though the asking price was vastly higher than we'd anticipated spending, and the house more dilapidated than any other we'd looked at, we took the plunge and bought it, moving into South Cornwall for good on a glorious day at the beginning of September.

Well, it was glorious when we left London, but by the time we arrived, quite late at night, there was a cold, dreary drizzle which did nothing to dampen our spirits. The movers had come a few days before, Ben shooting down to Treverny to let them in and to put the right beds in the right bedrooms and generally organize the move. When he finished the house was ready for our arrival. That is, as ready as we could make it.

Will and Amy were first through the door. They'd seen the house of course, but weeks before, and didn't remember much except that they'd be living by the sea. For a moment they stopped and stared, looking around at bare walls badly in need of both plaster and paint, at rough uncarpeted floors, and the few pieces of furniture we'd brought, looking forlorn and out of place in this new setting. Being kids and naturally optimistic, they recovered from the minor shock and ran off shouting to find their bedrooms.

Ben and I stood in the living room with our arms around each other, not speaking. 'Well,' I said finally. 'We've done it. Our new home.'

'Hmm.'

Even I, usually the cheery one, couldn't summon up the exuberance I'd felt after we'd finally found our new home. Not then, not at that late hour, with the drizzle turning into rain which was leaking down the side wall of the living room. Yes, we'd loved the house – but it was the house of our imagination, not the one we were standing in. This house was still the battered place used for years as a holiday cottage and a not very salubrious one at that. Not only had it not been modernized for years, but it also felt as if basic loving care had been withheld for the same length of time.

The work would be massive. And we were running out of money which was haemorrhaging away with all the many costs buying and selling entails. So we had decided to move in at once instead of waiting until some fundamental work could be done. The plan was to set up the pottery-painting business and work on the house at the same time, little by little, even if it meant we would be cooking on camp stoves in the courtyard. We were keen and enthusiastic, sure it would all work out.

Now, tired and a bit deflated, I looked around and wondered if Ben had been right all along when he'd voiced all those objections at the beginning. The enormity of what we'd done hit me like that blast of Cornish rain and wind nearly taking off the car door as we parked outside our new home.

We were all too hyper to sleep so I made tea and got out some nibbles. Will and Amy, having found their bedrooms, were now too excited to go into them. 'When can we go to the beach, Mum?' they shouted and 'Dad, are you going to take us snorkling tomorrow?'

We hedged, citing the bad weather, but Amy said, 'The rain's stopped!' Flinging open the front door, she called us to look.

Sure enough, as if by magic, the rain had not only stopped but the sky was clear, dotted only with stars and a miraculous full moon which turned the wet grass into thousands of sparkling diamonds. Jake, who'd been patiently sitting waiting for nibbles of his own, took advantage of the open door and leapt outside, barking his head off at the moon and no doubt waking all our new neighbours. Ben shushed him and got him in, as Amy said, 'Poor dog, sitting in the car all that long way.'

Without thinking I said, 'We'll go walk him on the beach. Right now!'

Ben looked at me and rolled his eyes. 'It's late. The kids are overtired as it is. It's been raining.'

'But it's not now, it's a beautiful night. So quiet and still.'

'Except for Jake,' Will shrieked as he and Amy fell about laughing.

'See?' I said. 'They're hysterical. A quick walk on the beach will calm them and Jake too.'

And us, I thought as we drove the short mile to Penwarren, the nearest beach – our beach now, a secluded sandy cove edged within a framework of rock pools and sheltered by cliffs. We drove the car down the narrow, windy road that leads straight onto the hard sand where we all tumbled out and began running up and down, shrieking with the relief of letting out all the delays, frustrations and stress of the past few months.

As Jake jumped in the water and the kids played games trying to avoid the small waves that splashed on the shore, Ben and I watched, our arms around each other. 'You see?' I said smugly. 'You see how *right* this move is? Even the Cornish moon is shining on us. It's an omen.'

Before I'd even finished speaking a sudden cold gust of wind came up like a demon from the sea, driving a fierce black cloud clear across that fickle moon and sending a shower of icy rain over all of us.

Running back to the car and already soaking wet, Ben muttered, 'Yeah, an omen. Great.'

Of all the things I'd imagined I might do when we moved to Cornwall, being a postwoman was certainly not one of them. I'm finding it all a bit of a struggle. Maybe pre-Christmas, the very busiest time for post office workers, wasn't the most brilliant time to start this job. But I had no choice. If this doesn't work out, I don't know what we'll do, we've tried everything else. Ben, for the first time ever, voiced what I'd been secretly thinking and dreading: the possibility that we might be forced to move back to London. He's as upset as I am about it. Despite his early reservations, he too is committed to finding a new happier life here. *Forget all that now,* I tell myself sternly. *You've got a job now at last, so quit brooding and get on with it.*

I concentrate on filling my huge Royal Mail bag with as much as I can carry. The post office in St Geraint is on the main street and I usually do one side of the village then come back to fill up for the other. However, there is *tons* of mail today. In December all the holiday brochures come out, as well as the gardening magazines so folk can start thinking about ordering bulbs. And of course not only are there Christmas cards but an inordinate amount of parcels all sizes and shapes, mostly from abroad: Australia, Canada and New Zealand, from Poland and Ukraine, Italy, France and even a huge one from China. All those folk not able to be with their loved ones this Christmas, I think sadly, but wanting there to be something for them to open on Christmas Day.

I ask Margaret if there is some kind of trolley to carry it all. She shakes her head, shrugs, and says something to the effect that there was but she thinks the wheel has come off and it's been stowed away somewhere. I don't pursue it as the post office has just opened and there is a queue of people waiting to buy stamps as this is the last posting day for overseas. Margaret, like everyone else, is working flat out.

I wonder what to do. It's already nine o'clock. Ordinarily I'd have finished this part much earlier but nothing is ordinary in the Royal Mail in these chaotic weeks before Christmas. I'll just have to fill my bag with as much as I can carry, then double back to get the rest. A nuisance, and tiring, and time-consuming, but it'll have to do.

Outside, it's finally a perfect winter's day. Cold, but windless and cloudless. St Geraint faces an estuary with a border of sea on one side and river on the other. The sky is brimming with tiny, fluffy clouds that obscure the sun for just a moment or two and the sea is that deep winter's blue that occurs when the sun hangs low in the sky all day.

The light in this place is amazing. The few clouds that breeze over the sun now and again make extraordinary shadows that ripple darkly across the aquamarine water then disappear, leaving the sea dazzling once again. Even on grey days, the vast expanse of sea and sky give a pale luminous light to everything that makes me catch my breath whenever I stop and look.

I'm doing that now, drinking it all in on this incredible winter's day: the fresh clean smell of salt and marsh, the sharp clear sky, the flecks of sunlight on water. As I walk along the main street of the town, which rolls along the seafront like a lazy sleeping snake, I smile a greeting at the shopkeepers as they open up. I pass the tiny chemist's, an old-fashioned clothing shop next to a smart boutique (both popular, which shows the diversity of the place), and several coffee shops. There's a very expensive art gallery as well as odd little places that sell local crafts.

I do a little skip as I walk – surreptitiously of course – for no other reason than it's not raining. The skip is a mistake. I trip over an uneven pavement, the heavy weight of my bag causing me to lose my balance so that I end up sitting ignominiously on the curb.

Lulu, the gorgeous young girl who works in the Spar, calls out, 'You OK, Mrs Posh Post Lady?'

'You can call me Tessa,' I say to her, not for the first time, but she seems to like giving me the full title. Where she heard my nickname, I have no idea. It seems to be spreading everywhere. Susie said, when I asked her, 'Word travels, bird. Glamorous new blonde, straight from Up Country.'

'Oh Susie, give us a break. Look at me. Glamorous? In this get-up?' I looked down at my shapeless uniform and Doc Martens boots.

She'd shrugged enigmatically. 'Well, whatever, but may as well get used to it, bird, word travels quicker than an eel round here. Folk heard all about you before they even set eyes on you.'

Posh is the last thing I'm feeling now as I struggle to maintain some shred of dignity and straighten my post bag. Lulu says, 'Mrs Posh Post Lady, let me help with bag. Ohhh, it is greatly heavy. It is magnificently heavy.'

'Sorry?'

'Maag-nee-feee-sont-lee,' she repeats, taking my bag, beaming at her use of a new word. 'Lulu like big new English words. Maaag-nee-feee-sont-ly. Wonderful.'

'Lulu's not really your name, is it?' I've been dying to ask her this for ages.

'Oh, no. It name I am loving. Lulu,' she sighs in delight. 'My birthday name too hard for English person to speak it without falling on top of his tongue.'

Lulu has not been here long and is staying with married cousins from her own country. She didn't know a word of English when she came over but she's picked it up fast.

I take the post bag from her. Lulu says, 'Oh, this be heavy. You be needing one of they I think.'

Oh Lord, she's learning English in a Cornish dialect. 'Needing one of what, Lulu?'

She grabs one of the small supermarket trolleys from the door of the Spar. 'Take! For borrowing. You bring back later, OK?'

It's a brilliant idea. I grab the trolley, throw my bag in, and I'm away. Pushing my supermarket trolley laden with post, I find I am smiling at people and they at me. The sun is actually shining today and it's amazing what a bit of dry weather does for this job. I'm feeling positively jaunty as I saunter up the road pushing my Christmas load. Leaving the trolley at the bottom of the steps up to one of the biggest houses in the village, I grab my post bag and lug it up to the front door. This road leading out of St Geraint has been nicknamed Millionaire's Row by the locals. The houses are huge and opulent, all facing the sea but with massive lawns and gardens on the slopes in front so that they cannot be seen by the likes of us commoners. The locals have nothing against millionaires, it's just that many of these houses are empty, holiday homes for the extremely wealthy, sometimes used no more than one or two weekends a year. Not long ago a helicopter circled one of them at the very edge of the sea, set in a secluded, private woodland. The place had just come onto the market. There was one passenger in the private helicopter. He took a quick aerial view and bought the property. There were rumours that he was a pop star or even royalty, for we have that here too, but it turned out he was yet another businessman looking for a second home to buy with his Christmas bonus.

It saddens me as much as it does the locals, for it's not just happening on Millionaire's Row. So many villages, especially near the sea, are filled with cottages of every size, modest as well as massive, that are empty all winter and only come alive in the summer months. I talk about this with Susie who is quite bitter, as are many other Cornish people. Susie's own two nieces, one a teacher and the other a dental assistant, can't afford to buy even a modest home in the county where they grew up. They're looking elsewhere for jobs, Susie tells me. Two more bright and talented young people leaving Cornwall. I don't say much when people discuss this, for I'm fully aware that I'm not local either.

'But you live here,' Susie said once, when she saw I had withdrawn from a conversation the other posties were having about the second-home owners. 'That's different, Tessa. You've moved here permanently.' Her words give me comfort. Maybe one day I'll be accepted by the Cornish, that they'll realize our real life is here now, not Up Country. We're not pretending to be part of this community – we really are, really want to be.

As I trudge up the steep steps of the houses on Millionaire's Row lugging my heavy bag, I think, *I'm too unfit for this.* At the farthest house on top of a particularly high slope, I'm exhausted by the time I climb to the top of the elegant, stone steps. It's a magnificent house on the hill with a stunning view, but the steps go on and on; they're a killer and too awkward to attempt with a trolley. The house has a letterbox on the road, a very large, smart one, and my first few days on this round were made so much easier by that postbox. But yesterday Margaret got a phone call from the owner, who is in Cornwall till after Christmas this year, saying that while she is in residence she wants her post delivered to the house.

So here I am at the top of the steps, panting and red faced after the exertion of the uphill slog carrying a heavy bag. The house looks unlived in and there is no letter slot in the door, nowhere to put the post. Though it is a dry day, there is a strong breeze and the weather changes from minute to minute around here. I can't risk leaving it somewhere to get wet or blown away. There is nothing for it but to ring the bell.

It's a good five minutes before someone comes to the door. I have rung a second time and am now about to leave the post under a terracotta pot with a miniature palm tree in it. If it rains, it can't be helped. There is a perfectly good letterbox at the bottom of all those steps.

The door swings open. A woman who can't be more than forty, dressed in designer clothes most of us can only dream about, is standing there looking irritated. 'Yes?'

I am a little taken aback. I'd expected someone elderly or infirm, someone unable to go down and up those endless steps for their mail every day, but this woman looks fitter than I do.

'Your post,' I say in my friendliest voice. After all, it's nearly Christmas and this is Millionaire's Row.

She takes it from me, gives it a cursory glance and says, 'Not worth the paper it's written on.'

Then she shuts the door in my face and that's that. *At least she didn't slam it,* I think as I practically fly down those hellish steps in a fury. *What's wrong with a quick thank you?* I'm shouting in my head *And what's wrong with your letterbox? Do you think that we posties are your servants? And shame on you if that's how you treat your servants anyway.*

At the bottom of the steps, reunited with my trolley, I take deep breaths and pause, standing in front of the low, wooden fence that separates the road from the beach. The water is striped with bands of indigo blue, turquoise, grey and black. The sun is dancing in and out of the clouds, creating a rainbow of colour on the water. Jutting out around the estuary on the left is woodland and I notice the trees, stripped of their leaves, are a rich, silvery brown. I can see fields too, rolling ones, still green and lush. There's a cove in front of the woodland with small boats moored and further out I can see the shapes of tankers, cruise ships and the ferry that crosses the river several times a day, taking passengers to other towns. On my right is the harbour, small, nestling and peaceful and in front, the sandy beach. A heron is standing at the water's edge between shore and woodland. As I watch, a cormorant skims over the sea.

I lean against my trolley and my mind calms. I have this every day of the year, I think, and that other woman for only two or three weeks. No one else sees her house for the other eleven months except the cleaner and gardener who come once a week. But me – I live here. I work here, as Susie has reassured me. My load suddenly feels lighter, the job easier.

I work here. How positive that sounds, and how Ben and I despaired of ever hearing ourselves say that.

Thank goodness it was different for the children. Will and

Amy have made the transition from urban kids to rural ones with the ease and resilience of the young. They love their new school, made friends quickly and easily, and the village is a delight, especially their own playground right opposite our house where they and their friends congregate after school to play. It hasn't been so easy for us.

We knew from the first day that things weren't going to be as rosy as we'd hoped, when we realized that the kitchen was in too sorry a state to patch up and would have to be completely redone. The cost was way above any of our estimates, so we had to plunge straight into our new business venture, the paint-your-own-pottery scheme, before we had intended.

It was obvious within weeks that the business wasn't going to work, that it was a daft idea for Cornwall. It was the children of the affluent middle classes, usually living in cities, who were clamouring for this kind of entertainment and artistic endeavour and a disaster for Cornwall, one of the poorest counties in England in that wages are lower here than anywhere else. We learned soon enough that Cornish parents were in general too strapped for cash to spend on such an extravagance as painting your own pottery. Especially as, ironically, there are probably more genuine potters in the county per head of population than anywhere else in England. And who needs to find entertainment for their kids when there's the sea and the countryside?

Despite all our intricate business plans, we'd not thought of these basic considerations. There was nothing for it but to drop our initial plan at once, before we plunged deeper into debt. Taking stock of our finances one evening, we were appalled to see how quickly our savings were draining away. We needed an income badly. The house was, as houses do, costing far more than we'd allotted for it to renovate, not to mention to buy in the first place. Then a plumber doing routine fixtures found the whole system corroded and needing replacement. Something similar happened when the electrician arrived for some minor work and we had to shut the power off at once as the wires hidden behind walls had been gnawed at by generations of mice. It was a wonder we hadn't been burned in our beds.

And so we started pouring over the local newspapers, looking at job adverts. At first we were optimistic because we were willing to take on anything reasonable. But then, after applying for quite a few – receptionist, secretary, taxi driver and super-market assistant manager were just a handful – we discovered that each job had dozens of applicants (unemployment is high in Cornwall and jobs scarce) and we were overqualified for nearly every job we applied for.

After this unexpected blow, we sat down again to try to think of something – anything – we could do to bring in an income. Luckily, Ben had a qualification we hadn't yet tried to make money from, something that we'd hoped to use in the future. Now, however, was the time. We were desperate.

Unlike me, Ben had completed the aromatherapy course that began the day we met and he had a valid massage diploma. He could offer his services not to the locals, most of whom could not afford them, but to the hotels that catered for the better-off visitors to the area.

The prime hotel nearby is the world famous Roswinnick, overlooking the estuary and sea in a prime spot in St Geraint. For several years now, the very rich and often the very famous find their way here for a weekend or week. Rock stars mix with royalty and wealthy Russian businessmen nod to their British counterparts in the exquisite dining room over the breakfast tables. They would be the perfect kind of customer, prepared to spend an enormous chunk of money to relax, de-stress and detox while enjoying stunning views and luxurious surroundings. So after an interview with the hotel manager (and a freebie massage for him), aromatherapy massage was added to the hotel's list of available services and Ben got his first call a week or so later.

I met him at the door when he came home, practically knocking him over in my eagerness to hear how the first session went. 'I hope it was a rich Eastern European princess who was so thrilled by your exquisite application of healing oils and massage that she gave you a huge tip well above your hourly rate,' I babbled as I dragged him inside to tell me all.

'Hardly,' He shook his head. 'She was an overweight, middle-aged sex worker from Manchester who'd won a packet on the lottery.'

I stared at him. 'You're joking, aren't you?'

'No.'

'Be serious. No one would admit to being a prostitute, lottery winner or not.'

'She never said she was a prostitute. Just said a sex worker.'

'She *told* you? She actually said it? I can't believe I'm hearing this.'

Ben began to grin. 'I couldn't believe what I'd heard either. I was half way through her treatment, getting on fine, I thought. She seemed to be relaxing though she didn't stop talking. That's how I knew about her lottery win.'

'And her line of work?'

'No, that came later. Suddenly she sat up and said, "Let's get to the nitty gritty now. Show me what you can do."'

'*What*?' I stared at him.

His grin was getting wider. He was certainly enjoying the telling. 'It turned out she thought aromatherapy massage was a euphemism for, well, the sex trade. Seems she advertises herself as a masseuse as well, back home.'

'So she wanted you to perform on her now that she could afford to be the client? I hope you walked right out.'

Ben laughed. 'She only wanted to learn some new tricks, she said. For when she's spent all her lottery money and has to go back to work. She's blowing it on travelling and has always wanted to go to Cornwall, so she started here first.'

'But if she's on holiday, why . . . ?' I trailed off, speechless for once.

'Why bring her work into it? I asked her that too. She said that while she was here, she thought she'd see what her Cornish colleagues are up to.'

I began to giggle. 'Was she disappointed when you explained what aromatherapy massage was?'

'She felt sorry for me. Said I probably made far less money than she did, and would I like *her* to teach *me* some good tricks to increase my trade.'

By this time we were both giggling so hard that Will and Amy had stopped playing in the courtyard and come inside to see what the hilarity was all about. 'Not for your ears, you two,' I said and shooed them back outside.

'How did you refuse her offer?' I narrowed my eyes at him, mock stern. 'You did, I hope.'

'I was very polite. So was she, actually. I finished the aromatherapy session and we ended up best of friends, though I'm sure she thought I was a sad no-hoper for not wanting to expand my business into the sex trade.'

Ben had no more clients quite like that again but he did have another unsettling experience at the Roswinnick. A few weeks later, he walked into a guest's hotel room and there, waiting for a massage, was an actor Ben had once worked with in London.

'It was so embarrassing,' he told me later, 'for both of us. Michael hadn't a clue that I'd moved to Cornwall; we'd lost touch ages ago.'

'What did he say? What did *you* say?'

'First neither of us could think of a thing, then we both started talking at once. Then there was another awkward silence until Michael started going on about what a coincidence it was to meet in such circumstances. I nodded my agreement and suddenly he looked stricken and started to say how sorry he was to . . .'

'To what? Go on, Ben.'

'Nothing. He just trailed off. I think he was going to say how sorry he was to see me reduced to living in Cornwall, doing what I was doing. Michael's the kind of guy that thinks anywhere other than London is unspeakable.'

Ben grew quiet after he told me this. I knew it had affected him, this chance meeting. I said, 'It must have been awkward.'

'It was, a bit. I asked him if he still wanted the massage and I could tell he didn't, that it would be embarrassing for him, but he insisted anyway. He didn't relax at all during it, though he'd said he needed to unwind, that's why he was in Cornwall for a few days. He's got the main role in a West End revival of a Pinter play.'

Ben was far away, no doubt thinking of the theatre and his acting days. They must have seemed very far away and unobtainable at that moment, especially as he had received a 'Dear John' letter from his London agent soon after we'd moved. Because he now lived in Cornwall, the agent regretfully could no longer keep him on the books.

'Horrid for you, Ben,' I said quietly.

He focused back on me. 'The worst of it all was that he gave me a huge tip. Far too much. That was the most embarrassing part.'

Ben carried on with the aromatherapy work but it didn't come often enough to pay our way in Cornwall. He managed to get a part-time job in a coffee shop in St Geraint, but the wage was low and the hours too few, so he was still looking for yet more work. Like most Cornish people, we were beginning to realize that to survive economically, sometimes it was necessary to have four or even five part-time jobs.

I desperately needed to find a job of my own. If Ben and I both worked, we might just manage to keep our heads above water. But I was beginning to despair as I was turned down by a supermarket in Truro (overqualified for a job as cashier); a dental assistant (no experience); and a waitress at a smart Italian restaurant (no experience, overqualified and also not Italian, or Italian-looking anyway).

Meanwhile our expenses were mounting. The water leaking through one of the outer walls that we'd seen on our first night in the new house turned out to be a sign of a crack in the bricks that needed professional mending. There was always something – except jobs. We were learning the hard way just how impoverished Cornwall still is, how hard it is to find work, to live.

Our golden dream was slowly turning to dust as we worried ourselves sick night after night. By this time we didn't even know if we could afford to move back to London, where we could at least find work. A move costs money and that was something we no longer had. As each job possibility fell through and our financial state grew increasingly dire with our debts mounting, we began to seriously despair.

Then, miraculously, I overheard a conversation which probably saved our lives – our lives in Cornwall, that is. It was afternoon on a balmy, early autumn day and I was waiting to pick up Will and Amy from the village school. As usual, a gaggle of mums sprinkled with a few dads were chattering as if they'd known each other for years, as they had, of course. And as I hadn't. I knew it had only been a couple of months since we'd moved to the village, compared to the lifetimes the others had lived here, but there were days when I felt as if I were not merely someone from Up Country but a creature from another universe. It's not that people were deliberately unfriendly, for they were all scrupulously polite to me, but nevertheless I got the feeling that they saw me as one who was definitely not on their planet and never would be. Luckily Will and Amy were fine, having merged, as children can do, seamlessly into school and village life. I liked the Cornish – we wouldn't have moved if we hadn't – but I was beginning to wonder if they really, truly, deep down would ever accept me, or Ben, or anyone who was not Cornish.

I felt it today as I greeted the other parents. Not wanting to be pushy and barge in on their conversations, I hovered around the edges. And that's when I heard the following:

'Did you know Ryan is giving up his job as relief postman?' this was from a short, exceedingly plump redheaded woman.

'No, really? He's only had the work these six months. Why?' The redhead's confidante was a vivacious young woman with hair in a long brown plait. She didn't look old enough to be anyone's mother but she had a baby in a pram with her.

'Bad hip, needs an operation. Said it wasn't his thing anyhow.'

'Shame. He's looking so much better since he got that job.'

'Too right. Lost tons of weight. He was getting right fat, sorry to say, but never would diet,' the redhead snorted disapprovingly for this lack of self discipline. 'All that weight'll go right back on now, you wait and see.'

They both looked grim, thinking no doubt of poor Ryan getting right fat again since quitting his job.

The redhead said, 'Means another postman coming again. Have to lock up Harriet. She eats postmen.'

I hoped Harriet was a dog and not some kind of Cornish carnivore I'd not read about yet. By now I was listening unashamedly.

The young mother tucked the baby's blanket tighter around her legs. 'Harriet's a right troublesome thing. Oh look, there she be now, the naughty beast.'

I looked down the path in the direction they were pointing expecting to see the Hound of the Baskervilles. Instead, a tiny Jack Russell terrier trotted into view. The redhead said, 'Harriet, you wicked dog, got out'a the shed again.' She held her affectionately by the scruff of her neck as the young mother went on talking.

'But not to worry, Ryan be around for a fortnight. New postie not hired yet. Margaret at the post office told me applications out now.'

I couldn't sleep that night. A postwoman, me? It was the most ludicrous idea I'd ever had in my overworked head and I've had some humdingers. Yet something had clicked when I heard that conversation. The pros and cons darted in and out of my brain like tiny arrows.

I was not a morning person. I could hardly bear to look at my beloved family first thing in the morning so how would I face strangers? I was not a physical person, not job-wise. I wasn't that fit and I knew post people did loads of walking, up and down hills. I'd never be able to do a job like that. But it was a job. A vacancy at any rate. A steady income, which could mean the difference between staying in Cornwall or whimpering back to London, broke, shame-faced and disillusioned.

I started to get excited. The timing was right too. I knew post people started early and usually finished around midday or shortly afterwards. We'd already had our first stroke of luck employment-wise – Ben had just got the role of Captain Hook in *Peter Pan*, the forthcoming pantomime at the theatre in Truro. He could get the kids up, breakfasted and to school before he had to go off for rehearsals and I could be home in time to pick them up.

In the midst of my excitement I started to despair. There had been so many jobs I'd applied for and none of them had materialized. Why should this be different? But maybe our luck was changing, first with Ben's acting job, now with this. Though the pantomime would get us through the next few months, the future was still bleak unless one of us, preferably both, found full-time employment.

The next morning I was at the St Geraint post office at nine o'clock. Margaret was at her usual place behind the counter. I knew her vaguely from buying stamps and other sundry post office business. I told her I'd heard there was a vacancy for a post deliverer and asked if she had application forms.

'You?' she stared at me incredulously and with more than a hint of suspicion.

'Yes, me,' I retorted. I hardly knew the woman; we'd barely exchanged any words except about the weather and here she was looking at me as if I'd said I wanted a job as a lap dancer.

'You want to deliver post?'

'Is there a problem?'

'Uh, no, no,' she slid an application form through the counter window. 'You'll need to take a written exam first. In Truro.' She said it triumphantly, as if the whole exam would be in the Cornish language and that would show me for being so pushy and presumptuous.

An exam? Written? The last test I'd taken had been for a driving licence when I was seventeen. What if I failed even before the interview stage? I'm sure she smirked as I took the application, folded it carefully and slipped it into my bag.

I didn't tell anyone, even Ben. I couldn't. For a start, we had been so positive when we'd started looking for work, so sure a job would be easy to find. We'd had so many disappointments, I didn't want to trouble him with yet another and what if I failed the exam? However the day came and I passed the first hurdle, the written test, which was basically no more than to see if I could read English, match up post codes, and work out times so that I could fill in my time sheet correctly.

When I was called for an interview, I finally told my family. There were howls of disbelief and laughter. 'Mum, you'll have to be outside all the time,' Amy said.

'I love being outside.'

'When it's nice. You hate the rain. And wind drives you crazy. And you're always cold in winter,' this was Will.

Ben asked, 'Do you really want to do this, Tessa?'

'Why not? It'll be fun!' I was trying to convince myself.

'You'll never stick it. It's not your scene.'

'I'll probably not get it anyway.'

'Probably not.'

I'll show him, I thought. *I'll show them all.*

The day of the interview finally arrived. I dressed soberly but not formally in a longish skirt, boots and a roll-neck pullover. My family, still disbelieving I could ever go through with this, nonetheless wished me luck and off I went back to Truro, wondering how many candidates I'd be up against and how experienced they were.

As I waited, my confidence began to ebb. Why on earth did I think that anyone would find me right for this job? No one else in Cornwall seemed to feel I'd be right for any kind of job, judging from the last few months. I was making a fool of myself even applying. No wonder Margaret had smirked when she gave me the application. Even the smartly dressed receptionist at the postal centre seemed to be smirking at me behind her computer as I waited for my interview.

I nearly left. I worked myself into such a dejected state that I was considering walking away before the interview when an older man in a suit and red tie called me into his office.

He didn't ask many questions, just the usual ones about work experience to begin with. I tried to make my executive job sound relevant to the Royal Mail but I saw him shake his head in disbelief as I spoke.

Then he asked the inevitable, 'Why exactly do you want this job, young woman?'

He sounded so stern that I couldn't think for a moment what to say. And then it came out. 'Because I'm desperate. Because we've just moved here and we love it and want to stay and I can't seem to get a job anywhere.'

There, I thought, *I've blown it*.

He looked at me thoughtfully then smiled. 'Fine. The job's yours.'

I froze. I couldn't smile back, couldn't move, couldn't think or speak. Finally I began to burble my thanks which he waved away with his hand. He came around from behind his desk and shook my hand.

'Sally my secretary will give you all the details, forms to fill in, when to start and so on.'

I thanked him again. But as I walked out I couldn't help asking. 'Why me? Sorry if I'm speaking out of turn but I can't help being curious. Why, out of all the candidates, did you choose me?'

He gave a small, embarrassed shrug. 'My dear, there weren't any other applicants. Five others were scheduled for interview, but you were the only one who showed up.'

There was euphoria in our home for days. I had a job, a permanent one. Ben also had work, work he loved in the theatre, and though it was temporary, maybe something else would come up in one of the rep companies. If not, at least with my job, he could look for something else without feeling frantic and stressed.

After the euphoria came the doubts, naturally enough. Could I do the job? It would require a lot of physical stamina that I wasn't sure I had. My friends in London never thought I'd last till Christmas. Annie, one of my dearest friends, hooted with laughter down the phone when I told her the news. 'Darling, I've known you forever. It's just not *you* for goodness sake. I give you a month before you come to your senses.'

Though he didn't say it, I think Ben thought the same, though once I got the job he encouraged me in every way, never letting on his doubts.

Now it is Christmas Eve and I have made it up to the cut-off point that was predicted for me. It has not been a great fortnight and there is a part of me that wants to go with the flow of predictions and simply quit the job. If we weren't so strapped for cash I probably would.

I have my own round now. Ten days ago Reg had to leave suddenly because of back trouble and I was given his round. He's not coming back, so a new relief post person will have to be found. Luckily I know his route quite well, already having done it when he was off for nearly a month.

Today I am in the van. It is sleeting, though it shouldn't last long, it never usually does in these parts. I have several rural deliveries to make, at farmhouses or isolated homes which were once thriving farms or workmen's cottages. I'm tired today. Too many late nights with some London friends who have been visiting for a few days. Hard as it is to combine this job with any kind of social life, I've enjoyed their company.

These dark cold wet mornings are beginning to get to me even when I go to bed early, which I do most nights. In fact the children and I go to bed at the same time. I wake at

4.30 a.m., sneaking quietly out of the bedroom so as not to wake Ben who is now busy every night with the pantomime.

My clothes are all the Royal Mail uniform so I don't have any problem deciding what to wear. Everything is ready and waiting for me in the kitchen where I wash and dress as silently as I can. I can't even use the bathroom as it is too close to my sleeping family in the bedrooms. There's no mirror here so I tidy my unruly hair using my reflection on the back of a soup spoon. Even Jake, from his basket bed in the corner, ignores me now, looking at me with one eye then going back to sleep. He knows he doesn't get his run outside until Ben is up with the children. All I have to remember is clean underwear which I slip on in the bedroom before rushing out to jump into my uniform. Will and Amy have made up a song which they sing when I'm getting my clothes ready for the morning:

> Postman Tess, postman Tess,
> Wears her own pants, socks and vest . . .

It's sung to the tune of Postman Pat, of course, and it sticks in my mind going round and round in my head as I dress.

I drive my car to the post office car park in St Geraint and pick up my van, glad I'm not driving to Truro. I only have to go there when I'm on the driving round, and today I'll be doing the walking one in Morranport. The van is behind the old boat yard, not a very salubrious place at 5.30 in the morning when it is dark and creepy, the old boat house creaking in the wind. It's a good thing I don't scare easily. These midwinter mornings there is a howling in the air that blows rain in from the sea and a kind of throbbing, pulsing rhythm to both land and sea which is eerie and almost primeval. I look across the estuary towards the river and the sea beyond, and can almost see those Celtic tribes arriving in their boats to conquer the Bronze

Age settlements on the peninsula. I feel as if I'm losing myself in time, slipping back a few thousand years and I lean against the van for a moment to steady myself. My cheeks are burning and feverish from the wretched cold I've had for days.

I force my tired, aching body into the van and begin the day. After collecting the post at St Geraint I drive to Morranport. The tiny square wooden post office stands on its own at the sea's edge. When the tide is in, it looks as though it too is bobbing in the sea, just like the boats moored in the small harbour. Right now the tide is out and the assorted rowboats, small yachts and dinghies are dotted along the wet sand, nestled into the seaweed like exotic sea creatures. Once these were sturdy fishing boats but now there are no fishermen in Morranport, their cottages transformed into B&Bs and holiday homes. Small seabirds are hopping their way around the stranded boats, sometimes flying away in a rush when the larger gulls come in to land and to bully.

Nell is there already though it's long before opening time. She spends more time here than she does at home. She is plucky and robust, with great breasts as magnificent as any ship's prow, and she's been working here at Morranport off and on for years, stepping in for the owners who travel extensively. Others have sometimes held the job when Nell gives up for a time, but now she's back.

Nell is small-boned and not very tall, with slender hips and shoulders, and skinny legs, all of which makes her grand, full bosom seem even more prominent. She reminds me of a plucky bantam hen.

'I've seen more than one retired major or ex-diplomat from Up Country be givin' Nell the old come-on when the wife's not been looking, though Nell don't give 'em a thing back,' Susie told me after she'd introduced us. 'And more than a fair few locals,' Susie had winked knowingly.

I'm sure some of those old badgers tried it on with her too, for Susie's a pretty woman in her mid-forties and a flirtatious one too. She's never married, but she's never without a boyfriend, or so Reg tells me. I think Reg would like a go himself, confirmed bachelor though he claims to be.

But now I'm asking Susie about Nell. 'Isn't she married?'

'Widow some twenty-odd years.'

Today Nell is wearing brown cord trousers and a white mohair turtle-neck jumper which shows off her bosom to advantage and matches her snow white hair which frizzes messily around her wrinkled face. Instead of looking unkempt, it makes this octogenarian look trendy.

'Morning, Tessa. All right, me handsome?'

'Just fine, Nell, and you?' I sidle by her to where the post is stacked.

She sighs. 'I be poorly.'

I look at her. She looks ruddy and healthier than most women half her age. 'What is it?'

'Feeling rheumaticy these days,' she stares out of the window at the sea. The light half-sleet, half-rain is falling and dissolving into the waves which look black and unfriendly.

'Sorry to hear it.'

She turns and looks me sternly in the eye. ''Tis too much for me now, this job. After Christmas I be off. Retiring. 'Bout time, you be saying.'

I know Nell enough now to realize she's not accusing me; it's just her way of talking. 'Don't be daft, Nell. You run this place like a sea captain runs his ship.'

'Be that as it may. I be poorly. Some younger bloke or maid can take over come January.'

She looks so determined, standing there with her frizzy hair, chin up and bosom heaving. Poorly she does not. But what do I know? She could be in agony with her rheumatics.

I'm sorry she's leaving, though. I've not known her long, but I've grown to like her in this short time. She's feisty, honest and fun.

'I'm sorry, Nell, that you're not well, and that you'll be going. But if that's what you want to do, fair enough.'

She narrows her eyes at me. They are deep green, like the sea in autumn or early spring when the sun comes out briefly but the air is still bitterly cold. ''Tain't what I be wanting, 'tis what must be. You'll be saying I be a quitter now.'

I have to smile at this, it's so outlandish. 'Nell, that's the last thing anyone would say about you and you know it.'

She snorts. ''Tis enough talkin' 'bout me. Now let's be getting back to work. Got the parcels? Oh, and there's another in the fridge.'

'The fridge?'

'Aye. You be thinking I should of put it in the freezer, but 'twould be foolish as you'll be delivering it today.'

I stare at her snowy mohair back while she rummages in the big shop fridge. 'Nell, I'm not thinking anything. I don't know what you're talking about.'

She turns and thrusts a large, damp, limp parcel into my arms. I shriek and nearly drop it. 'Yiii . . . iiikes! What the devil is it? Feels like dead flesh. Yuck.'

'Dead fish. Same sort o' thing. 'Tis the sea bass.'

'What?'

'From old Joe Yeovil. His mum's the one looking after the great-grandson's dog.'

'Oh, the one with the vicious dog with the daft name, Batman.' Much to my discomfort, the little hamlet with all the dogs and the feral cat is now on my regular beat, not Susie's, after some minor route changes have been made by the post office.

'Aye? Daft name, you say? I think it be a good name meself.

66

And *I* never had no problem with Batman.' She plants her feet firmly apart and looks ready to debate the issue all day. Solidarity amongst the Cornish is a frightening thing to be up against.

'Never mind the dog's name, Nell. Why is her son sending her a frozen fish?'

'Not frozen, fresh. Wouldn't of put it in fridge if it was frozen but in freezer. Had it come the weekend mebbe I'd of put it in freezer instead of fridge. Keep 'im fresher in freezer than fridge, if you know what I mean.'

'Yes, well, sort of. So why does he send a fresh fish by post when she lives so near the sea?'

She looked at me as if I were the dotty one. Maybe I was. Maybe I was missing something here. Finally she said, slowly as if explaining to a dunce, 'He be a fisherman.'

'Well, couldn't he just give it to her?'

Now Nell sighed, a great sigh that shook her bosom and made the waves behind the post office quiver. 'He be living at other side of county. 'Tis easier and cheaper to post than to drive it clear across Cornwall.'

The fish, wrapped in slimy plastic and soggy brown paper, was oozing seawater and fishy secretions down my arms and onto my uniform. It was also smelling a bit, well, fishy. Nell, noticing, said, 'Better get on then, afore he goes off.'

I went out of my way to deliver the fish first, which meant picking up the van again. Batman luckily was locked inside the house, his owner out, so I left the fish in the garden shed, as Nell had told me. 'She'll find it, don't fret; she knows it's coming and twill be looking every day for it.'

The roads are slippery now, wet rather than icy, thank goodness. I drive out to my first drop, a tiny village with a stunning view overlooking the sea. It has a pub that doesn't seem very welcoming but then again I only see it in the morning.

I slow down near the 13th century church which, unlike the

other churches in the area, looks unkempt and almost derelict. The churchyard is neglected and overgrown with weeds. Ivy scrambles over everything, climbing the scrub oaks, the crumbling tombstones and old broken mausoleums. I've never seen the church open, even later in the day, though I've peeked inside the windows. It looks plain but still in use, despite a cracked window or two.

The church which, unusually, stands outside the village on its own, is a stark contrast to most of the old stone Cornish houses which I drive to now. They're all smartly painted and recently renovated. A few still look a little careworn but no doubt when, or if, the owners sell they will be tarted up and modernized just like the others and probably bought by second-homers. A week ago most of the houses in this village were empty but now, on Christmas Eve, some are lit with fairy lights and candles as the residents leave their primary homes Up Country to holiday in their second homes.

Those who are up and about greet me civilly, wishing me a Happy Christmas. No tip though but then why should they? They're not here most of the time. One young couple come to their door flushed and excited. 'Just tried to light a fire but the chimney keeps smoking,' the man says, laughing. He's handsome in a prosperous, polished way in his casual cashmere pullover.

'We just got here,' the woman tells me, laughing too. I feel like a grump but I can't help wondering what's so funny about a smoking chimney. Maybe because to them it's not real, they're just playing house. Their real life is somewhere else.

The woman goes on, 'Drove all night. God, it's good to be out of the City.'

I make a sympathetic face but secretly I'm envying her clothes: trendy, stylish, 'Toast' country clothes. She has swinging hair so well cut I instinctively put my hand up to my straggling pony tail. I used to look like that, I want to tell her. I used to get my hair styled at the best salons in London and buy my clothes at the trendiest boutiques. And I gave it up for *this* I want to add, just to see the expression on her face. But even as I think this I feel wistful. And then I remember just why we did it, and what we're striving for here in Cornwall, and the feeling goes.

Behind the woman I see a couple of kids, a boy and a girl of about six or seven. They are squabbling furiously. The girl is holding something orangey which I think at first is a stuffed toy and the boy is pulling on it trying to get it away. 'Keep it down, twins,' the woman yells at them good-naturedly.

There is an almighty screech coming from the stuffed toy.

'Jamie, let go of Marmalade. You too, Anna.' The man lunges at the kids and grabs a ginger cat from the girl's arm. The cat is hissing and snarling and the twins are crying now.

When all calms down, the cat having run into the kitchen with the children following, now shrieking with laughter, the man turns back to me. 'Sorry about that. They're over-excited. So is Marmalade, he hates long trips in the car. Do you know anything about chimneys? My name is Adam, by the way and this is my wife, Elizabeth. We're fairly new here. Live in London, only bought this place last summer and haven't had a chance to use it much.'

Smoke is hurtling out of the front room and into the corridor where we're standing. The couple seem kind enough but I can tell I don't register as a person to them even though they politely invite me in for a 'Christmas drink'. I wonder if that means coffee or a Bucks Fizz, given that it's still morning, but I don't ask, say I'd better be getting on. I notice my voice is hesitant but they don't insist or perhaps I'd have changed my mind. I could do with a bit of warmth, a hot drink and some cheery company for a few minutes, but I know the invitation was not meant to be accepted. They wish me a Merry Christmas and close the door before I've barely turned around.

As I leave I see Marmalade in the front window, no doubt wishing he'd been left behind in the peace and solitude of London. In my febrile mind he seems smug, there in the warm if smoky house and me out in the cold on this Christmas Eve morning.

Though it's stopped sleeting, the wind is nearly gale force. My face is stinging with it and my nose is running. I rummage about in the van for some tissues, unable to stop sneezing. This cold I've got is worsening and I hope it doesn't turn to flu. Just what I need, being ill at Christmas. Ben is cooking me a surprise meal, a special Christmas Eve supper when the children are in bed, as the theatre is closed tonight. It's to be our night, just the two of us, before the pandemonium of the big day itself. The way I feel now, I just want to go to bed with a Lemsip.

First there's another small village to deliver to, this one still fairly full of permanent residents. Everyone here I speak to asks where Reg is. I tell them he's left his job for good and their obvious disappointment at losing Reg and gaining *me* doesn't exactly make me feel cheery. I know Reg has been around a long time, but still . . . As I drive down a long tarmac road to my next customer, I'm relieved that it's my next to last stop.

Trelak Farm has been a B&B for a couple of years now but before that the land had been farmed by the Rowland family for generations. Small farmers, they couldn't withstand the falling prices for their stock, rising costs of feed and the masses of paperwork necessary as one new EU directive after another was issued in the last ten years. It's happening all over Cornwall now. Small farmers have nearly become a thing of the past, like so much else.

Susie told me that Emma and Martin Rowland didn't want to stop farming and go into the tourist trade at Trelak but they had no choice. It was that or move out of the farmhouse and they couldn't bring themselves to do that.

Martin hates doing B&B, I've heard, and seems to have modelled himself on John Cleese in *Fawlty Towers*. But it's not an act. He loathes strangers in his house and resents every minute they are there.

As I get out of the van at Trelak Farm a sharp gust of wind slaps me in the face and makes me lose my balance and I nearly topple over into a muddy pool of rainwater in the old farmyard. It's a lunatic wind, whipping around the skeletal trees and bowing them down with its fury. A common sight here in Cornwall, trees bent permanently in one direction, away from the constant gales from the wind.

'Fresh,' one woman told us when we were looking around for houses to buy, standing on the hillock behind the garden of a cottage near the sea. ''Tis healthy air. Fresh,' she repeated as we were nearly bowled over by a gale of nearly cyclonic proportions.

I'm thinking of this and of something I read in a book about Cornwall by Daphne du Maurier where she quotes a writer in the early 1600s speaking of the climate here, 'The air being cleaned with frequent Winds and the Tides, is pure and healthful, so that the Inhabitants are rarely troubled with infectious Diseases.'

So far so good, but the writer goes on, '... yet the wind being sharp and piercing, such as have been sick, especially Strangers, recover but slowly.'

Exactly. How long have I had this wretched cold? I sneeze again and I blow my nose, feeling my icy fingers touch my burning cheeks and feverish face. I feel the gale hammering against and through my Royal Mail waterproof jacket, chiselling through my flesh to get to my very bones. *Such as have been sick, especially Strangers, recover but slowly.* Terrific. No wonder whatever I've got refuses to go away. I'll be lucky if I'm better by spring, especially if this weather keeps up.

There's a letter slot in the door at Trelak Farm, or Trelak Farmhouse Bed & Breakfast as it now is. I stuff the one last lone Christmas card into the slot and turn to go but the door suddenly opens in my face. 'You're early,' the voice is gruff, accusing and loud.

'Sorry?' I step back. Martin Rowland, tall and lanky just like John Cleese, is breathing fire like a dragon over my head.

Or so it seems – it's probably just the sudden blast of heat coming from the open door. It makes me long for home, for our own warm house, for Ben and Will and Amy.

We stare at each other until he takes in who I am. 'Emma, 'tisn't them, tis only the postman,' he bellows over his shoulder.

'Post*woman*,' I say but he's not listening.

Emma, tall and lanky like her husband, joins him at the door. She's wearing a quilted raincoat, boots and hat. Martin too has a jacket on. 'We're just off to get a few last-minute things in Truro before the shops close for the holidays,' she says. 'Martin thought you were the guests, arriving early.'

'You're open on Christmas Eve?'

She nods, looking stressed. Martin says, 'Can't believe she's letting a room out on Christmas Eve.' He looks belligerent.

'They were desperate, Martin, I told you. Everywhere else is shut, and they're having some kind of family reunion in Morranport. Some long lost cousin or other, only there's no room in the house for any more relatives.'

'No room at the inn,' Martin mutters.

She puts her hand on his arm. 'Exactly,' she says softly. 'How could I turn them away?'

He nods. There's no answer to that one, not today.

I like this couple, whom I've only met twice before while doing Reg's round. He's blustering and loud, but I think that hides the pussycat inside. From what I've heard, Emma knows how to handle him. She seems down-to-earth, kind but practical. She's not Cornish but she's lived here twenty-five years, since she came as a young teacher at the local primary school then met and married Martin almost immediately.

I know they're in a hurry to get out so I say goodbye, wish them a Merry Christmas and get back into the van. As I open the door it nearly blows off its hinges, the wind is so strong. When I try to shut it, it doesn't seem to close properly. I must remember to report it when the holiday is over.

My last stop is down a potholed dirt road to the smallest house on my beat, a tiny stone cottage that looks as though it belongs in a storybook for children, one about wicked witches living in a deep, dark, spooky forest. I stop in front of a broken wooden gate, get out of my van and walk the short distance to the front door. The garden is brambly and neglected. An old apple tree, some unpruned shrubs and a couple of ancient scrub oaks grow wild and unruly in the tiny space.

I knock on the wooden door as there is no letterbox or slot anywhere. The door was once painted a cheery blue but it has long faded and begun to peel, as have the window frames. I stand in the wind which is making a weird sucking sound in the tall pine trees behind the house, the kind of sound that can drive a person mad.

It seems I'm waiting at the door forever. Hooray for the Royal Mail waterproof, windproof tent coat that I was so disparaging about at first. It flaps around me like the sails of a boat in a storm but at least it's kept me dry from the earlier sludgy sleet. And now it's raining, great fat heavy drops that are not quite snow but not far from it.

Finally the door creaks open and Mr Hawker, whom I've

never met, is greeting me with his wobbly smile. It's a strange, sad smile, sincere but tenuous, trembling too. It's as if he's not sure if he really has the right to smile.

I can't blame him, not in his circumstances. I know a lot about Mr Hawker, from Susie, Reg, Nell and the others. He lives alone, has never married and has no family as far as anyone knows. He came here from Penzance years back as a ten-year-old lad, looking for work. He got a job on Trelak Farm, working for Martin Rowland's grandfather, sleeping in a room no bigger than a closet and then, when he was grown and had some importance on the farm, he was given the farm cottage he lives in now.

'Managed to buy it eventually, years and years back,' Reg said when telling me about Mr Hawker. 'Guess he had nothing else to spend his money on. Good thing too for 'im, cause when Martin and Emma had to sell up the land, the cottage would've had to go too and no way he could of afforded it then.'

Mr Hawker opens the door wider. 'Come in, come in. You be saturated standin' there. I heared tell that there be a new post maid, with Reg ill and all.'

I step inside the door onto old linoleum flooring. The smell of decay and urine is overwhelming. I try not to flinch and force myself to smile. 'Not much post today, Mr Hawker.' I don't call him by his first name; no one does, though no one seems to know why.

'No.' He looks at the flyer, some advertising for an insurance company, with longing on his face. Reg says he's never delivered any personal letters here.

But Mr Hawker is ninety-one. I supposed any friends he might have had once are gone. Anyway, he's always been a loner, Susie said, painfully shy when away from the farm and his own territory.

He has let me in because both Reg and Susie have told him

about me. I guess being a postman or a woman isn't a threat.
Chatting to us is a way of making contact without having to
have social know-how.

Apparently Mr Hawker never goes out, not even to shop.
Emma and Martin up at Trelak pick up his pension and buy
his few provisions. He won't let them do anything else, though.
He says he's healthy and fit enough to look after himself. It's
just that he's a tad bit nervous out of the house, he's told
people. Can't get used to the modern world, he says, so he
may as well stop at home.

I am standing there dripping over his linoleum but he doesn't
seem to mind. This is his main room, for there is no front
porch or hallway in this tiny cottage. There are no rugs, only
this dull brown floor covering which makes the dark room
with its tiny windows even dingier. There are no lamps either,
only one dull overhead light. Two lumpy armchairs of indeterminate colour and a plain wooden table and chair are the
only furniture. A box of corn flakes and a half pint of milk
sit forgotten on the table.

I see a massive spider's web in the corner over the ancient
wood-burning cooker.

We talk for a few minutes about the weather and then there
is a silence as we stand awkwardly facing each other. I'm not
sure how to leave. How can I wish this lonely man a Merry
Christmas? He'll be here at home, as usual, eating something
out of a tin. In the past a few of the kindly folk in the nearby
village have invited him to Christmas dinner but he's always
refused, with such a mixture of longing and terror in his eyes
that people stopped asking. 'Much to his relief,' both Susie and
Reg have told me. Emma and Martin too have tried to do more
for him, have tried to invite him over to the farmhouse, but
it's no use. He won't accept either help or hospitality, fearful
of losing his fragile independence.

The stench in the room is so stifling I'm having trouble breathing. The air in the place is odd, at once that horrid damp cold that goes straight to the bones, yet stuffy, with the wood stove pumping out heat and an acrid smoke that is making my eyes water.

'Goodbye, Mr Hawker, must be back on my rounds.'

Before I can go he shoves his hand in his trouser pocket and takes out a piece of lined paper wrapped around a small hard object. He shoves it awkwardly into my hand and says, 'For the post. Christmas and all. I be thanking 'ee.'

It feels like a coin. I don't want to accept – I know how small his pension is but I can't refuse. I feel tears welling up and blink to stop them. This is my first and only tip this Christmas.

Mr Hawker's fifty pence piece wrapped in a piece of lined writing paper is one of the loveliest Christmas gifts I could ask for. I thank him profusely and say goodbye.

Poor man. As I get into the van I see he's still standing at the door, waving at me as I start up. I nearly weep, he looks so forlorn. He's wearing a long grey cardigan over several pullovers; I can see the sleeves of different colours poking out of holes in the dingy cardigan. The hand he raises to wave me off is swollen and knotted with arthritis.

I wave back. 'Merry Christmas,' I whisper. I watch him through the rear view mirror as he stands waving until I am out of sight.

And now I'm finished, for today at any rate. And then there is the holiday. I'm wet and cold and ill and starting to feel feverish. But I've got this far. I've lasted till Christmas. As I drive I take one hand off the wheel to pick up the crumpled paper and coin that Mr Hawker gave me and squeeze it like a talisman before putting it down again on the seat next to me.

* * *

Back at St Geraint I park the van behind the boat yard in its usual place but I don't get out, not yet. The van is facing the sea and I sit and watch the foamy waves, the squally spray, the grey and purple sky ripe with storms. There are massive rocks on the edge of the shore, half covered by the surging water. There's a legend here that a holy man, a saint, sat daily on one of those rocks round about AD 550, giving lessons to the fishermen after their day's toil. The story goes that a seal used to clamber on a rock nearby, not to imbibe Christianity but to bark at students and teacher. Perhaps the seal was a dissenter, well ahead of Wesley and the other Methodists who would one day inhabit Cornwall, or perhaps he was doing no more than barking his approval of the saintly man and his lectures. Whatever it was, the preacher could no more tolerate this seal than he could a recalcitrant student. He smacked the seal's nose as he would have smacked the hand of a disruptive child and the seal slunk back chastised into the sea.

I look for seals now as they are not uncommon in this estuary, sunning themselves on the rocks when the weather's warm. But it's crazy to think I'll spot one now as they'll all be hiding from another storm that's fast approaching from the sea. There's a lull now after the wind, sleet and rain, but out over the sea the midday sky is bruised and blackened, with ominous clouds. It's time to go home. Ben will be waiting, and so will the children.

On the drive back to my family, the light changes as the storm nears, becoming a strange feverish yellow which is growing darker by the minute. I don't know if it's the eerie light or the fact that I'm light headed with illness and exhaustion, but I take a wrong turning and find myself on a strange road. It's narrow like most of the roads around here but it seems to be running down into a wooded valley. There are no villages or farmhouses, no sign of any kind of habitation as

77

the road winds and curves in the valley. There is thick woodland on either side: ash, beech and oak with a few conifers. The bare branches of the trees are coated by the sulphurous light looking beautiful and ominous at the same time.

There are no turn-offs, no buildings, nothing but this winding road through the wooded valley. I've lost all sense of direction and don't know where I am, or where this road is heading.

And then the woodland disappears and I'm on a marshy plain, the road crossing a little stone bridge over a rushing river where a single swan is floating slowly and elegantly, framed by the sudden expanse of purple and yellow sky.

I have to stop. It's so breathtaking, this scene. I get out of the van and stand below the old bridge, looking at the wet expanse of grass and moss on either side of the river. It's like a vast marshy meadow right out of a fairytale, with what looks like an egret in the distance standing pale against the dark lavender-grey of the sky.

Is it really an egret? I've seen them before, but only in Florida. I've heard they're appearing in Cornwall but no one I know has seen one. It's smaller than a heron and pure white, startling against the green moss of the meadow. The swan, unafraid and unthreatening, swims up to the edge of the water just in front of me as if trying to grab my attention away from the egret. I feel I must give it something, in honour of the season. I've just received a special gift, a fifty pence piece from an old pensioner, and I want to give something in return.

I search my jacket and trouser pockets for a biscuit or another titbit but nothing is there. 'Wait a minute,' I whisper and run back to the van.

The swan waits as if understanding every word. The storm seems to be waiting too, for it has not yet broken despite the blackening sky.

I find the remains of a cheese sandwich I had for lunch and

throw it to the swan. It seems to nod its head in acknowledgement before consuming the bread and looking at me
expectantly. 'That's all,' I murmur.

The swan appears to accept this and begins to swim silently
away. I stand for several minutes, savouring the moment. The
egret is still there too, poised like the statue of some ancient
nameless god. It is so silent. I can't remember ever feeling a
silence so intense, so moving. It is, after all, Christmas Eve.
Silent Night, Holy Night.

Finally I go back to the van, decide to carry on further along
this strange road before giving up and turning around to go
back the way I came. To my surprise, I find I've driven a
different way to the neglected church outside the village which
was my first stop this morning. I know where I am now.

I pass the overgrown churchyard, the broken side door, the
cracked windows. But this time there are lights inside, shining
through the stained-glass windows. Out front several men and
women are hanging coloured lights on a tall Christmas tree
which wasn't there earlier. The wind is blowing them about
like paper cut-outs and it seems to me to be a crazy thing to
do, with such a ferocious storm brewing, but they are laughing
and determined, shouting instructions and encouragement at
each other as they struggle to keep the string of lights from
blowing away in the wind.

I love their spirit, their optimism in the face of all odds. I
slow down to watch them and as I pass that ancient dereliction
of a church, a trick of the lights in the windows and shining
through the cracks in the battered door, makes it seem like the
old church is smiling, grinning like the carved face of a jack-
o-lantern. I smile back and make my way home.

January

There are primroses out in the lane behind our house. It's a sun trap there. On the coast and hills the weather is still Arctic with freezing winds, but along our lane, and in little pockets all over Cornwall, it's summer.

The daffodils have been out for ages, appearing not long after the New Year and of course there are snowdrops everywhere. The rain of November and December has stopped, at least for now, and we've had days of blue sky interspersed with gentle, floating clouds.

The older farmers on my round, when I comment on the rare fine weather, suck in their cheeks, purse their lips and take a sharp intake of breath. 'We be paying for it later, me handsome,' they say ominously.

At the post office in St Geraint, Margaret has more time to be chatty, as we all do. I haven't had a chance to talk properly to Margaret since the Christmas rush began. Now, there's a lovely, relaxed feeling amongst all of us, with our busiest season over. We're taking more time to gossip and dawdle. The great weather makes it easier too.

I'm glad I haven't quit the job – well, today I'm glad. I'm not naïve enough to believe either the good weather or these gentle post-Christmas weeks won't end, but I've stuck through those awful early weeks and I'm starting to feel at ease with my colleagues and with the job. Not entirely, after all I've not been at it long, but I'm getting there.

I'm collecting my post as Margaret and I talk, about nothing in particular. I have to leave our conversation for a minute as another customer comes in to buy stamps. I carry a load of parcels and letters to my van parked outside and go back into the shop as the customer leaves. 'Such a relief, Christmas being over,' I say idly.

She looks up at me. 'Must be for you especially. Tough time to start this job. You done well enough, though.'

This compliment sets me up brilliantly. I smile radiantly at her but she's already dealing with another customer.

Later I'm in the post office at Morranport, talking to Nell. 'It's going to be odd, you not here,' I say to her.

'Me? Not here?' Nell stands up straight, her bosom facing me with indignation.

'Yes, well, you leaving and all.'

'Who's saying I'm leaving here?'

I'm confused. 'Actually, Nell, it was you who said it. Before Christmas. You said you're retiring.'

'Oh that,' she waves her wrinkled hand at me, brushing off such a ludicrous suggestion. 'Changed me mind, I did. Now why would I do that, you be saying to yourself. Well, a woman's got a right, true? And I be thinking, now what in the good Lord's name would I be doing, at home?'

Standing there with her formidable eighty-odd year-old bosom, clad in a scarlet pullover today, with her short scruffy white hair all over the place, Nell looks indomitable. 'You're right, Nell. What indeed *would* you be doing at home?

I'm delighted you're not retiring. Royal Mail needs you, that's for sure.'

She looks keenly at me to make sure I'm not mocking her. She's no one's fool. Finally, satisfied that I meant what I said, her look softens. 'Well, maid, I could of said they be needin' you too. You done well in the mad rush up to Christmas.'

Two compliments about my work in one day: I'm overjoyed. I've passed the test, I've arrived, my colleagues are happy with me. I'm a true proper efficient postwoman at last. It's ridiculous how much satisfaction this gives me.

It's not just the rare January sun and the compliments that cheer me this month but the fact that all our London visitors are gone. Since we've moved to Cornwall, we've had a rash of guests. It is a well-known fact of life that whenever one moves to an idyllic place, both friends and acquaintances descend like magpies. This is fine in the case of good friends, like Annie and numerous others who have visited us, but we soon learn that people we thought we knew are quite different when actually living in our house. We'd had a couple of colleagues from The Body Shop visit in the autumn as well, and that was fine, but then there were the others.

Seth and I had worked together for my last few years with the company and we'd got on well. When he phoned to say he'd like to visit us and bring his girlfriend, I thought it would be a fun weekend.

They arrived by car at noon the day after Boxing Day. To our surprise, Seth, who is usually outgoing and gregarious, seemed distracted. Introducing us to Samantha, he hardly responded to our greetings, being too busy fussing over the slight but curvy woman wrapped in a white, fake fur coat, her long, shiny, blonde hair hanging over it artfully.

'Samantha's ill,' Seth whispered, his tone hushed as a priest announcing the Pope is dying. 'She needs quiet.'

I was solicitous – at first, until it soon became clear that Samantha was hungover in a major way. I wouldn't have minded if she'd got that way at our house, it wouldn't have been the first time that friends appeared slightly the worse for wear at the breakfast table, but the fact that she'd brought the hangover with her to inflict on us rather irritated me.

However, trying to be sympathetic, I showed Seth the guest room and together we got Samantha under the duvet. Throwing her arm weakly over her face, she mumbled something to Seth. 'What is it?' I asked.

He didn't even look at me. 'D'you have any Alka Seltzer?'

Luckily, we did. I brought her up a glass of the fizzy stuff. Seth, still sitting at the side of her bed, tried to coax her to drink it. I started to creep out of the room but Seth called me back. 'Er, Samantha feels cold.'

I brought blankets – not enough. And filled a hot water bottle.

'Oh, Tessa, d'you mind making it a bit hotter? Samantha's shivering, poor thing.'

After sending Ben out to the shop to get some sparkling water as Samantha didn't drink plain tap water, and me to make peppermint tea when the sparkling water left her feeling cold again, the invalid finally fell asleep and Seth came downstairs.

'Well, that's a pity,' I said. 'I suppose she doesn't want lunch?'

Not only did Samantha not want lunch, she didn't want dinner either, though she sent Seth downstairs around six for 'some brown toast with just the tiniest sliver of butter.' A few minutes later, he was back down with it untouched, asking if the bread could be slightly less toasted and with a bit more butter and perhaps some cheese?

Seth pulled himself away from Samantha's bedside long

enough to scoff the special seafood risotto I'd made for them, then rushed off without offering to help with the washing up so that he could make sure Samantha was comfortable.

We never did meet her, for they left at noon the next day as planned and Samantha hadn't once come downstairs. Seth made a half-hearted apology, but he was far more concerned about her than he was with inconveniencing us. All evening, when he wasn't upstairs, he sat moping. Ben, the lucky one, was back at the pantomime, so I had the brunt of Seth's company. He drank copious amounts of wine and got tipsy and maudlin, telling me how wonderful his new 'beloved' was, but how fragile she was too, like a hothouse flower. Yes, he actually said that. Seth, my old workmate, my colleague, once full of fun, drooping over a hungover hothouse flower.

When they left she managed to flutter her fingers at us and say something that might have been thank you, or sorry, or more likely, just plain old goodbye. I couldn't hear as she was muffled up with scarves and a furry hat and didn't even turn around to look at us.

'She's feeling so much better,' Seth called out from the open car window as they drove off. 'Isn't that great?'

All our holiday visitors are now gone and it's an exceptional January day. I take my postbag and walk along the seafront at Morranport. I love delivering on this street, with the sea on my left and a row of Georgian fisherman's cottages on my right. At this time of year the wrought iron balconies are empty and the tidy neat gardens which are bright with buddleia and palms in summer look wintry and rather desolate. I try to imagine what they were like when the fishermen still lived in them. The last ones to fish here had to move uphill away from the sea to Poldowe where house prices were cheaper, years ago when the small harbour village was first discovered by holiday makers. Now they're all gone from there as well. People I've talked to in the houses up the hill are worried about this, wondering what it will mean to their children and for the future.

My bag is light as most of these cottages are empty, their owners back home after the holiday break. I walk briskly, revelling in the cold but windless fresh air, the tangy smell of sea and stone. It's strong today. There are mounds of dark brown and green seaweed swept up on the rocks and beach after the last high tide. Gulls squawk in the sky and on the ground, bickering with each other over snippets of food. The small boats in the tiny harbour cling to the sand like limpets. Some are quite scruffy and in need of a good coat of paint, worn out after a hard winter of being pounded by sea and storms. In between the boats a couple of young boys are prodding the rock pools with small nets attached to long sticks.

Winter's not over yet, though. Despite the deceptive sun and pockets of warmth in sheltered spots, there is a wintry feel still in the air. And over the horizon, black against the bright blue sky, there are clouds looming, biding their time but gathering strength.

I shiver despite the sun as a tiny breeze begins, as if to remind me that it's not spring yet. I walk even more briskly. I've lost half a stone since I started this job, and that's over the Christmas holidays too, when I didn't stint myself on food. It's hard to believe sometimes that I'm actually getting paid to exercise, when back in London I had to pay a personal trainer to get me into the shape I'm in now. I feel fitter and healthier. The lingering cold has gone, vanished without a trace by Twelfth Night. I've got more energy than I've had for years.

Ben does too. The pantomime is over but it was a great success, the seats sold out every night. He's enjoying acting again enormously and is now feeling that wonderful glow of having done a job you love well.

What he'll do now, we're not sure as my postie job is not enough for us to live on. There's the café to fall back on, and the aromatherapy, and I'm optimistic now, sure something else will turn up. We'll worry about it when the time comes. We're learning to live day by day and not get stressed about the future.

I walk on, feeling jaunty and spry. At the end of this row of houses, the village peters out into the coastal path. There's a small, whitewashed, stone cottage on a promontory jutting out over the sea; a salubrious romantic place for a cottage if there ever was one. It gives me great joy that the couple who live here are locals, even though they are not fisher folk. But they come from generations of fishermen. The owner, Archie Grenville's father was one and so were his grandfather and great-grandfather. This was the house he was born in.

Archie and his wife are retired teachers, having met and married in Truro where they both taught at the grammar school. Often on my rounds I see them together in their front room which overlooks the sea. If I climb the stile into the fields and the coastal path, and look back at the village, I can see into the side window of that room, see them sitting on the sofa either reading together, or animatedly chatting while they look out over the water.

I feel like a voyeur when I'm standing watching them but sometimes I can't help it, for a minute or two anyway. They look so calm, so contented, this couple in their seventies, still together after fifty years. And what do they have to say to each other with such enthusiasm on their faces, after all this time?

I watch, fascinated. Jennifer Grenville is standing at the window and Archie comes up to her, puts his hand on her shoulder, points with the other hand to something out at sea. They stand motionless, watching whatever it is, as I watch them.

Suddenly, I'm punished for my nosiness, for intruding on

someone's private moment. As I stare into the Grenvilles' house a sudden gust of wind takes me by surprise and the letter I was about to deliver to them flies over the stile, over the stone wall at the side of their house and into the sea.

I shriek and run after it. The noise brings the couple scurrying to the door. I'm shaking my head, gabbling something inane, telling them I'll be back in a minute with their post, while I scurry over the low wall onto the rocks below. Luckily the tide is out. I'd probably have jumped in anyway and killed myself in the process.

I'd like to say that my first thoughts are for the two old folk whose letter I'd lost. What if it's a longed-for missive from a friend, a son or daughter or an ancient relative? What if it's a notification of a huge Premium Bond win? I'd not looked at the letter at all as I was too busy ogling them. What if in my carelessness I've destroyed what for them would have been a life-changing letter?

I don't think any of those thoughts, I'm ashamed to say. Or not until later. Right now I'm thinking, *Oh hell, there goes my job.*

I'm balancing on a jagged rock trying to reach the letter which is bobbing about in the foamy waves. The tide is coming in fast and the water is quite deep in places. I'm aware of the Grenvilles hanging over the sea wall and calling out something to me. I can't hear a word they're saying. A wave brings the letter closer and I make a grab for it, nearly falling in. The shouts from the sea wall are becoming more hysterical.

I'm soaked from the turbulence but I don't care. I want that letter. Now I hear someone else, a younger voice shouting and I look up to see the young lads I'd passed earlier. 'Try this,' one of them yells as he throws down his net.

It lands near enough for me to grab the pole without falling into the water. I make repeated stabs at the letter but I miss it each time, causing a crescendo of a groan in my audience.

It's still maddingly near and at least it hasn't been swept out to sea but I'm getting angry now and feel like drowning the damn thing instead of saving it. And then another wave crashes in and brings the letter with it, leaving it stranded high, but unfortunately not dry, on the rock behind me as the water recedes.

There's an almighty cheer from the sea wall, where at least a dozen people have gathered. I try a heroic leap from my rock to the other one and topple off, scratching my hands badly. There's a collective gasp from the crowd but I've grabbed the letter, pulled myself up before anyone can try to help. I stand on the rock, waving the soggy paper like a flag. Another cheer from the crowd and I bow modestly before stiffly, inelegantly, clamouring back over the jagged rocks to hand the dripping mess of paper to the Grenvilles.

Jennifer and Archie – we're on first name terms now – ply me with hot coffee, wash out the scratches on my hand and give me a pair of baggy but clean, track suit bottoms to put on while they dry my trousers. The letter which I'd so heroically saved is drying on a radiator. It is an advertisement for loft insulation.

'Never mind, dear,' Jennifer says when we discover this fact. 'It was a brave, if foolhardy, thing to do.'

Archie echoes the bravery bit. 'We'll write a personal letter to the post office, commending your integrity and sense of duty. They should be proud to have women like you working for the Royal Mail.'

Three days later, I kill a cat. Not intentionally, of course not. The cat runs out into the road and dives under the wheels of my van like the most maniacal of suicide bombers.

I stop and rush to the poor thing but it is dead even before I get there. A slight trickle of blood is running from its furry mouth and its spine is twisted oddly. It is ginger coloured with a white tip on its tail and a white face. I recognize this cat: it's Marmalade.

By now three or four people have gathered around me and the dead animal. There is a lot of tut-tutting and shaking of heads but no one is making a move to notify the cat's owners. I'm trembling all over, upset and near tears.

'Please,' I say to the woman nearest me. 'Can you tell the Johnson's – you know, Adam and Elizabeth, they're called, their house is across the road there – can you tell them what happened?'

No one moves.

'It's their cat,' I explain, wondering why I have to do so. In such a small hamlet, everyone knows what animal belongs to whom.

Still there is no volunteer.

I'm becoming agitated. 'Right, I'll do it myself.' I stand up, holding poor dead Marmalade.

'Take it easy, maid,' a white-haired man leaning on a cane hobbles up to me, pats me on the shoulder. 'Ain't no rush.'

'But there is. They've got kids, it's their cat, we've got to tell them before they come out and see the poor mangled thing. They'll be shattered.'

The man holds me back as I start for the house, 'They be gone.'

A woman with a scarf knotted under her chin continues, 'Gone Up Country, back to their own home. Don't live here-abouts, not except for holidays.'

'I know that but they were here over Christmas and into the New Year. They wouldn't have gone without their cat.'

The two begin talking at once. They tell me that Elizabeth, Adam and the twins left a few days ago but had to leave Marmalade as the cat had disappeared.

'Looked all over fer it. Kids howling an' bawling, Ma and Pa frantic-like. Finally had to go without the cat. Asked us to keep watch fer it.'

We stand there for a moment in silence, me still holding the stiffening creature. There is blood on my Royal Mail fleece. Finally I say, 'I'd better phone them, let them know. Does anyone have their number?'

The woman with the scarf does as she looks after the house while it's empty and cleans it before and after their visits. She comes back with the number and with an old towel. 'To wrap it in,' she says.

I assume by this that I am to take the cat away, as no one else offers to dispose of it. So I wrap poor Marmalade in the towel, an old thin beach towel with a faded palm tree on it, and place him with the post in the back of the van.

It isn't far from Morranport so I drive back to use Nell's phone. I have my mobile with me but there's no signal anywhere around here. Nell is sympathetic and insists on seeing the dead cat, no doubt checking that I've got it right, that the animal really is dead and not moribund. I tell her how awful I feel. I've never hit anything, not even a squirrel or a vole, before.

'Not your fault, maid.'

'I know, but I still feel awful. I suppose I'll have to be the one to bury it too. But I'd better ring the owners first.'

I gabble my apologies on the phone to Elizabeth Johnson as I break the news about Marmalade. She is upset but tells me I'm not to blame. Marmalade never was a cat for looking both ways before he crossed a road.

I say, 'Your children will be devastated.'

'Oh my God, the kids! Yes, they will, they will.'

'I'm so sorry,' I say for the hundredth time.

'Oh dear.' She sounds more distraught now than she did

when I first told her the cat was dead. 'They'll never forgive us if they can't have a funeral.'

'What?'

'Oh, you know, a proper burial, funeral hymns, prayers, speeches, that sort of thing. The kids love it. They had a big one for the gerbil and one for the terrapin too.'

'Oh. Right.'

'Look . . . sorry, I didn't get your name?'

Just call me Mrs Postie, I nearly say but I don't think she'd get irony right now. 'Tessa Hainsworth.'

'Look, Tessa, I can't deprive the children of their funeral. Could you do us a big favour, and hold the cat until we get down to Cornwall again?'

I think fast. The next school holiday is not until the end of February and it's only the beginning of January. For a hysterical few seconds I imagine myself driving around with a dead, decomposing ginger cat in my van for six or seven weeks. Things like this never happen to Postman Pat, that's for sure.

Elizabeth goes on, 'If you can just put it in your freezer . . . ?'

I am so relieved by this idea that I agree. Somehow, goodness knows how, I find myself saying, 'Fine, we'll keep it for you. No problem.'

When I hang up Nell looks at me, a hard look. I stare back. 'Well, maid,' she says. 'Your freezer or mine?'

We both grin then start to giggle and soon we're laughing so hard we can hardly wrap hapless Marmalade in a plastic bag before placing him at the bottom of the big shop freezer in the back of the post office.

'Fish in the fridge, cat in the freezer – I'm starting to get the hang of this job, Nell,' I sing out as I leave the post office.

"Bout time,' she hollers back with a cheery wave.

I finally forget about the cat when I go back to my beat, for I'm now on my way to Trescatho, a place of cob, stone and slate, accessible only by a narrow lane with high hedgerows on either side.

The fine but cold January weather has held; the sky is blue glass and the sea is jade green. I park the van by a gate leading into a field where early Cornish lambs are skipping in the grass while their mothers, Dorset ewes, graze alongside them. I lean on the gate a few moments and gaze at the sea in the distance, the animals not far from me. They gaze back with momentary interest then return to their munching, oblivious to some starlings quarrelling amongst themselves in the nearby trees until they fly away and the quiet returns.

As usual, I'm overwhelmed by the stillness. Perhaps more than anything it is something I'm aware of in Cornwall, something I'm awed by. I guess it's those years of living in cities where you live with noise, all day and all night. Here, I seem to go from pocket to pocket of calm, quiet, broken only by the beautiful warble of a wren, or the singing of skylarks.

I remember the first time I heard the larks, as I was parked one morning at Creek, having a last look at the estuary before carrying on my round. I heard what I thought was ethereal music, lovely sounds I couldn't recognize, coming from somewhere in the sky. Looking up, I saw tiny bird-shapes and realized the songs were coming from them.

I sat there for ages, joyous to have this blessing of birdsong, yet sad that the traffic, the noise of London had prevented me from hearing it for all those long years.

Here in Trescatho, the silence is even more intense. Every time I come, I feel I've stepped back hundreds of years in time. The village seems isolated and cut off from the 21st century. Its position helps to create this feeling, with the high cliffs going down to the sea on one side and the precipitous hill falling to the river on the other. There's only one narrow road leading to it and it's a cul de sac which ends at the village.

Once it was a lively community, with an inn, a blacksmiths, a tiny shop and even a one-room village school. Now there are only a cluster of stone houses.

It seems a million miles from anywhere, this place, and the fact that it's so quiet, so empty of people, adds to the feeling of timelessness. Even the stone barns alongside the farmyard seem frozen in the past. There are no signs of animals, yet hay and straw are stacked up in an open-ended shed. I haven't seen a tractor but there's an ancient plough in the corner. I keep expecting to see the oxen that pull it.

Yet this doesn't seem like a ghost town. I know these houses aren't empty; I see names on the post I deliver and smoke rising from chimneys, smoke from wood-burners and the old Agas and Rayburns I sometimes glimpse through half-curtained windows. I drop the post in letterboxes, in sheds, in boxes hidden from the rain, and even into a few front porches with doors left ajar for me. But I've never seen another soul. Well, only one and he was so odd I'm beginning to wonder if I imagined it.

It was the first time I'd delivered the post to Trescatho, early one foggy morning. A lone sheepdog somewhere behind the farm at the edge of the hamlet barked once then stopped, and an owl hooted loudly, making me jump. I had to walk down a narrow footpath of old cobbles, grass growing in between, to a nest of cottages clustered around a tiny square, a postage stamp village green. I kept expecting to hear the sound of horses' hooves on the cobbles.

The mist dipped in and out between the houses and a full moon still shone through the dark and fog and the coming dawn. I felt like I had stumbled across Brigadoon, the sleeping town said to wake and appear only once every hundred years. If a man in a shepherd's smock and a woman in a crinoline and bonnet had appeared in one of the doorways I'd not have

93

been the least surprised but I sure as hell yelped when someone came up behind me and put a heavy hand on my shoulder.

An apologetic voice said, 'Sorry, miss, if I frightened you.'

Turning, I saw a man towering over me and I do mean towering. He must have been well over six and a half feet tall, probably more. He had thick, long, black hair down to his shoulders and he held one hand in front of his mouth even when he talked. I murmured something back but noticed his other hand was still on my shoulder.

We stood there for a few moments and my fear was coming back despite the civility in his voice. He seemed in no hurry to speak so I stammered, 'Uh, can I, uh, help you? Do you have a letter you want me to take?'

This flustered him. 'Oh no, no no no, thank 'ee anyway. It's just that I'm needing to get by. Bit of a hurry, y'see.' He nodded towards the cluster of houses ahead of us, shrouded in the heavy mist. A light shone from one of them but it was eerily muted, looking more like candlelight or a gas lamp than electricity.

I suddenly realized that because the path was so narrow, there was no way he could get past me unless I squeezed myself up against one of the stone garden walls. This I did and he hurried by, finally dropping his hand from my shoulder and the other one from his mouth. It was then I had the second shock of the day. His two eye teeth were as long as fangs. He looked like every picture I'd ever seen of imaginary werewolves.

I don't know if I yelped again; I hope I didn't. I do know I stood there frozen with fear as I watched that huge lumbering creature disappear into the house with the light. Then I delivered the post – luckily there was none for that particular house – and scurried out of the village as fast as my little postie legs could take me.

When I got back, I nonchalantly asked Susie and Reg,

who was still working at the time, if there was anything strange about Trescatho. 'No, why?' they both replied, looking at me as if I was the weird one.

I've never seen him again, whoever he is. Or was. And I've never seen the people who live in that house. The name on the odd letter they get, mostly advertisements, is a common enough name, so there are no answers there.

I used to scorn all those books I saw on sale when we moved here, about 'haunted' Cornwall and 'mysterious' Cornwall but now I hold my tongue. This place makes believers in elves and fairies of all of us at one time or another, I'm beginning to think.

Trescatho is no less mysterious today, in a strong morning light and under a cold blue sky. I've long since given up trying to solve the mystery of my 'werewolf' but I indulge in lighter fantasies: I am a time traveller and this is my favourite stop-off back in the 16th century. I do this all the way to the red posting box which, if not exactly 16th century, is pretty old. It's embedded in a Jack and Jill herringbone stone wall, part of the one that surrounds this cluster of houses on the green. The old postbox has been cemented in, though the rest of the wall is dry stone – or Cornish hedging as it is known here. Unlike these walls in other counties, the stones are thin and are laid flat, one narrow stone above the other. In Devon, the next county up, the dry stone walls are made with larger stones and look totally different.

I unlock the Royal Mail postbox to collect the letters and that's when I see the first sign of life in this mysterious hamlet, clustered in a heap at the bottom of the collection box: snails, about six or seven of them, looking as if they've lived there for decades. I smile to myself. *Snail Mail.*

I run my fingers through the letter slot to check if the brush is still there, those soft bristles which are supposed to keep spiders and other crawling creatures out of Royal Mail property. Yes, it's still intact. Staring at the snails for a moment, I wonder how they got through the barrier before I take the few letters and gently close the box, leaving the snails where they are. Another mystery, but one I'm contented not to solve. Let the snails live amongst the letters in peace.

As I drive away I wonder if, the moment the van is out of sight, the people of Trescatho all come tumbling out of their cottages and get on with the lives they've been living for the last few centuries, the lives I'll never see, never know about, no matter how many times I deliver their letters and parcels.

The stillness doesn't last long. Soon I'm back in my van, going up the hill to do a few more deliveries. I've finished my round but I'm doing part of Susie's. It's her birthday today and she's taken the day off, so I and the other deliverers are sharing out her round for this one day, along with our own.

I go up the road to Eleanor Gibland's house, parking at the creek where I had tried to find the rainbow's end that time. It seems years ago now but it was only last November. I get out of the van, stare idly at the water gurgling and rushing over stones and pebbles, spilling over onto the mossy grass along-side. Then, unable to resist, I paddle out into the shallow creek to take a look at the hunk of rock where I saw the glint of gold that crazy day as the sun shone through the storm clouds. Is it really a yellow stone or was it an illusion created by the strange sky and stunning rainbow, that November morning? Perhaps there was something underneath the pebbles that caused that golden colour?

I lean over and start turning the stones over, forgetting completely where I am and what I'm supposed to be doing.

A prissy voice brings me up short, 'Still looking for that pot of gold, are you?'

I flush. How did she know what I had been up to that

morning? I never told her I was following a rainbow. No doubt
Susie did, though. I'd told her the story, laughing at myself as
I did so. The story must have spread all over our postal area
by now. I really must remember how nothing is either secret
or sacred around here.

I'm handing Eleanor some flyers for a bath shop, an advertisement for computers and what looks like a bank statement,
when the quiet of this tranquil spot by the creek is broken by
the loud noise of a motor. I look around, startled, but there
are no vehicles driving up the narrow road to the house, nor
are there any tractors in the fields alongside.

Eleanor says, 'Helicopter.'

We look up, and sure enough, there's a huge helicopter
heading towards us. In moments it is right above us, circling
us like a buzzard homing in on carrion.

I'm getting nervous. The helicopter is so low, so close and
so noisy, that Eleanor and I have to shout at each other. 'What's
happening?' I yell. 'It must be looking for something.'

'Or someone,' she shouts back.

I can't bear the noise any longer so I wave goodbye and jump
into the van to get away from it. As I look up again I see people
inside, waving their arms. It makes me jumpy as I don't know
what's wrong, what they're after. Are they warning me about
something? Has there been an accident? Has some serial killer
armed to the teeth escaped from prison somewhere? Could he
be hiding in a Royal Mail van? Is he in mine?

I drive at top speed out of the drive and head back along
the cliff road to St Geraint. To my horror, it seems that the
helicopter is following me. Is it the police, I wonder? Did
someone report me for leaving their post in a leaking shed? I
slow down, stop at a lay-by overlooking the cliffs and sea. The
helicopter hovers overhead, circling the van. I rev up again,
drive into town and into the boat yard parking area. I'm almost

too frightened to get out but I tell myself not to be so silly. I open the door and look up. I can see the pilot and co-pilot inside, and other people too, still waving and shouting at me. What do they want?

Tentatively, I raise my arm in a kind of salute. This acknowledgement seems to be what they have been waiting for as the helicopter circles one more time and then flies away in a rush of whirring blades and overwhelming noise.

My ears are still ringing when I meet Susie in the coffee shop. I wish her a happy birthday and plop down next to her and Eddie, our new relief postman. Eddie's a lively, energetic young man with thick ginger-blond hair and endearing freckles. Already he and Susie have a great relationship going, though more like brother and sister than work colleagues, one minute thick as clotted cream and the next sparring with each other. Luckily for the sake of peace in the post office, the sparring is always done in a joking way and neither of them take it seriously.

I order a latte, another coffee for Susie and tea for Eddie. When that's done I say, 'So, Eddie, who was that pretty young woman you were showing around in the van yesterday?'

He grins, cheekily. 'Her? Oh, she's history. Never showed up at the cinema yesterday evening, stood me up.'

Susie grimaces. 'Don't blame her. Wouldn't want to be one of your women for sure.'

Eddie sighs, rolling his eyes. 'Can't help the way they run after me, maid.' He winks at me and I smile back. There's something about his slow easy confidence that's appealing.

Susie gives him a mock slap on the wrist then turns to me. 'Is everything OK, Tessa? You looked flustered when you came in just now.'

'I was.' I tell them about the helicopter following me all the way from Eleanor's house.

'I saw it,' Susie says. 'Just as we come in here.'

'Coast Guard,' adds Eddie.

'I wonder what it was up to? Terrified the life out of me. Can't be looking for someone lost at sea, not up around Eleanor's place anyway.'

Susie grins, 'Course not. They thought you was me, is all.'

'What?'

'They do it every year, me mates in the Coast Guard. To wish me a happy birthday. Didn't realize I took the day off today. Usually work on m'birthday.'

I am still looking confused. 'The men in the helicopter thought *you* was *me,* Tessa.' Susie has that slow patient *I'm talking to a dumbo* tone of voice that seems to be the one many of the locals use with me more often than is comfortable. 'Those blokes know my round better'n I do.'

Our drinks arrive before I can say anything else, but what is there to say, anyway? By now Susie and Eddie are talking of something else, going out for a meal together that night by the sound of it, as if the instance of a Coast Guard helicopter circling a post office van to wish the postwoman inside a happy birthday were a normal everyday Cornish occurrence.

And well it might be, I think as I take a sip of my latte, wondering what this bizarre job will have in store for me next.

February

Up Country it is still winter but in Cornwall spring is well underway. The camellias, which were budding last month, are in bloom. For days their white, pink and red petals have been strewn like confetti all over the village. The gardens are filled with camellia bushes, some of them fifteen feet high, and every time there is a high wind the air swirls with colour. The petals stick to my red van like tiny, colourful stamps.

In January, the fields along the roadside began to fill with the daffodils that will be sold Up Country. I've heard there is trouble finding pickers now, since so many Eastern European countries have joined the EU and the workers go to the towns where the money is better. Only the Latvians and the Estonians still seem to be regulars.

I love driving up and down the hills in my petal-splattered van between sunny yellow fields, revelling in the colours. My old friends in London tell me that despite a few early blooms, the city is still grey and gloomy. Here, the magnolias are beginning. Though the February breeze is still cold, I roll down the windows to get a whiff of their perfume when I deliver the post to some of the houses along the sea. The vanilla scent of magnolias mingles with the smell of salt and seaweed; they look so exotic in these seaside gardens, those bare branches with gigantic blooms. In the sheltered valleys the trees grow huge. They were brought back by the famous plant hunters of the past and every time I see them I am transported back to a different time, a different place.

Today is Friday and I'm looking forward to a whole rare weekend off. Last night Ben and I were up late, cleaning the house in anticipation of Annie's visit. I love it when really good friends come to stay. It takes away the sting of some of our other visitors, like Seth and Samantha, and another couple, Morgan and Glenda, who ate us out of house and home without once helping to peel a vegetable or wash a dish; who offered to take us for a pub meal and managed to turn their backs so Ben was forced to pay; and whose two hyper-active children so antagonized Will and Amy that they were enraged for ages afterwards. But those visitors were not my dear old London friends. Those, I miss terribly. Annie is a special one, sharing all those intimate girlie talks that can only occur with close female friends.

Though I've made loads of acquaintances here, I don't feel any of them have become friends yet. There are some in the village I'd like to get to know better and once or twice I've sensed a breaking through of that thin but strong line between acquaintances and friends. Somehow before it happens, before that line is crossed, there seems to be a pulling back – not from me but from the villagers. It's all very polite but I'm acutely aware of the exclusion.

Yesterday was a prime example. I was in the village shop, buying some Cornish cream for Annie's arrival, when Daphne, who farms along with her husband a few miles from the village, came in. Daphne's children go to the same school as mine and we've met at PTA meetings and other school functions. We've talked loads and I've sensed a common interest between us despite our different backgrounds.

At the shop yesterday we began to chat. I told her about Annie's arrival, how I intended to clean the house from top to bottom before she came.

'For a friend?' said Daphne. 'Goodness, my friends have to take me as I come. I hate cleaning.'

Another thing we have in common, I thought, and said, 'Oh, I hate it too. And Annie wouldn't mind what the house looked like, of course she wouldn't, but she's allergic to animal hairs. Our house is covered in them.' I groaned, thinking of all the animal fluff poor Annie would have to contend with. There's not only Jake but the fur and fluff of rabbits as well. We've acquired two since Christmas, and though they live in a hutch outside the door, they're tame enough to come inside and cuddle on the sofa with the children.

Daphne commiserated when I told her about my friend's allergies. Then, encouraged, I started to confide in her about Annie, about how much I've missed her. Around us the life of a village shop went on, with a pensioner coming in for a single stamp, a young man picking up some beer for a party later, and a couple of mothers with babies buying milk and bread and stopping to chat for ages over the dairy products.

By the time Daphne and I finished talking, I felt like we'd known each other for ages, so I said, impulsively, 'You'd really like Annie, y'know, and she'd like you. How about joining us for the evening, going to the pub or something, just the three of us? Or coming out to my place? Ben is working most evenings this week so Annie and I will be on our own.'

She refused, politely, saying she had a lot on that week, and I'm sure she did. I knew Daphne was a busy woman, but she didn't give me another opening, didn't offer to get together with me after Annie left.

Well, fair enough, I thought, as I walked slowly home that day: Daphne has the farm, the kids, her own full life. She probably doesn't have much time to see her own old friends, let alone make new ones. But there have been other examples of this. People are friendly enough on the surface, but that's as far as it goes. I know it all takes time. But for now, I can't wait for Annie to get here.

I'm shivering as I drive along the empty roads to my first delivery. There's a cold wind today and the heater in the van is not working properly. It's 5.30 a.m. and the fields of daffodils are radiant in the early morning moonlight. I've had to clear my windows of the ruffles of camellia petals; the van is still covered. I like it – it feels festive and celebratory.

And then there is a moment of horror: a loud thunk against the windscreen, a dark shape hitting it, flying up and landing on the bonnet of the car. My heart thumps as I screech on the brakes and pull over to the side. Luckily there are no cars behind me; there's been no traffic at all on this road since I set out. I look at the inert form lying still on the bonnet. It's an owl.

I'm distraught. I love owls. This one was minding its own business, out hunting food on a lonely road and I came along, headlights blazing, confusing it totally as it flew into the lights and then into the darkness of death.

I feel bereft and tearful. I want to call Ben, talk to him, hear his warm words of understanding, but he'll be asleep. Everyone I know is asleep and I suddenly feel lonely here in this isolated place at this unspeakable hour in the shortest, and at times the most difficult, month of the year. All the doubts that racked me last autumn come flooding back. Did we do the right thing moving here? Will we survive financially? Will we ever make true, lasting friendships? Will I really be able to stick this job till the coming of spring when light mornings and warmth make it easier?

Even as I think these glum thoughts I know I'm over-reacting, taking the owl's demise personally, letting its death release all the fears I've managed to submerge so far in this New Year. Things are better for sure but we're still on the edge despite my job, despite Ben's several part-time jobs. We're holding on, but it's still pretty tenuous.

I succumb to tears as I take the owl tenderly, place it on a grass verge at the side of the road and sprinkle it with some camellia petals I've scraped from the van. Then I pull myself together and go back to work.

The wind is so strong that by the time I reach Morranport, I have a hard time holding the van door open. I park by the beached boats next to the post office and pick up the sack of mail for this stretch by the seaside which I deliver on foot. The sea is foamy and turbulent as the wind whips it about. I can feel my hair being pulled out of its band and beginning to stand up on top of my head.

By the time I arrive at the Grenvilles' house at the end of the road I'm a frozen, dishevelled mess of a postwoman. It's 7.30 by now but low cloud cover is blocking any dawn that dares show its sunny head.

Archie Grenville greets me at the door, a cup of steamy hot coffee in his hand. I'm not surprised to see him as he and Jennifer are early risers. Since I rescued that lone letter from the sea in front of their house and dried off in their living room, they're always offering me refreshment when I come delivering.

Today I take him up on the offer and follow him gratefully into the warm, cluttered and cosy kitchen. As he pours me a coffee and adds the hot milk already waiting on the stove, he tells me his wife is upstairs, still asleep. 'Or, I should say, Jennifer is sleeping at last. She's had a poor night; her arthritis was bad. It's this cold wind, I think.'

I've been in this kitchen a few times since the episode of the nearly-drowned letter, growing fond of this old couple with their dignified, kindly togetherness. They have their own world in each other yet somehow do not exclude others as some couples do. I feel embraced by them both every time I go into the house.

The windows of the kitchen are steamy inside and wet from the sea spray on the outside: the wind is driving the spray further than usual. There are plants everywhere, on every surface – arum lily, spider, a few cacti, an African violet – and on the wall there are paintings, rather good ones which are all portraits that Jennifer has done of friends and family. 'Some folk take photos, I paint,' she'd shrugged me off when I'd praised her work.

Most of the walls in this room that don't have portraits on them are lined with open shelves filled with books. I've had a glance at them before, mostly history books, and many on Cornwall. I've wanted to ask Archie about them for some time, for there's always one open on the kitchen table when I go in. Some have scraps of lined paper, with writing in longhand, carefully placed in certain pages.

'Ah, you've noticed the books,' Archie says now. 'Since I retired, I've discovered a passion for the past. Because I'm a selfish old codger, it's my own past, or Cornwall's past, that interests me most. Same thing, I suppose.'

I point to the sheets of paper. 'Are you writing your own book?'

He laughs and the sound rings around the warm kitchen naturally. 'No, no. What I've done, see, is jot down the most fascinating bits, for me anyway, trying to put them in some sort of order. Maybe our children will be interested one day – it's their heritage too,' he turns serious. 'And it's disappearing fast.'

I look over my coffee cup at the two books on the table. One seems to be about early farming and fishing in the county, the other myth and superstition. Seeing my glance he says, 'Aye, it went hand and hand around here, still does, y'know. The rational and the irrational. I know for a fact that some of the old fishermen still throw a bit of bread into the sea before they begin the day's fishing, as they did centuries ago. For luck.'

I nod, 'I can understand that. A libation for the gods, to appease them. Keep 'em sweet.'

'That's it. The Romans did it with wine, always poured a drop or two on the ground or the table for their gods.'

'Well, I don't blame the fishermen for using any good luck charm they can, the seas around here being what they are.' We both look out at the waves foaming and snarling across the horizon.

Archie says, 'Not only the fishermen, though. Only yesterday I heard that one of the locums at the surgery – I know him, retired ten years ago but still comes out when one of our regular doctors is ill – recommended a local charmer for a lad's warts.'

He sees my smile and acknowledges it with one of his own but says, conspiratorially, 'He maybe said it tongue-in-cheek but I wouldn't bet on it. The thing is, there really are charmers still around, left over from the old medicine men.' Now he shakes his head. 'I've heard folk talk of witches, too. Oh, they say it mockingly, pretending they have no truck with such beliefs, but old superstitions die hard, believe me. It's bred in the bone, y'know.'

Reluctantly, I stand up to leave but before I go, Archie picks up a sheet of paper. 'Have your children had the measles yet?'

I shake my head. 'Well then, you'd better have this, for when they do.'

I read it quickly. It's an old remedy apparently. You take a freshly-killed chicken, pluck out its feathers and hang it upside down in the patient's bedroom. Within a day the measles transfers itself to the bird which turns rotten and nasty as the patient is cleared of all infection.

I shudder, 'Poor bird.' I am thinking too of my poor dead owl.

'I know, not very nice for it.' We're silent for a moment. 'And d'you know, that remedy's been used within my lifetime. I saw it used on one of the fishermen's sons when I was five or six.'

Soon I'm on my way home driving along the same road where I started my round this morning, thinking about all the old Cornish stories of magic and witchcraft, a slight smile no doubt on my lips as I ponder the gullibility of people. Just when I'm starting to feel most rational, I see a black cat lying dead near the centre of the road.

Once again I pull over. I'm shaken not so much by the fact of the dead animal – I see more road kill than I care to remember on these lonely tracks – but because it's exactly the spot where the owl flew into my windscreen this morning.

I get out of the van and pull the cat into the grass at the roadside. It's not that long dead either, the car that hit it cannot have been far ahead of me. The creature has no collar and I don't recognize it; there are no houses on this stretch of the road either.

The owl is still there, the camellia petals stuck to its feathers like tiny drops of pink and red blood. I drag the dead cat next to it, cover it with petals as well and stand for a moment, feeling a bit goose-bumpy as I wonder whether this is a message from the spirits of old Cornwall warning me not to be such a sceptic.

The Owl and the Pussycat. I know it is a bizarre coincidence, hitting the owl then finding the cat in the same place on the same day but that poem has long been Amy and Will's favourite. I used to read it to them before they learned it by heart. Even now we still sometimes recite it together as we're driving along somewhere.

All the way home, the beginning of Edward Lear's poem about the owl and the pussycat goes round and round in my head until finally I turn on the radio and blare up the volume to drown it out.

Annie arrives in a whirlwind of city scents, tastes, sights. As she tumbles into the house I think I can detect, underneath the delicate perfume she wears, a whiff of London – a mix of diesel fumes, Indian takeaways and the damp of thousands of woolly winter coats. She's looking great as usual, her short, dark hair sleekly cut, her trim figure clad in a crisp, white shirt tucked into belted, well-cut jeans. The soft, oversized, woolly cardigan she's wearing is a Donna Karan piece of knitwear that makes her look both sophisticated and feminine.

She's as excited to be here as I am to see her, going from room to room commenting on the changes we've made to the house since she saw it last autumn. 'It's looking terrific, you've been so busy!'

The first thing Annie wants to do is see my van. 'You, a postie, I can't believe it,' she cries, yelping with delight. 'Why aren't you in uniform? I'm dying to see you in it. Are you really a postwoman or are you making it all up?'

I assure her that it's all true and to prove it, on Monday I take her to work with me. I can show her the Cornish country-side while she helps me on my round.

'Oh, this is so funky, wait'll I tell everyone back in London,' she shouts above the van's roar. Then she begins to sneeze.

'What is it?' I look at her anxiously as her whole body shakes with sneeze after sneeze. I suddenly remember that I've sometimes had Jake with me in the van. And of course Susie's cat rides in here too. I apologize but Annie makes light of it.

'I'll just take another antihistamine,' she says, groping about in her handbag.

I drive her to the sea, to the thin strip of sandbar on the estuary where I often stop for lunch. 'This is my canteen,' I tell her, parking the van on the hard sand at the edge of the shoreline which overlooks the bay.

It's an idyllic day. The cold winds of last week have eased and a warm front has enveloped the country. February and it's a spring day, balmy and blissful. The water is a deep blue-green and I look out across the rocks for seals. Surely they'll be sunning themselves on a day like today.

No seals but there's a cormorant, nose-diving into the sea. The sun flashes on the patch of white feathers on its face as it hits the water. I wait, and watch, and sure enough, it's been lucky this time and bobs up with a small fish. Further on, standing with one foot in the shallows, is a heron, and closer to us about half a dozen sandpipers are strutting about.

I start to point out these things to Annie but she's deep in a reverie of her own, so I keep quiet. She's standing next to me facing the sea, inhaling deeply. She's wearing her Ugg boots and a nifty little, skintight rollneck jumper tucked into those marvellous jeans. She looks terrific with her new hair-cut. 'Toni & Guy?' I'd asked her last night when I commented on it.

'Yeah, new stylist at my branch,' she touches her short, sleek hair which I notice has deep red streaks in it. 'But yours looks good too.'

I grin, 'Model night at Toni & Guy's in Truro. They need

to get the experience and I need not to spend a fortune on hair. Great compromise.'

Standing here facing the sea, Annie looks like a telly ad for some posh new shampoo with her slim body and good looks. In fact she works for the BBC, in research and programme development. She's bright, sophisticated, talented and also more allergy-prone than even I, her best friend, knew when we lived in the city. She's started to sneeze again and to cough as well. 'Sorry,' she mutters between gulps of air. 'Something's tickling my throat. Must be the salt air or something.'

'You're not allergic to the sea,' I say. 'You can't be, nobody is.'

She can't answer as her nose is blocked and her sinuses stuffed, the coughing and sneezing goes on and on. I hand her another antihistamine as we climb back into the van.

Annie raves over the countryside in all its spring glory but her allergies are getting worse. After stopping to picnic in a grassy meadow, she breaks out in an itchy rash all over her legs. After smelling an unidentified wildflower in a hedgerow, her eyes swell up.

We drive into St Geraint to buy eye drops, nasal sprays and more antihistamines. After our purchases we stop at the café on the seafront where Ben is now working part time. It's called the Sunflower Café, an appropriate name on days like today, with the sun shining in through the large picture windows and the sea sparkling right in front. We're the only customers there so after he's made and served our cappuccinos, Ben sits down with us. While Annie takes herself off to the loo to repair the damage done to her face by the Cornish countryside, I ask Ben how things are going.

'Slow,' he says. 'But then that's the way it is, in winter. My hours might be cut even more till things pick up in the spring.'

Another worry. My salary is certainly not enough to keep the family going; we need Ben's as much as mine. Thank goodness for my postal job, though, at least it's full time and I've got a contract. I've even signed the Official Secrets Act – how much more job security can a person need?

After our coffee Annie and I wander onto the jetty. The ferry for Truro is about to leave so we listen to its horn as it chugs away, watching it disappear into the distance. A few seagulls watch too. 'I guess Paul and Paula have already gone, on the early ferry,' I say.

'Who're they?'

'Didn't I tell you? Paul and Paula are seabirds, turnstones, and a few years back they began commuting on the ferry. They catch the 8.15 from here every morning and come back every evening.'

Annie turns to me and stares, 'You're making that up.'

'Not at all, it's true. The locals noticed it first and named them. Paul and Paula always get the last ferry back, every day, and the next morning they're on that first ferry again.'

Annie still looks disbelieving. 'I suppose you're going to tell me that they have a great day in Truro, getting their feathers done at Toni and Guy's and buying knickers at Marks and Spencer before coming home for the night.'

I grin, 'Don't believe me if you don't want to, but it's perfectly true. Ask any of the locals.'

She actually does. We go into the tiny bakery right in the middle of the harbour. It's no bigger than a garden shed and looks like one too. After I buy my bread and a few cakes, Annie asks Millie and Geoff, the elderly couple who have owned the bakery for years, about Paul and Paula.

'Oh, 'tis true alright,' Geoff says. 'Every mornin' we see 'em on that 8.15 ferry.'

'And every evening, back they come,' Millie adds. 'I'd be that worried if they wasn't on that last ferry home.'

Annie searches their faces for signs that this is an elaborate joke that country folk play on innocent city visitors, but their kind homely faces assure her it's not. She takes out a thin moleskin notebook from her oversized Mulberry bag and begins to write. 'I've got to remember this, to tell all your old friends back home,' she mutters while she scribbles.

My week with Annie goes by too quickly. Despite the allergies, Annie plunges into country life, treating it like a rare adventure to a lush but alien landscape. She's determined to make the most of it.

Because she can't have a dog of her own but loves them, she takes Jake for long walks while I'm working. The chemist in St Geraint must be running out of allergy medicines as she continues to sneeze, swell and itch at an alarming rate, but this doesn't deter Annie from fussing over Jake. He adores her and tries to sit on her lap in the evenings, clawing at her posh jeans as he tries to kiss her. She reaches for the tissues and takes another pill.

And then one day I come home from work to find Annie in a state. 'What's up?' I ask.

She's looking dishevelled and sweaty and a bit grimy, so unlike my immaculately groomed friend. 'I've had quite a day. I've just got back from the police station.'

'What?'

'You wouldn't believe it, what people do. Some people just shouldn't keep pets, shouldn't be allowed. I think I'll write to my MP.'

'Annie, calm down.' I make a big pot of mint tea and sit her down at the kitchen table. 'Now drink this and tell me what happened.'

'Well, I was walking down to the shop and on my way back I saw this dog, this beautiful apricot poodle, wandering along the road.'

I am busy pouring tea so don't reply. She goes on, 'No owner, no collar, nothing. Just *wandering*.' She says the last word as if wandering were a synonym for doggie drug abuse.

'Yes?' I'm becoming a bit distracted, thinking of how I need a hot shower after the day's work before I get going on dinner.

'Well, I was absolutely appalled. I marched right out, gave the poodle a few of Jake's biscuits then got him into my car and took him straight to the police station.'

'What!' All my attention is focused right back on Annie. 'You *what?*'

'I knew you'd be upset too, you're an animal lover like I am and it breaks your heart too to see stray dogs wandering the streets. Imagine, such a gorgeous dog and her owners letting her get away like that. Why she could have been killed or abducted or . . .'

I didn't wait to hear the rest. 'Annie, that dog is a bitch called Annabel. She's not a stray, she belongs to one of our neighbours on the other side of the church.'

'But she didn't have a collar.'

'No, she's got a skin allergy. You should know about that.'

'And she was just wandering . . .'

'Annie, this is the *country*. That's what dogs do. If they're docile and friendly, they wander about the village and nobody takes any notice. Sometimes Annabel has even come inside our garden when the gate is open. Jake loves her. I'm just surprised you haven't seen her before.'

'Oh dear,' Annie looks chagrined.

'Never mind, you can't help having a city mindset.' I pat her hand kindly. 'I suppose Annabel is home now?'

'Ah, no. Actually not. I took her to the police station in Truro and left her there. I don't know what they've done with her.'

I race out of the house, behind the church and to the neighbours. They're not in. I phone the police station.

Yes, Annabel is still there and no, they haven't found the owner yet. I explain everything and say I'll be right over.

I leave a note for the owners in case they get home before we do. Forgetting my shower and tonight's special dinner I was making for Annie's last night, I drive to Truro in heavy traffic and a heavier mist that has suddenly fallen. Annie, crestfallen and quiet, goes with me. Annabel licks us both all over when she sees us and Annie reaches for the new inhaler she's acquired since coming to the countryside.

'I'll take us all out to dinner tonight,' she announces when we return Annabel to her rightful place in the village. 'To make amends.'

She does and after a glass or two of wine, we're all laughing hysterically over the incident. But not as much as I laughed when, sitting in the car, I watched and listened while Annie apologized to Annabel's owners and tried to explain her actions. The bemused look on their faces, the tolerant rolling of the eyes and shaking of their heads as Annie turned to walk away from them, had me in stitches all the way home.

The last week in February is half term, and once again most of the second-homers are in residence. When I get to Adam and Elizabeth Johnson's house, I'm relieved to see them. 'Good to see you back,' I say to Mrs Johnson when she answers the door.

She looks distracted. Behind her, there are the shrieks and hollers of two children seemingly murdering each other. 'So sorry, it's the twins,' she says and shouts at them to stop whatever they're doing at once.

I hand her the post and she takes it, thanks me and starts to shut the front door. 'Er, Mrs Johnson, about Marmalade?'

'What?' she's hardly listening to me as the noise inside the house starts again.

'Marmalade?' I repeat.

'Oh, uh, no thanks, I brought all those basics down with us from London.'

Before she can shut the door again I say quickly, 'I meant your cat, Marmalade. He's still in our freezer back at the post office.'

She looks at me as if I were a lunatic until the penny finally drops. 'Oh, *that* Marmalade, of course. I'm so sorry, I'm not quite with it today. Such a chore, getting organized to come down here. And Adam not able to get away until the weekend.'

'I'm sure it must be,' I say, trying very hard to be sincere. Having a second home is such a burden, I want to say, I'm so glad we haven't that worry.

We stand there looking at each other for a moment. I'm waiting for her to tell me when she's going to collect her frozen cat but she doesn't say a thing, only stands there politely waiting for me to go. Finally I say, 'You wanted us to keep him until half term so your children could have a funeral. So will you collect him yourself from Morranport? Or would you like me to deliver him with your post?'

She looks horrified. 'Oh dear. Oh no, God no.'

'That's fine then. You can collect him any time from nine to five. Nell will be there at the post office, she knows where to find him.'

But Mrs Johnson is shaking her head. 'Look, uh, oh sorry, I've forgotten your name . . .'

'Tessa Hainsworth.'

'Tessa, I'm so sorry to put you to all this trouble but the children seem to have forgotten all about Marmalade. In fact we've already got another cat; he's in London with Adam. So if you don't mind disposing of the, uh, carcass, I'd very much appreciate it. Now, if you'll excuse me, I must go and sort out the twins.' She closes the door firmly without another word.

Back at Morranport Nell says, 'I've got a good mind to go meself to that fool of a woman and leave the body on the doorstep. What she be thinkin' of?'

'I don't know but it looks like we're stuck with a frozen cat in the freezer indefinitely.'

She glares at me. I shrug, rolling my eyes.

And then, as we usually do in ludicrous situations like this, Nell and I begin to giggle, then laugh, with such abandon that a customer walks into the shop, takes one look at us and walks out hurriedly.

'We've got to stop this,' I gasp when I can talk again. 'You've just lost a customer.'

'Must of been a stranger,' Nell gasps when she can speak again. 'Anyone else would of stayed on, found out what be goin' on so he could join the fun.'

No doubt others did. The tale of frozen Marmalade was all around Morranport by the next morning.

March

I'm feeling so settled into my job now that I've decided to make a real effort to fit into the community. The first thing I do is to get involved in an after-school gardening club for the children at our local primary school.

I run it together with Daphne. My relationship with her is still the same, confined to a chat in the village shop and at school functions. Once or twice I've hinted that we meet more often but she pretends she doesn't get it. I'm resigned to it by now though it still saddens me.

The gardening club idea came to us while Daphne and I were waiting for the children one afternoon. We were standing near the wonderful garden attached to the school which was unused and overgrown. Daphne and I agreed that it was a waste, all that lovely space gone to seed, and that was how it all started.

Twenty-five children sign up for our club. First I'm excited then worried. What do we do with them? What will we grow? Where will we get all the seeds, the young plants, the compost, the pots? But first things first, I tell myself.

Daphne has a couple of cows calving and she's unable to concentrate on the gardening club during this time so I'm on my own the first day, with twenty-five eager young faces gleaming at me ready to be inspired.

By me? I panic. I can already hear Annie's giggles as I tell her about this. She knows I've never been a gardener who knows what she's doing but there's a first time for everything, isn't there? It's a cold cloudy day but at least it's not raining, not yet. A strong sou'westerly is beginning to blow but I'm determined to keep the troops' morale high. 'Chocolate digestives, children,' I shout, brandishing the biscuit packet high above my head. It nearly blows out of my hand but before my audience can dissolve into anarchic laughter I cry, 'And orange squash for all! Let's picnic before we start, and when we finish we'll have more treats.'

Biscuits crunched and drinks downed, the youngsters set to work with spades and forks, setting into the overgrowth like a wraith of pint-sized furies. It takes a number of after-school sessions and the help of several parents we've roped in before finally the ground is cleared and dug over, ready to be planted when the planting season is upon us. Right now it's wet and freezing but it won't be long till spring.

'Miss, what will we plant?' one of the more precocious children asks me.

'Not sure.' I hadn't thought that far ahead. I was far too concerned with getting the ground prepared while the rains held off. Just as well too, for it's pouring now. Wildly I look around for Daphne but she's just gone home. The rest of us have all run inside the school house where we are waiting for the storm to let up.

Others are taking up the chorus. 'What will we plant, Mrs Hainsworth? What are we going to grow?'

'Runner beans!' a bright-eyed sprog of a child shouts. The others start to add their penny's worth.

'No, peas. I love peas.'

'Onions! Great hu-mun-gous onions to make the girls cry!'

'Shut up Alan, I bet you cry as much as girls.'

'Don't.'

'Do.'

'Sunflowers! Let's grow lots and lots of sunflowers.'

'And pink flowers and red flowers and blue and yellow and . . .'

'And onions!'

'And beans to make the boys fart!'

'We never!'

This is getting out of hand. 'SHUSH EVERYONE.' I put on my stern no-nonsense voice. 'We'll grow everything we can. IF you all behave yourselves.'

Foul weather hits Cornwall so our gardening project has to move inside. Daphne and I get everyone to write recipes for things we'd like to cook with the vegetables we'll grow. We draw pictures of gardens and make paper flowers. We collect yogurt pots to fill with compost and plant seedlings. The trouble is, we have no compost, no seeds or seedlings, and no money to buy these things. And so I take my problem to my customers.

By now I'm getting to know them quite well. Mr Hawker, my poor, dear, sad, old man, has become almost a friend in that we always chat for at least ten minutes, sometimes more, when I deliver his post. I've discovered he likes KitKats so every week I take him a pack of six small ones. He thanks me solemnly and profusely. He gives me things too – an old women's magazine he found in one of his cupboards some-where, an apple left over from a box that Martin and Emma Rowland gave him last autumn. I accept all these things with the same profusion of thanks and solemnity he gives me when I present my KitKats.

Other customers are beginning to give me things too – the odd bunch of early spring flowers, a jar of home-made marmalade, some frozen blackberries in an old margarine carton. Susie told me at the start not to refuse anything, no matter how mouldy the fruit, or how many jars of marmalade I already have gathering dust in my cupboards. 'You'll be hurtin' their feelings bad,' she said to me gravely, 'if you don't take their gifts.'

Now I am going to beg for gifts. I tell all the customers I get a chance to talk to about the school's gardening club, tell them how we're on the scrounge for supplies. By the next week, people on my route are waiting outside as I arrive to give me half-filled bags of compost, plastic pots, ceramic basins and cuttings from favourite plants.

When I deliver to Trehallow, the 'doggie' hamlet as I call it in my head, I risk Batman's wrath to accept sprigs of rosemary from his keeper, my favourite little old great-grandmother. Batman is usually inside when I arrive, howling his huge canine head off. 'He likes you,' Great-grandmother tells me. 'That's his bark when someone he knows and likes comes around.'

Silly me, not recognizing a happy bark, I think as I go away with the cuttings. Pity Royal Mail didn't add How to Talk Dog in their induction.

Others in Trehallow are generous too. Lily, the border terrier who is on a perpetual diet, is actually allowed three green biscuits while her owner rummages in her garden shed and comes out with a tray of leek seedlings. 'The luck o' the Irish to you, maid,' she says as she always does. I've given up wondering why this Cornish woman always wishes me Irish luck and just accept it gladly.

Blackie, the next door's mongrel, hears me and is yapping for her biscuit before I even get to the garden gate. It's bone-shaped yellow biscuits for Blackie and as I drop them into her salivating mouth her owners, the roly-poly Tweedledee and Tweedledum, come waddling out and say in unison, 'Oh Tessa, we be hearing 'bout your garden club.'

They, and Blackie, herd me into their greenhouse and by the time I leave, my van is full of marvellous cuttings and tiny plants: courgettes, runner beans and lettuce, ready soon to be planted out into our newly prepared soil.

When I tell Martin and Emma Rowland about the school gardening club, they're more enthusiastic than I am. Since they lost the farm and had to open the B&B, they've taken to gardening in a big way. 'Never had time for it when we were farming,' Emma told me. 'But I find time now, even during busy season. Soothes my soul. Soothes Martin, too. He's never got over not working the land, so working a garden is at least next best.'

When I next deliver to them, they're both waiting for me. They too start filling my van with all sorts of plants and cuttings, mountains of them. They add some organic fertilizer – 'We've got loads' – and even some old tools that they say they don't need any more.

I try to thank them but Martin scowls, trying to look blustery. ''Tis nothing, maid.'

Then his face lightens. A pick-up has arrived and in the back, sitting on a clean pile of straw, are two small brown goats. 'Look, the little 'uns are here,' he beams at his wife.

He takes them out, one by one. They've just been weaned, the farmer who brought them tells us. Martin is already talking to them, calming them like his own children, as he leads them to their waiting field and pen.

Emma says, watching him, 'He does miss his animals so. I thought if we got a couple of goats, it would be something. He can go out and talk to them when the guests drive him up the wall.'

From Trelak Farm, I go to Mr Hawker with one lone envelope, obviously a circular. He hears me coming and is standing at his open door waiting for me. We exchange a few words about the weather then he stiffly, awkwardly, thrusts something out at me, obviously wanting me to take it. 'I heerd tell from Martin you be doing a garden thing with the kiddies. Here be some seeds fer it.'

I take the two packets of runner bean seeds. They're covered with dust and grime; the packaging looks old-fashioned, the colours faded. Mr Hawker must have dug them out from a shed or cupboard where they'd stood for years, maybe even decades.

'Why thank you, Mr Hawker,' I say, moved once again by this kind old man. 'This will certainly be a help.'

As I drive away I turn to look at him. He's still standing in the open doorway, his hand up in a slight wave.

I bring my loot to the school and Daphne smiles while the kids hoot and cheer. 'My goodness, Tessa, haven't you done well,' she says.

'Not me, my customers,' I tell her.

During the next week, while the weather remains foul, we put plants in pots, cuttings into compost and plant seeds in long planters. We label and make notes with all the enthusiasm of those early Victorian plant gatherers.

And then, when the weather improves, it's time to put some of the plants out, early though it still is. For this is South Cornwall where things of a seasonal nature happen far earlier than anywhere else in England, like plants growing and birds nesting. Which they're doing now, some of them. I hear them in the early morning dawn, making their birdsong. Blackbirds, robins, skylarks, doves – the sky seems full of melody as winter turns slowly into spring. Often these days I stop the van on lonely country lanes to listen and watch. In London my only connection with these marvellous feathered creatures was the odd bedraggled pigeon but here you can't help but be a bird lover. We've even learned to love chickens. Impulsively, longing for free range eggs, Ben and I have bought half a dozen point-of-lay chickens, beautiful brown Rhode Islanders with yellow legs. Ben built a house for them in the back garden and we've fenced off a section of lawn where they can roam freely and happily. I can't wait to start eating the eggs.

Easter comes at the end of March this year and there is a school fête to raise money. It's a Saturday afternoon and the whole village turns out: children, parents, grandparents and siblings, dogs and cats and even a pet rabbit on a lead. It's another balmy day with the March winds mercifully at bay today. Ben, the kids and I walk to the school and as Will and Amy go on ahead, we linger at the kaleidoscope of colour in the village. The magnolias are in full bloom and are now joined by rhododendrons and azaleas. The colours are dazzling – bright blues and purples, pale pinks and creamy whites, oranges of every shade from pale marmalade to dark amber. It will go on like this next month and the next, this chaos of colour.

We get there early as I'm going to man our gardening club stall while Ben runs a 'Pluck the Pheasant' stall. He's made a free-standing wooden pheasant cut out with feathers he got from a gamekeeper's wife, and the child that plucks a feather tipped with red nail polish wins a lolly. There are food stalls and tea stalls, great tables laden with clean quality used clothes for a jumble sale, an assortment of games to play – guessing how many coins in a bottle, throwing hoops and tug-of-war.

I have several young helpers on my gardening stall and they're doing just fine, so I let them take over while I roam around. Daphne stops to say she'll take over our stall for the last hour, to free the youngsters. She's with several of her friends from the village, all laughing and talking easily. I watch them as they go off and mingle with the crowd, thinking of what several non-Cornish residents have told me, that it takes about twenty years to be accepted, so it's early days yet.

I go back to our stall which was crammed with all the seedlings and other plants we didn't have room for in the school garden. Unfortunately, the labels the children had so carefully placed on everything had smeared, so that no one knew what they were buying. Despite that, everything has gone, even the dozen small pots with the rosemary cuttings dipped in root powder that I'd helped the kids to plant. 'Ah,' I say when I realize they've gone. 'Oh dear.' I'd put them aside when I saw that the rosemary hadn't taken, that these were all small pots of dead stalks. 'Well, it was for a good cause,' I mutter to myself, counting the great wad of money we'd just made for the school.

That night, flushed with success – Ben's stall had made a huge profit too – we go down to the village pub for a drink after dinner, taking advantage of the fact that Will and Amy are staying overnight at a friend's house. The pub is packed, with lots of folk from both our village and the neighbouring ones. We stop to chat to people at the bar before weaving our way through the rowdy crowd looking for a table for two.

On our way we pass Daphne and her husband Joe, sitting at the long low oak table in the corner with three other couples. 'Well done, Tessa,' she says. Then, to the others, 'The gardening club's produce raised the most money at the fête today and the whole thing was Tessa's idea.'

While I try to protest that Daphne was as much responsible as I was, everyone praises me, saying complimentary things and sounding as if they really mean every word. I feel touched by it all. But then there's an awkward moment when the talk runs out and we're still standing there. Joe asks us, belatedly, to join them, and Daphne nods her head, smiling. Somehow it's too late. Though perhaps sincere, it doesn't sound natural.

They've got a closed group, a group of old friends with years of shared experiences. To join them would be to alter their dynamics; we would feel intruders. So we say truthfully that there's no room and that anyway we're not staying long. No one tries to dissuade us.

We find a corner with a table for two and have a drink, some crisps. The pub is like countless others both in Cornwall and all over England – low ceiling, oak beams, horse brasses, beer-smelling, dark but pleasant – and comfortable enough. We talk about the fête, about our jobs, about the children, and then decide to get home for an early night. Everyone waves cheerily as we leave.

Easter also brings the first wave of 'emmetts', the Cornish word for tourists. In Devon I've heard that the word is 'grockles'. The two counties are careful of these distinctions; I know that people who live in Devon can be quite as sniffy as the Cornish when both places are lumped together as a vague West Country entity. Everyone is quite clear that when you cross the Tamar River, you cross a line from one world to another.

Some of the differences are obvious from the start. Like the anti-litter signs: in Devon it's 'Keep Devon Ship-shape', while here in Cornwall you see a smiley-faced bin-bag that states, 'Mrs Baggit says take your rubbish home'. Recently I've heard Devon visitors commenting on these slogans as a sign of the sophistication of Devon compared to its southerly more unsophisticated neighbour, but I've retorted that they just haven't got the sense of humour we do. I realize that I'm starting to think like a Cornish woman.

The emmetts that arrive first are what I call the pink shirt brigade, the high-powered City types who own second homes along the sea fronts and the tiny villages near the coves and beaches. They like to think of themselves as part of Cornwall, a breed apart from the day tourists or the campers or holiday makers who only rent, rather than own a piece of the county for themselves, but the locals don't see this distinction. They're still visitors here, transients boosting their economy.

Easter week is at the end of the month and I'm walking along the seafront to St Geraint post office. A spate of warm weather predicted for the weekend has lured not just the second homers but day trippers as well to the town. You can usually tell the difference: the ones here for the day are ambling along, eating ice cream and feeding the seagulls, though there are strict rules against doing so as the birds have become aggressive over the years. I've seen a gull swoop down and take a sandwich from a man's hand as he stood on the harbour waiting for the ferry and another one snatch an ice cream cone from a little girl's fingers. They have sharp claws and beaks, and have become a menace. Especially in June and July, when they're protecting their young, they can be vicious and dangerous.

The second homers are too busy to eat ice creams and loll about the seafront, though they take a moment in their busy lives to frown at the day trippers as they throw a crumb to the gulls. The men in their Armani casuals keep surreptitiously consulting their blackberries or desperately trying to get a signal on their mobile phones while they try to figure out how to open the toddler's pushchair, something they've never had to do before. Meanwhile the women, in their Boden knits and cords, steer the men up the side streets where there is a boutique or two selling unusual designer frocks and Dr Hauschka organic skin cream.

It never varies, as we discovered on many visits to Cornwall before we finally moved here. As I walk briskly along I'm reassured that it's all beginning again. The second homers are back in their cottages, soon they'll be back on their yachts. Life in South Cornwall goes on as usual.

Susie joins me before I get to the post office. 'Buzzing, isn't it,' she mutters as we try to pass two supremely obese women eating pasties as they walk. I notice a couple of the pink shirt brigade staring disapprovingly at them. The day trippers are giving 'their' town a bad name, all that eating in the streets and letting oneself go to seed.

Susie giggles; she's noticed it too. We look at each other and raise our eyebrows. All of a sudden I'm feeling I've been here forever, being able to grimace at all the assorted visitors with the assurance of a local.

Outside a small office, we stop to chat with Harry, who has recently started work for one of the accountants in town. Harry, with his partner Charlie, moved down from London around the same time we did, buying a small cottage in the next village to ours. Ben and I met the couple right after Christmas at a party given by some mutual London friends who had rented a cottage near us for the New Year. That night, Harry and I discovered we had other acquaintances in common and since then have struck up an easy friendship, meeting every now and again for coffee or lunch and a chat.

He's outside his office now, rolling a cigarette. 'Hey Tessa, Susie. Looks like summer's early this year.' He rolls his eyes in mock horror.

Harry is in his mid-thirties, tall and lean, devastatingly good-looking. In London he too was part of the pink shirt brigade, a high-powered accountant for one of the most prestigious firms in the city, but, like me, the stress finally got to him and he moved to Cornwall last summer.

Charlie, on the other hand, is Cornish born and bred. He was born in Morranport, the son of a fisherman. Unwilling to come out to his family, he left home for Up Country, worked at odd jobs here and there before ending up as a hair stylist in a trendy salon in Kent. He and Harry met in Canterbury when Harry, visiting friends, popped into the salon for a haircut. The couple have been together since.

'It was me that was desperate to come to Cornwall,' Harry told me when we talked one day, on a wet January morning in St Geraint. I'd finished delivering the post and was in the Sunflower Café trying to get warm before going home when he joined me. 'Daft name for a café, with the rain beating against that huge glass front,' Harry muttered as he warmed his hands on a hot cup of rich chocolate. 'But at least it's warmer here than in my office. Something's wrong with the heating. I have to pop out here to get warm between clients.'

Even with a nose red with cold and hair slick with rain, Harry looked ravishingly gorgeous. Curious, I asked, 'How did you end up here? Surely there were more job opportunities in Truro.'

He'd shrugged. 'I'd had enough of big firms, believe me. I really did want to downsize in every way.'

I nodded. 'I know what you mean.'

'So when Charlie heard through the village grapevine about this opening, I applied straightaway.'

As we sat huddled over our hot chocolate that icy day, Harry told me more about how he'd got here. 'I've always loved Cornwall, used to come here on holidays with the parents. I think that's why I first fell in love with Charlie – the rugged Cornish-ness of him.' He looked dreamily out of the window.

'Didn't Charlie want to come back?'

'He was torn. Missed the place, yes, but knew he'd have to come out if we moved here. Was a bit nervous of that. His family didn't know.'

'And is it all right now with them?'

Harry had looked pensive. 'Yeah, more or less. It wasn't easy, telling them. A small village – it's hard. But they're OK with it now.'

After a brief chat, Susie and I wave goodbye to Harry and wander on towards the post office. We pass the old clothes shop that has apparently been there for decades. A stark contrast to the trendy boutiques, it has clothes in the window that would have been old fashioned in the Sixties. I've rarely seen it open. There is a sign on the door, written in pencil: Closed until I can be bothered to open it again. I've seen this sign often, but sometimes it changes to: Open until I get bored. Mostly, though, the shop is closed.

I asked Susie about it when I started the job. 'Oh, that place. Owned by an old bloke. Poor man, partner died a year or so back, tries to run the place hisself but his heart's not in it.'

Obviously not. I take another look through as we walk past. The sign is as faded as the pleated wool skirt and the beige nylon blouse in the window.

In the post office, Margaret greets us cheerily. 'Junk mail issued today, ladies,' she says, indicating mounds of it in the sorting room. 'But of course I should have said "business mail" as we must officially call it. Have fun.'

I look sheepishly at Susie. I've already learned the trick of putting it aside to be delivered the next day, when I'm not on. We all do it, surreptitiously of course, pretending we don't. It's just such a chore and so pointless too. The number of people I have who give it right back to me, or mutter 'firelighters' when they see it, is phenomenal.

On the way home I stop at the little supermarket for some milk and butter. It's packed today.

Lulu sees me. 'Mrs Posh Post Lady, how are you?'

'Fine, Lulu, what about you?'

'Oh very fine too. I am liking very much this place in sunshine.'

The woman she is serving, flashy in her town clothes, her pink and yellow patterned town wellies, stares haughtily at her, for daring to chat to the customers. Behind us, there is a queue of second homers, some I recognize, having already delivered to them. They're talking loudly and Lulu and I stop talking to listen.

'Do you think the chicken is *really* fresh? I'm not so sure. Wouldn't be surprised if it's been frozen.'

'We should have brought one from home.'

'Yes, we should have stocked up in Waitrose. Pity there's not one here.'

Lulu looks at me and shakes her head. I pack up my milk and butter while the couple behind me pay for the dubious chicken.

As they leave I hear them say, 'She wasn't very friendly was she, that foreign girl who served us.'

'Rude, if you ask me. You'd think they'd train the staff properly, wouldn't you?'

I scowl at them as they go out. I can just imagine them telling their friends Up Country how rude the post office staff is too.

A few days later I am in St Geraint again, planning to meet Ben for a hurried lunch, not in the Sunflower Café but somewhere quiet where no one knows us so we can relax and talk. A new tea shop and lunch restaurant has opened on the edge of town and we've decided to try there. It's behind the Roswinnick which is full now with guests. I've heard there's an English dame who is a well-known actress staying at the hotel this week, as well as one of the stars of a long running soap, but so far I've not seen any of them roaming around town.

The Easter break has remained warm and dry and it's not yet April; I hope this bodes well for summer but you never know. St Geraint will empty for a time after this spring holiday but the hordes will be back as soon as summer starts. Earlier even – the May Bank Holiday is usually the beginning.

As I approach the Roswinnick I see a crowd of people gathered outside. At first I think they are trying to spot the celebrities, though the locals are usually fairly blasé about them and don't pay them much attention.

As I get closer, I hear a noise in the sky and look up to see what the excitement is about. An air ambulance is about to land on the thin strip of shoreline in front of the hotel.

I see Harry amongst the onlookers and ask him what's happened. 'A builder, working on a house a few miles from here, on his own in the middle of nowhere, apparently fell off the scaffold. Nearly ripped his arm off.'

'Oh how awful. Where is he now?'

'On his way here, to St Geraint. Luckily some walkers heard his cry for help or he'd have been there all day. Apparently they've put him in his car and are on their way here with him now. It's Ian Franks, you probably know the guy.'

'Only vaguely, he's not on my normal route.'

Eddie has come up behind us and says, 'He's on Susie's round but I've seen him lots when I've done relief for her. Nice bloke, has a couple of kids, little maids not even big enough to go to school.'

'Is he bad?'

Eddie's face is pale under his freckles. 'Don't know.'

We look over at the air ambulance, now on the ground. The tide is coming in fast and everyone is anxiously waiting for the car with the injured man. It's a real race against time, for the helicopter will have to leave without Ian if the tide comes in before he gets here.

There's a sudden cheer from the crowd. A Volvo estate is driving furiously up the street, escorted by the local police. The rescue operation is completed just in time, the helicopter, with Ian safe inside, is barely up in the air before the sand bar is covered with water.

Later, over lunch in the small back-street café, I say to Ben, 'Poor Ian, there's talk of his losing an arm. It was a nasty accident, apparently.'

'So I heard. Poor guy.'

Next day, people are talking of nothing else. Everyone is distressed. 'God knows what Ian will do if he can't work,' Martin Rowland says to me. 'He's a bloody good builder, one of the best, done it since he worked with his father as a young kid.'

Emma gives me a brown pot with a heavy lid. 'Can you drop this off at his place? His wife and kids might be glad of it. It's only a stew, but they might be needing something hot when they get home from hospital.'

I don't tell her that the family isn't on my round. It's not far out of my way to drop by anyway. At other places, I'm given daffodils to take to Ian, a couple of flowering plants, some fresh fruit, magazines. Even Mr Hawker, who has nothing to give, hands me a sliver of lined paper on which he's written, 'Dear Ian, I hope you get better soon. I knew your grandfather; he was a good man.'

I put all the offerings into Ian's unlocked front porch, as no one is home. The goodness, the sincerity of these people and their gifts, touches me to the core. The generosity of those who have very little has not stopped amazing me since I moved here.

We learn soon that Ian's life isn't threatened but his arm is. It's been operated on but apparently it's touch or go if the operation will save the arm. What will he do, how will he live, how will he support himself if he loses his business? I'm asked this a dozen times, not that anyone expects an answer.

It isn't until a few days later, when the good news spreads that the operation is a success and not only will Ian not lose his arm but will fully recover and be able to work again, that people heave a collective sigh of relief and finally are able to let go, to turn to other things.

April

Annie comes down again at the beginning of the month for a long weekend.

'I've come to remind you of your roots,' she says as I meet her from Truro train station. 'So that you don't become too bovine.' She's carrying her laptop as well as her weekend bag. 'Had so much work to do, that's why I didn't drive this time.'

I smile smugly. 'I remember those bad old days, when I had to lug my work home with me every weekend. Not any more.'

'OK smartie.' She makes a face at me. 'You have an answer for everything since you've moved down here.' As usual she looks stunning, a smart belted trench coat over her designer jeans and a perky little wine-coloured beret on her sleek hair.

I lead her to Minger, the name we've given to my old car. It's a far cry from the smart company car I once had. Minger is a little white Peugeot that used to be a police car. Since we moved it's been the 'beach' car and smells of wet dog, salt and seaweed, potato crisps and peanuts, hence its name. It's full of sand, which we return now and then to the beach, and there seems to be some kind of irrigation system going on in the boot as after a rainfall, we hear sloshing water noises every time I go around a bend. Will and Amy discuss whether anything would be able to grow in the dark recesses of the boot; we all hope for cress, so that we can have yummy egg and cress sandwiches to eat on the beach.

Annie says, 'You've still got this death trap?'

'Minger might be deteriorating, but she's safe. Passed her MOT first go.'

Annie gets in sceptically and immediately starts to sneeze.

'Now what is it? I left Jake at home and even mucked the car out, in honour of your visit.'

'I know, I know, it's me,' she wails. 'Who knows what it is this time. I'm probably allergic to Cornwall.'

Whatever it is doesn't get better. I make the mistake of forgetting about our new hens and taking Annie in through the back door which means passing the chicken run. Although they're getting used to us, the hens are still a bit nervy. They set to, squawking and flapping their wings when we walk by.

'Aaarrgghh!' Annie yelps, jumping like a hare in headlights.

'Sorry, I should have warned you. It's the hens. We've only had them a short time and they haven't completely settled.'

I make soft chucking noises to the chickens, as I've tended to do lately when I feed them. In the short time we've had them, I've grown to love my hens: the way they cock their little heads to the side as if wondering what I'll do next; the way they scuffle about in the straw; the funny little cluck-cluck noises they make.

'You talk to them, do you?' Annie asks with a grin.

'Calms them down, I hope. They were quite scatty when they first arrived.'

By now the hens are getting excited, expecting food. I open the tight lid on the metal container where we store the layers' mash and give them a small handful which they rush upon with delirious squawks.

Annie says, 'Is that all they get?'

I grin, 'No, of course not, this is a bit extra but we do have to be careful with overfeeding. Anything left over and the rats will move in.'

Annie shudders. 'Life in the country, eh?'

'Don't worry, they're not here yet.'

A few feathers float down to land on Annie's shoulders. She sneezes again and starts rubbing her eyes. 'C'mon,' I say hurriedly. 'Let's get you inside.'

In spite of all the antihistamines, by late afternoon Annie is covered with raised lumps all over her arms and face.

Ben sees her and freaks out. 'Annie, your whole face is swollen. C'mon, I'm taking you to the hospital.'

I feel awful for not noticing how bad she's become but we've both been talking a blue streak and trying to ignore her escalating allergies. I say I'll take her to hospital while Ben cooks dinner. We've discovered a lobster fisherman down here who will deliver a whole lobster, freshly cooked, straight to our door for only £6. We couldn't believe it at first but now, when guests come from Up Country, we always have a lobster evening. They think we've struck it rich and are astounded when we tell them the price.

At A&E in Truro, Annie is given a massive injection and told to go home and stay away from whatever has caused the allergy. 'It's Cornwall,' she tells them peevishly. 'And I can't avoid it; my best friend lives here.'

The lobsters are a great treat. 'So there are some advantages to this rural life, I guess,' she says when we finish. 'That was delicious.'

'And at that price,' I add. 'We might not be able to afford to get rid of Minger but we can eat lobster now and again.'

'I suppose it's worth it, giving up stuff, if you can get food like this.'

'What d'you mean? What sort of stuff?'

'The kind of things we have in the city. Like, well, like Pilates.'

I look at her incredulously. 'What do you mean, give it up?' Annie and I used to take a class together in London. 'I've got a brilliant teacher in St Geraint.'

'You're kidding. Here? In Cornwall?' She says it as if it is in outer space.

'We've got everything here, Annie. Everything we need, anyway.'

Later, Annie and I drive down to Penwarren Beach. It's dark and quite chilly but the stars are out. Annie's swelling has gone down and her face is only partially lumpy. Her once immaculate hair has been messed up by the trauma of allergies, of coping with Cornwall and is poking up in odd places around her head, falling now and then into her eyes. She shakes it back nonchalantly, barely noticing. She looks good, I think, despite the lumps: relaxed and at ease.

We sit on the damp sand, watching waves breaking on the shore, catching the flickering lights of a boat out at sea. I've brought a blanket from home that we wrap around us, hoping there's no dog or rabbit hairs, or chicken feathers on it.

'Maybe you've got something here,' Annie murmurs, her soft voice blending with the sound of the waves.

'Something more than lobsters?' I tease.

'Hmm, maybe. Maybe you're not so crazy after all, moving here.'

At the post office in Morranport, Nell is threatening to retire again. 'Let the rightful owners come back and take over this place, it's theirs, in't? Travelling the world like they do, not at all fussed about us poor old folk having to face all this.'

'All what, Nell?'

She gives me a look that tells me how pathetic she thinks I am, then hands me a newspaper clipping from one of the daily South West newspapers: '40,000 fear axe as Royal Mail goes high-tech,' shouts the headline.

I read it while Nell watches, making sure I don't skip a word or two. She's looking magnificent today, her bosom clothed in a purple, cotton, long-sleeved tee-shirt, a shell pendant nestling cosily in the middle. Her short hair is standing on end as usual, seemingly without any artificial aid.

The article is about some revolutionary sorting machine that will make all postal workers either redundant or reduced to part-time work when it is in place. I hand it back to Nell. 'We've heard all this before,' I say. 'There's always something threatening but it never comes to anything. I bet this won't either.'

She sniffs, 'You be thinking I'm getting all in a twitter about nothing, are ye?'

'No, Nell, not at all. Of course you worry, we all do. It's just pointless, isn't it, to worry about it, when there's nothing to be done.'

She sighs, ignoring the customer who is gently knocking at the door of the post office, pointing at his watch to politely suggest it's past opening time. 'Like the closures. You be telling me I should forget about them too.'

'Rumours of this place being shut have been going on for years, since Ben and I used to holiday here. You're still here, Nell, and so is the post office. It'll be here for ever.'

She grunts, disbelieving, turning her back on me and letting in the customer, saying breezily, 'What's your hurry, me handsome?'

The burly white-haired man that comes in apologizes for rushing her, even though it's ten minutes after opening time. He buys some stamps and some Polo mints and stays for at least fifteen minutes chatting to Nell while I sort in the back room.

When he goes, Nell says, 'D'ya know who that was?'

I tell her no. 'I've seen him around, though. Isn't he a fisherman?'

'Yep, one of the last around here actually working. Soon won't be any fishing boats about, what with the sea all fished out.'

'It's not too good for them, I know.'

'And what fish there be left in the ocean, those monster trawlers – now't but factories on the sea, they be – are swallowing the lot. No room at all for the small fisher folk.'

'Like the small farmers,' I say.

She nods. 'No room for the little blokes, not no more. Not in anything, even post offices.'

I say, to steer her away from her favourite topic of the injustices done to rural post offices, 'So who is he? That man? Other than a fisherman?'

'He's Charlie's dad. Arnie, name is.'

For a moment I'm not sure who she means. She sees my bewilderment and says, 'You know, Charlie, the hairdresser, works in Truro. The gay one.'

'Oh, Harry's partner. So that's Charlie's dad. I heard he was a fisherman.'

'Poor man. Poor dear man. The kindest soul you ever be wanting to meet, and his heart broken like that.'

I look up sceptically from a pile of parcels I'm trying to sort, trying not to get drawn in. 'He seemed quite cheery to me. He obviously is very fond of you, Nell.'

She brushes that aside with a sniff, 'You be telling me next I don't know what I'm talking about, eh?'

'No, Nell, I wouldn't dream of it,' I sigh loudly and succumb. 'OK. So what broke the poor dear man's heart?'

She pauses so that I can fully comprehend the tragedy of her words. 'His son. That young lad, Charlie.'

'He's nearly forty, Nell. Well, late thirties, anyway. Old enough to lead his own life.' I'm remembering Harry's hesitation when I asked how Charlie's family coped when he came out of the closet.

'Mebbe so.' Nell's voice is dark, her face stern. 'But however old, a lad can still break a parent's heart, believe you me.'

She stares at me again, daring me to disbelieve her.

'Nell, for goodness sake, Charlie can't help being gay, it's what he is. He didn't choose the life simply to break his father's heart.' I slap a package into the sorting box.

Nell pulls herself up from behind the counter to peer at me. 'Gay? Who said anything about being gay? His dad don't be caring about that. It be because Charlie isn't a fisherman that's breaking his heart.'

Harry and I talk about Charlie's family a few days later. We're sitting on a rickety wooden table outside Millie and Geoff's tiny bakery on the harbour, which the couple have set up so that they can serve tea and coffee with their simple but delicious cakes and biscuits. It's not quite warm enough to be outside but the sun is shining, there's no wind and we can't bear to be indoors.

There's not much activity on the harbour today. The long Easter break is over for the schools and most of the second homers have gone home. It's a weekday, so there are no day trippers about. The sea is still and unruffled. A shearwater is skimming stiff-winged above the slight swell. As it alternates its flight between showing its dark upper and white under side, I'm thrilled to be able to recognize it. After years of only the depressed pigeons and scrawny sparrows on the dirty pavements of London, I'm still awed when I see birds living in their natural environment.

A few seagulls sit on a post eyeing us hungrily and we're careful not to spill a crumb of our blueberry muffin to encourage them to come closer. That's the one bird I cannot bring myself to love. I've seen one draw blood, claws catching a bald man's head as the bird swooped over him to grab his crisps.

Harry brings up the subject of Charlie and his father. I'd asked him why he seemed out of kilter that morning, a bit distracted, even glum. 'Oh, it's Arnie again. He and his mum came over for Sunday lunch. It was all going really well – Charlie's a great cook, does a mean roast dinner – when I made the mistake of asking Arnie how the fishing was going.'

'Ah,' I say knowingly.

For a moment we're distracted by a pushy seagull that flies perilously close to our table, trying to grab the remainder of my muffin. We shout and shoo it away then Harry goes on. 'Yeah, I should have kept quiet. Kept off the subject.' He lapses into a morose silence.

I say, finally, 'So are you going to tell me about it?'

He looks at me with his stunning green eyes and thick black eyelashes. I could sit and admire him all day, he's so gorgeous. Sometimes, when I make a delivery to their cottage, I stop and have a cold drink with Charlie as their place is the last in a row of cottages on a steep hill.

Since moving back to Cornwall, Charlie has discovered a talent in himself for creating wonderful and original works of art, all based on the sea. During the Easter holidays, one of the craft shops in St Geraint sold some of his tiny boxes decorated with seaweed and shells, painted an exquisite pearly blue. The shop wants more and so does an outlet in Truro, so Charlie now works only part time at the hairdresser's to concentrate on his artwork.

When I stop at Charlie's on my round, we always have the

same routine. First I admire his latest creation – last time it was a rainbow of multi-coloured pebbles, each one carefully picked for its unusual colour, nesting in a tiny octagon of thinly carved driftwood – and then we sit in his workshop, their mad terrier hopping about between us, talking about Harry.

'I can't believe my luck,' Charlie says again and again. 'He's not only the most beautiful man I've ever laid eyes on, he's also a sweetie.'

I don't know about the sweetie bit – I haven't known Harry that long – but I agree about his beauty.

'Don't know what he sees in me,' is Charlie's next refrain.

I smile, knowing it's useless to try to tell Charlie how necessary he is to Harry. Hopefully when they've been together for longer than the two years they've had so far, he'll realize how much Harry needs him.

Charlie, with his rugged, chunky body, his wayward hair, his open and honest face, is as different from Harry as a mackerel to a dolphin, but he is beautiful in his own innocent way. Though Charlie is the artist and Harry the accountant, Charlie is the practical one, Harry the dreamer. They complement each other better than most heterosexual couples I know.

Harry tells me now about the disastrous Sunday lunch. 'So there we were, our bellies full of this succulent spring lamb, cooked with rosemary and garlic, and lemon potatoes like we learned to cook in Greece – oh man, did I ever tell you about the chef we met in Rhodes, what a cool guy . . .'

I interrupt hastily, 'Not now, Harry, later. What happened after the lamb and lemon potatoes? Other than the pudding, that is.'

Before he can go on, Millie comes out with a huge, brown, ceramic teapot, refilling our cups without being asked. Right behind her is Geoff, carrying a plate covered with a paper napkin. 'I've brought you another muffin, Tessa, on the house.

I be knowin' when you've skipped lunch, me luvver.' He sets the second mouth-watering muffin on my plate while Millie urges Harry to finish his and she'll bring him another too.

When she's gone, Harry says, 'Arnie went ape-shit when I asked about the fishing. Went on and on about the plight of the small fisherman, how none of the youngsters want to do it any more because it's so hard now, with the big trawlers taking all the business and quotas getting difficult and the price of diesel – you know the kind of stuff, we hear it all the time, living here.'

'But Harry, it's all true. Every year there are fewer and fewer fishermen. The small boat owners are being squeezed right out.'

'Listen, rationality went out the window with Arnie. Started going on about how some of his fishermen mates have sons – daughters too – who'd love to take over the boats despite the difficulties but can't because the cost of living is so high now in Cornwall. They can't afford to buy a house anywhere near the sea, or even rent one that isn't a holiday cottage, so they just say sod it and move Up Country.'

I shake my head, 'Harry, you can't blame him for going on about all that. It's so terribly true. He's worried sick about the future.'

Harry, who has been glaring absentmindedly at another encroaching seagull, turns his mesmerizing green eyes on me again. 'I know, I know. Deep down I feel sorry for the man, but then he went on about *his* son being lucky enough to have a cottage not far from the sea and yet he turns his back on it.'

'But Charlie hasn't turned his back on it. He loves the sea. All his art work is about the Cornish coast, the water.'

Harry sighs, 'Tell me about it. I know, you know, Charlie knows. Even his mum does. She tried to calm everyone down, when things got out of hand. Charlie finally lost his temper,

after holding it in for nearly a full half hour while Arnie ranted.'
He throws a small pebble at the persistent seagull, now only
a few centimetres from our feet, but the bird doesn't move a
feather, just cocks its head aggressively.

I don't know what to say, wondering how often this same
scene is repeated throughout Cornwall. I feel sorry for Arnie
but sorry for Charlie too. I say, 'Did Charlie ever consider
following his dad's profession?'

'Yeah, he tried it way back, but it didn't work.'

'Why? Does he get seasick?'

'Actually he does but that's no big deal. Charlie says lots of
fishermen do. They live with it.'

You learn something new every day, I think, and say out loud, 'So
what made him give it up, in the end?'

Harry stretches out his long, lean legs clad in faded jeans,
nearly toppling the tenacious seagull still waiting for a handout,
or the chance to steal our crumbs. It squawks indignantly but
still refuses to give up its watch at our feet, head cocked up
towards us and eyes glowing malevolently.

'Hissss,' Harry snarls at the seagull. 'Go away you well-fed
scavenger monster. Go back to the cliff tops where you belong.'
He hisses again. The seagull refuses to move. Its tiny marble
eyes glitter in the sunlight.

Harry gives up and turns back to me. 'The simple, and I
suppose the only, reason that Charlie isn't a fisherman is because
he hated it. Doesn't like boats, doesn't like being out on the
water even in good conditions and especially doesn't like the
job of catching fish in any way shape or form. So he trained
to be a hair stylist, which he liked loads better and now is as
happy as can be doing it part time and his art work the rest
of the time.'

I never get a chance to answer this because another seagull
has landed near the first one and the two begin squabbling.

There is such a raucous flapping of wings and squawks that even Millie and Geoff come out to see what's up, though they're used to seagull battles outside their shop.

Then, while the two birds shriek at each other at our feet, a third one swoops from the sky, seemingly from nowhere, and scoops up the second muffin Geoff had put on my plate before I have a chance to take even one bite.

'Bloody gulls,' Harry says darkly as we settle down again. 'Makes one almost want to go back to London.'

'Except for the pigeons.'

'Yeah. Bloody pigeons. Can't win, can you.'

'Nope. I think I'll take the gulls, when all is said and done.'

We get more muffins only this time Harry stands guard, swatting the *Guardian* he bought at the newsagents at every encroaching seagull, looking so fierce and Viking-like with those green eyes and tall body that I have to stop between each bite to admire, the way I'd admire a beautiful painting or an exquisite sculpture.

South Cornwall, I've discovered, is like a lush tropical jungle. Plants and blooms and flowering bushes seem to double in size overnight, overwhelming me every morning as I set out on my rounds. The magnolias are still flowering and the colours of the rhododendrons and azaleas dazzle me every day; I never get tired of filling my eyes with the spectacle. I remember how in London I used to primp over my tiny, pitiful plants, worrying about every cold wind and excessive rainfall, coaxing and cajoling them into growing. Here, I feel like I'm in the Amazon, as blooms and foliage spring riotously into life after the winter months.

It's a drizzly day today and has been for nearly a week, the early spring balminess long gone. As I drive along the coastal road I can't even see the sea, it's so shrouded in mist. Instead,

I look out over the damp green fields where a few sheep are idly grazing. I'm not thinking of anything, which happens increasingly since we've moved here. In London, my mind was always racing, always one step ahead of the present, thinking of things that needed doing or planning, figuring out how to order the future instead of concentrating on *now.*

Here, I'm beginning to live in the moment and it's bringing me a peace and happiness far beyond anything I've known before. Though I've always been happy in my marriage, with Ben and then the children, it was a joy tinged with worry about our future, worrying about not having enough time together – worrying about life, basically. Now I feel as if I'm *living* life instead of hassling about it.

As I slow down around a bend I see a magpie at the side of the road, then a second and finally a third. The old rhyme about the birds goes through my head: One for sorrow, two for joy, three for a girl, four for a boy . . . and so on up to ten. But after ten I pause; what comes then? Was there ever a verse that tells us what seeing eleven magpies means? I start to make one up. Eleven for coffee, twelve for tea, thirteen for you, and fourteen for me! Not exactly Shakespeare, but what the hell. I amuse myself by carrying on like this until I reach twenty-three and I'm at my next drop.

So much for clearing the mind of thoughts, I think ruefully. Mine just flew away with the magpies. But I don't care. At least it wasn't fretting and stressing about work, or the family, or the state of the world. It was merely idling, enjoying life, as I'm starting to do more and more.

Getting out of the van, I pick up a wad of thick envelopes, some padded. One or two of the flimsier envelopes have long, tough strands of dark hair poking through. When I first saw these arriving, for there were several every week, I wondered if some kind of witchcraft was going on. Archie had been telling me bizarre stories about ancient times in Cornwall – old curses, spirits, hauntings, and I'd let it get to me.

My imaginings were made worse by the house the envelopes were going to. It's a converted grey stone chapel, set on its own in an isolated spot in a creepy, wooded valley. At least it seemed creepy the first time I saw it, on a dreary winter's day, when I first began this job. It was drizzling that day, like it is today, but then it was still pitch dark in the early mornings when I delivered. The woodland surrounding the house was gloomy and dripping, the water running off the deep green needles of the conifer trees into a muddy mass below.

I parked outside an old wooden gate leading into a soggy garden and then on to the house. The granite stone of the old chapel gleamed like a malignant talisman in the soft rain and the ivy covering much of the walls seemed to me to be suffocating not just the house but whoever was brave enough to go inside.

I hesitated, not wanting to get out of the van. It hadn't been long since my meeting with the man I still think of as the werewolf, in my Brigadoon village of Trescatho. I was still a little shaken by it, despite knowing my imagination was running amok and had to be brought under control.

So I tried to control it then and there. 'Right,' I said aloud, scrambling out of the van, clutching the sheaf of letters for the house.

I jumped a foot when a loud caw pierced the air. Looking around wildly, I saw a raven perched on a fallen tree trunk at the edge of the woodland next to the chapel. Well, I think it was a raven.

Annie, when I told her this story on the phone that night, said, 'You're making this up. You wouldn't know a raven from a rave. Or a pigeon for that matter.'

'Annie, it's the truth. That is . . . maybe it was a crow?'

'What's the difference?'

'Uh, not sure. I know a raven's a big crow but since there was only one, I had nothing to compare it with. Like, if there were crows about, or rooks, I could have compared the sizes . . .'

'Tessa, you're raving,' she started to giggle. 'Get it? Raveing? Raven-ing?'

'That's not the remotest bit funny.'

When she finished laughing over her pathetic joke she said, 'So go on. There was this deserted chapel . . .'

'Converted, not deserted.'

'And a raven or a crow or a rook.'

'Not a rook. Rooks are more gregarious. This one was on its own. Besides, they have baggy trousers.'

'What? Who has?'

'Rooks. Long feathers on their thighs. They look like funny pixies in baggy trousers.'

There was a long pause in London. Then Annie said, 'Tessa, I think you should come back to the city for a while. You're really losing it.'

'Look, forget the raven. Let me tell you what happened next . . .'

So I did. I told her how, at the same time as I heard the raven, or whatever it was, I noticed that the top envelope in the stack I was holding, a long white one that looked a bit crumpled and smudged, had several long heavy, black hairs sticking out of the hastily sealed edges. I stared at it then leafed through the other post. One other had the tips of some brown hairs poking out of the envelope and two others, when I felt them, definitely had something that felt like the same thing.

As goose bumps began creeping up my arms and neck, I looked at the address. All the envelopes were addressed to Cassandra France, The Old Chapel, Morranport, Cornwall.

Cassandra. My thoughts spun wildly out of control as I tried to remember the smattering of Greek myths I'd learned in school. Wasn't she some sort of witch? A fortune-teller or something? Was this *human* hair in the envelope and was it sent to this person living in this deconsecrated chapel so that she could cast wicked spells on the poor unsuspecting victim?

I told myself not to be such an idiot but I slumped back into the van, unwilling to open the bleached wooden gate, soggy with rain and go to the door of the chapel. How fitting, I thought, that the witch works in an unconsecrated church; did she choose it deliberately? And those heavy pines, drip-dripping with the rain . . .

I stopped my lunatic mind, told myself to stop imagining gothic horrors in an innocent converted chapel and stomped through the mud to the house to deliver the post. The first obstacle was the lack of a postbox.

I started grovelling around looking for a plastic container, bucket, something to put the post in, but there was nothing. I hadn't been to this place yet, though Susie had pointed to it when she was showing me the route that first week. 'No post for the old chapel for a while, Tessa, the owner is away visiting family for a month. But the house is right up through the woods,' she'd explained.

There hadn't been post until now, so this was my first delivery here. I wished fervently the owner had stayed away, at least till spring. The misty rain was smearing my face and I was getting impatient. By now I was used to all the strange containers people used for their post but there was nothing at all suitable here. I looked for the doorbell but there was only a heavy brass knocker. Although it was barely seven in the morning, I had no choice but to knock.

After what seemed a very long time, but was probably only a few minutes, the leaded window next to the door opened and a hand with blood-red painted fingernails thrust itself out at me. A deep guttural voice croaked, 'I'll take that.'

I never saw the face, never had time to do anything more than put the hairy envelopes into that scary hand because even as the witch – or rather the woman – spoke, a jet black cat jumped out of the window and landed on my shoulder with a yowl loud enough to raise the devil himself.

I screamed, the cat hissed, the witch-woman shouted something and somehow I managed to get back to my van unscathed. I risked a backward glance as I drove away but the window was closed, the cat vanished. All I could see was the ancient chapel glowering in the mist, the branches of the thick pines brushing against its slate roof.

Against her better judgement, Annie was intrigued once I'd got this far. 'How bizarre, Tessa. You're a braver woman than I am. I wonder if she really is a witch? I don't believe in them of course, but Cornwall is so weird anyway, I wouldn't be surprised to find anything that goes bump in the night appear there.'

'Annie, hold on until you hear the rest of the story . . .'

When I got back to the post office at St Geraint I found Susie in the sorting room and bombarded her with questions. 'Who lives in that scary chapel? Who's this Cassandra France? Some French throwback to the Inquisition? What's with these human hairs sticking out of the envelopes that I had to deliver to her?'

Susie looked up from the letters she was sorting. Margaret, who had just finished serving a customer, began to laugh. I said, 'What's so funny? D'you know who I mean, Margaret? You wouldn't be laughing if you'd been delivering there today.'

Now Susie too began to grin as I described what had happened. 'All right, what's the joke, you two?'

Susie said, 'Cass is a homeopath. She works from home

but most of her customers are from Up Country and can't get to her.'

I snorted, 'What, so they send her a lock of their hair?'

Margaret said, 'No, idiot, they send her their horses' hair.'

Susie tried to explain, 'Cass has been a homeopath for years but she's always said she feels more at home with animals than people so that's what she began treating. Horses are her speciality. She says she can prescribe remedies just by analyzing the horse hair, so that's what she does. She's quite famous in the world of animals and alternative therapies.'

I mulled over these facts while Margaret sold a book of stamps to a customer. 'I hope you didn't say something daft to Cass,' Margaret said to me when the customer had gone.

'How could I? I never even saw her, only her hand reaching out of the window. She hardly spoke, just croaked something at me, like a frog.' I stopped, then added, 'A French one at that.'

Susie and Margaret were laughing so hard by the time I finished the last few words that I could hardly understand Susie when she began to speak. 'For a start, m'bird, she sure as hell's not French. You be jumpin' to conclusions again. Just because her last name is France don't mean a thing. She be English, West Country born, though I don't recall exactly where. Dorset, I think.'

'With a name like Cassandra?'

'It's Cassie, actually, but the other sounds better for the customers.'

'Oh. All right then. So she's not a witch.' I found myself feeling a tad disappointed. 'But she's not exactly friendly. Stuck her hand out for the post and hardly said a word.'

Susie and Margaret exchanged long-suffering looks for the stupidity of posh posties from Up Country. Susie said, 'She be ill, Cassie is. I just got a prescription from the chemist's to take to her on me way home. She's got laryngitis, can hardly talk, and a chest infection too. Can you blame her for not wanting a conversation?'

A couple of months have passed and I'm at the old chapel again. Although it's drizzling this early morning just as it was on that day last winter, a weak sun is breaking through the clouds and shining fitfully on the conifers which look a shiny bright green today. I take the bunch of envelopes with the horse hairs poking out of some as they did on that first day I delivered here. I open the door of the chapel and leave the post on a ledge inside the front door as I've learned to do. Tobias, the black cat, sits behind a jasmine bush in a big terra-cotta pot and purrs at me when I stroke him.

As I turn to go, Cass comes out wearing a red dressing gown that matches the red of her fingernails, to exchange a few pleasantries before I go off again. She's a woman in her late forties, with a cherubic face, a pleasant, rotund body and curly, light brown hair speckled with grey. She's got freckles on her small snub nose and is about as witch-like as Winnie-the-Pooh. My face reddens every time I see her, for she is not only down-to-earth but as nice as a homemade scone and Cornish clotted cream. I hope no one has told her about my off the wall imagination and the story I concocted about her before I knew her but the way she sometimes smiles at me, in a kind of knowing manner, makes me wonder.

Now that the busy summer season is approaching, there are more jobs about so Ben has got a Saturday one doing change-overs. Holiday cottages are let from Saturday to Saturday, so when one group goes, there has to be a quick clean-up job to get the places spick and span for the next lot. Ben is in charge of doing this for a couple of cottages in St Geraint, so when I'm working on that day we try to meet for a quick lunch.

Luckily the children have a swimming club they go to on Saturdays and Ben takes them to the local pool, drops them off with the instructor then goes off to work, while I collect them later.

When we have some free time together Ben and I tend to go back to the tiny café and snack shop we found on the outskirts of St Geraint as it's well away from the sea front and not filled with people who know us. Ben's doing several jobs to keep the cash flow going. He still does an occasional aromatherapy massage at the Roswinnick, the part-time work at the Sunshine Café and now the change-over job on Saturdays.

As for his acting, he's now got an agent in Cornwall, though there's not much work down here. It's been frustrating but we knew when we moved, and his London agent dropped him, that this was what it's like in the world of acting. If you're not based in London, it's tough to get good acting jobs. I know Ben misses it.

The new agent got him some voice-over work after the pantomime stint ended, and has promised more in the summer. There's talk of a new television series in the pipeline set in Cornwall and there might be a small role in it for Ben. We're not counting on anything, though, just enjoying living from day to day with what we've got. So far we are cogging along, making ends meet and slowly putting down our roots.

Ben arrives at the café first, sitting at our favourite corner table. It's an ordinary place, basic, untrendy, unlike the Sunflower Café which has geared itself to the demands of the second homers for basil and mozzarella salads, a dozen varieties of green or herbal teas, and perfect lattes. This one, called simply Bill's Place, serves Cornish pasties or a savoury no-nonsense steak and kidney pie if you want food, and PG Tips tea or plain filtered coffee if you need a shot of caffeine. I wonder how long it will last in a place like St Geraint.

We talk about the children, about our morning, and then stop talking to dig into our pasties. Bill's Place must get them from a local bakery, for they're spicy and tasty. You can't beat a good Cornish pasty every now and again, especially after a hard morning's work delivering the post or mucking out a holiday cottage.

As we drink the remains of our tea, I see one of my customers come in. We nod and say hello, but for some reason he looks startled, probably because he's seeing me out of context. This has happened before. Customers see me in ordinary clothes at a village fête or in a café and can't quite place me. But I'm wearing my uniform now, so I can't make out why he's looking so surprised. I find out the following week.

Susie corners me on a thundery Friday morning to say she needs to talk to me, 'In private.'

This sounds odd, but I say, 'Let's have a quick coffee at the Sunflower before we do the second half of our rounds.'

'Don't know, bird,' she tries to sound casual. 'Ben be working there today?'

'No, not till this evening.'

'That's OK then. As long as it's not too crowded and we can talk private like.'

That's the second time she's used that word and I'm starting to get nervous.

It's nearly empty in the café and Susie looks relieved. She still leads me to a table on the opposite side of the room away from the only family in there, even though they are out-of-towners, that neither of us knows.

We order coffee but don't speak until it comes and the waitress has gone. I can't bear the suspense any longer. 'Susie, what's wrong? Is it one of the customers? Have I made some great glaring boob of a mistake that I'm not even aware of?'

Susie can't look me in the eye. She stares at her untouched

black coffee. 'Don't know how to say this, bird. Without being blunt.'

'So be blunt. Just say it.'

'Just a warning, like, OK? Cause I like you, y'see?'

'A warning about what?'

She still won't look at me and starts, maddeningly, to stir another sugar lump into her coffee. I say, 'Susie, if you don't spit it out I'll scream.'

'Right. Fine. Sure, me bird, blunt's the word. OK.'

She looks around fearfully. Then whispers, 'You've got to stop meeting your lover in St Geraint.'

I'm so speechless she takes this to mean I know what she's talking about. Hurriedly she goes on. 'Look, what you do is your concern. Not for me to say what married folk do in private, not being married meself, see? Two sides to every story, is what I tell folk when they say things, but you been seen, bird, and the talk is flying. Ben'll find out if you don't be careful like.'

It takes some time, and two coffees, to unravel this mystery. It turns out that I have been seen at Bill's Place not once but several weeks running, holding hands with a man. The last spotting was on Saturday.

I say, 'Susie, the man I'm meeting is Ben. My husband.'

She looks more shocked than if I'd admitted to a lover, 'Ben? But why?'

'Why? Because we like each other, why do you think?'

'But you can see him at home.'

'Not always, with all his jobs, and the kids, and my odd hours. With this change-over job it's great to snatch a lunch hour together on Saturdays.'

She's still not convinced. 'But why such an out of the way place? Why not the Sunflower?'

'Because we know too many people who go in there and we want time on our own now and again.'

'Oh.' She looks crestfallen. 'Oh my, I do believe I've dropped meself in the shit. Sorry, Tessa, shoulda' kept me big mouth shut. Thought I was doing you a favour.'

I reach over and squeeze her arm in a reassuring manner. 'Susie, you have, you've done me a huge favour, believe me.'

I mean what I said. I've just learned in a big way how small communities work, how people talk, how rumours spread, how even the slightest oddity is discussed, analyzed and magnified out of all proportion. It's good to know this. Still, it's hard to believe that of all the customers who spotted me having my clandestine lunches with Ben – and according to Susie, there were several, though I only noticed the last one – no one seemed to entertain the thought that he might be my husband.

I suppose that would be far too mundane. No doubt I'll be a great disappointment to them, when Susie starts putting the truth around about my so-called 'affair'.

I'm learning more about small town life every day, and a great deal of it is through Susie, who watches everyone and everything with wise benevolent eyes that don't miss a trick.

But one day at the end of the month she comes into the St Geraint post office looking both angry and hurt. Margaret and I stop what we're doing and ask her what's up.

'It's Eleanor. We had a row. A big 'un.'

I'm shocked and so is Margaret. Eleanor has been on Susie's round for years and they've become friends. I found this out when I took it over the first time. I remembered Eleanor had made it pretty clear that she couldn't wait for Susie to come back.

It's hot in the post office and there is hardly room for the three of us in the sorting room. Susie says, 'Look, Margaret, you've got customers, I'll tell you about it later.' Turning to me she says, 'Let's go sit on the sea wall, get some fresh air.'

We walk down past the harbour to find a quiet stretch of

stone wall to perch on. The tide's out and there's a mass of seaweed on the wet rocks being pecked over by oyster catchers. The last two days have suddenly turned hot, way too hot for April. I mention this obvious fact to Susie as we settle down on the wall.

Susie says, 'That's what be doing it. It all be too soon, making people do daft things.'

'What? I don't understand.'

'It be this heat. Near 80. Unnatural.'

'Hmm. Nice though.' I turn my face to the welcoming sun, close my eyes before saying, 'What daft things exactly?'

'That Eleanor. I get up to her place, all set to stop for a cuppa and a good natter. She be out in the garden, fussin' away with her azaleas. I be admiring 'em when all of a sudden she whispers in my ear, in that bossy headmistress-y voice she uses, "Susie, I have found the solution to my problem with that tree."'

She mimics Eleanor's voice so perfectly that I have to giggle. Susie doesn't join me, though. She goes on, 'The tree she was talking about ain't just any ole tree, y'know. It be a handsome forty-year-old copper beech and that Eleanor be killing it dead. And it don't belong to her either.'

I turn to her, intrigued. 'Why? I can't imagine Eleanor doing something like that.'

'HAH.' Susie says this in such a thunderous voice that the near-by oyster catchers fly off warily. 'Well she is. Killing it dead.'

The last three words are spoken so loudly that some day-trippers sitting near-by turn to look at us.

'Start at the beginning, Susie. I haven't followed any of it yet.'

She does. Apparently the copper beech is in Eleanor's back garden; that is, many of its branches are and now some of its roots are beginning to creep under her greenhouse. But the tree itself is firmly planted on her neighbour's side of the fence.

'He be that ole boy Perkins, the one always in overalls. Widower fer years, he be, decent enough bloke but stubborn as Eleanor be herself. They two been fighting over that tree for years. Eleanor says the shade be blocking the sun and her greenhouse is practically useless. Perkins says she be exaggerating. Been going on for years, their bickering.'

'So what's happened now?'

Susie tells me. It seems Eleanor confided to her the fact that she had furtively encircled the trunk of the tree with a thin copper wire. 'It's so thin that Perkins will never see it,' she had told Susie gleefully, 'but it'll cut into the bark, stop the tree breathing. Get rid of it once and for all.'

'Oh dear.' I am all attention now, and so are the day-trippers next to us. Susie hasn't thought it necessary to lower her voice. 'Does that really work? Could a bit of wire really kill the tree?'

Susie shrugs. 'Never heard tell whether it works or not, though I've known a fair few folk who've tried it. I doubt if Eleanor knows for certain either, but she sure be giving it a try. Anyway, that's not the point. The fact is, she's giving it a go. I told her that it's attempted murder, what she be doing, that it be an underhanded and nasty thing to do.'

'And she said – ?'

'She said what about her greenhouse!' Susie practically snorts with indignation.

'Oh dear,' I say again. Then, 'Well, what about her greenhouse? I mean, of course I think it appalling that she's trying to kill the tree, especially as it's not even hers, but Eleanor does love her greenhouse I know.'

Susie looks at me scornfully. 'She could move her greenhouse. And I told her so. She told me to mind my own business and get off her premises if I didn't like what she's doing. I said I be going straightaway as I be wanting no truck with a tree killer anyhow. She said if I ever came back she'd call the police and I said if she did I'd expose her to all of South Cornwall as the tree-killer she is.'

I'm quite stunned by the vehemence of Susie's anger, as well as such an unfortunate outcome to this long-standing battle between neighbours. I say, 'Well, however you both feel, you've still got to deliver the post there.'

'No way. Either she puts a postbox on top of her lane, or she be getting no post from me, for sure.'

We are silent for some time. The day-trippers, sensing there will be no more colourful stories of life in rural Cornwall, get up and move away. I feel languid in the heat, despite being upset by Susie's story. Finally I say, 'Are you going to tell Perkins?'

She stares at me in some surprise. 'Tell him what?'

'Why what Eleanor has done to his tree.'

'You be getting as daft as everyone else in this hot sun. Course not. T'ain't my conflict now is it? Nothing worse than getting involved in someone else's feud. Just ain't done, bird.'

On Susie's day off a few days later, I start to drive up Eleanor's lane and there, tied haphazardly to a branch of a beech tree at the edge of the track, is a plastic container. On top of it are the words POST written bluntly in red letters.

I saw Susie this morning at the Truro sorting office and she said she'll never forgive Eleanor for attempting to kill the beech tree, even though it seems that Perkins discovered the sabotage and removed the wire.

Now, seeing the new postbox, I doubt if Eleanor will ever forgive Susie for telling her what to do in her own garden. I have a sense that this new breach will not be mended for a long time.

Another lesson I've learned about rural communities, I think as I put Eleanor's post into the precarious box. Feuds can flare up without warning and last for ages. People can hold grudges for just as long here as they can in the city, or maybe longer, with less busy-ness to distract them. Already I've heard of families at odds with neighbours because of some squabble their parents had years ago.

I wonder if I should go to see Eleanor Gibland, try to plead Susie's case, tell her the good things Susie's said about her. Or try and remind Susie of how much she has always meant to Eleanor. But even as I think this I know it's an idiot's thought. As Susie said, there's nothing worse than getting involved in someone else's feud.

Before long I'm whistling again, thinking that on a warm day at the end of April, there's no better place to be than driving down a rural road in a postal van in Cornwall. There's a blue sky above with a couple of buzzards circling, there's the sea to my left, and on my right, a mass of rhododendrons blazing pink and purple. I'm happy as a skylark, and if this is being bovine, as Annie accused me of being last time she was here, I'm the most contented creature on God's good earth, and that's a fact.

May

I'm having a clothes crisis this month, thanks to the bizarre weather. Some mornings I wake up to freezing rain and a sharp wind that makes me grab my heavy Royal Mail waterproof and wear it over a thick woolly. Then by the time the first light breaks, the sun is gloriously warm and I'm sweating in my wintry gear for the rest of the day.

Often it goes the other way, when I wake up to a balmy dawn and think: *Hurrah, summer is here.* Tugging on nothing more than a red polo shirt and a pair of ghastly Royal Mail shorts which reach my knees and make me look like a bag lady, I skip outside merrily humming jolly songs about summertime and the livin' bein' easy. Then of course the wind shifts, clouds snarl over the horizon and the temperature drops twenty degrees.

I'll be glad when the weather turns warm and stays warm for a bit, not just for my sake but for the sake of my whole family. On these unspring-like days when a cold wind blows, we've got to put on extra layers as we read or watch telly or relax in the sitting room, for we can't close the main window.

A swallow has made a nest there and if we shut the window we'll crush the three speckled eggs we've spotted. Already the newly painted wall is dappled with swallow guano but we don't care; all of us are thrilled that this delightful family is making a home with us.

Luckily the windows are tall, and high up, so that Jake can't get to the nest. The mother bird seems oblivious to his noisy presence both inside and outside the house; she seems totally at home here. I wonder if perhaps our window has been a favourite nesting place for generations of swallows. I hope so. I tell Amy and Will that we must make them as welcome as we can, to keep them coming back to us.

Annie came down for a very brief weekend after the swallows had made their nest. Shivering as a blast of cold wind came through the open window, she pulled her cashmere cardigan tightly around her. We were all huddled in thick fleeces and blankets, watching the late news on telly. Annie, her teeth clattering with cold, muttered, 'This is why I come down here so often, y'know. To get more stories about you barmy people to dine out on.'

Annie's not the only one who has taken to coming down often. To our consternation, Morgan and Glenda, and their two children, came back for a second time. When Glenda rang to inform me of the impending visit, I didn't know how to say no. She didn't exactly ask, I realized when I got off the phone, but had informed me they were coming down, in such a way that somehow I couldn't demur.

This time they hadn't forgotten the wine, though it was a far cry from the 'exquisite' wine Morgan had promised us (but never delivered) last time. It was actually cheap plonk from Tesco, which still would have been fine if Morgan hadn't ordered a very expensive Chianti at the Italian restaurant he took us to in Truro. 'The dinner is my treat,' he'd said expansively. 'I looked the restaurant up on the net, supposed to be good.'

It wasn't bad – cheap and cheerful – and Morgan did pay. We only had one course, because Glenda said, 'I've heard they do huge portions here, so we mustn't order a starter.' And after we'd finished, Morgan boomed, 'That was filling! You'd have to be a glutton to want dessert. Shall we go back to your place for coffee?'

When the bill came, Morgan paid for the food but seemed to expect Ben to pay for the wine, even thanked him profusely for offering to do so. Rather than making an awkward scene, Ben let it go, but with the exorbitantly priced wine, of which we'd had two bottles, plus the babysitter I'd booked to look after the four children (who were squabbling even more this time than they had last visit), it was the most expensive night out we'd had for months.

The really galling thing was, Morgan and Glenda kept referring to 'that great little restaurant we took you to' for the rest of their stay, making sure they didn't have to open their wallets, or help with the preparation of any of the other meals for the rest of the weekend.

Never again, I think, remembering that visit. I forget them, and everyone else, as I drive around the quiet lanes. This morning the dawn seems earlier than ever, the light haloing the pale, delicate green of the new leaves, glittering on the spider webs still wet with dew on the fresh grass.

It's so beautiful, so tranquil, that I stop the van and open the door to feel the early warmth, smell the damp grass, hear the skylarks. They're out in full voice today, their harmony and song as pure as the new morning.

I sit and listen for ages, until I can hear the sound of a tractor approaching and know I must move; he's probably going into the gate I'm blocking. But the larks will be here tomorrow, I think as I drive away. And so will I.

When I worked at The Body Shop, we had to do a community project – called Walk the Talk – which entailed some kind of social service, like working with the young, or the elderly, or with animal rescue groups. Anita Roddick believed strongly in keeping communities alive; she used to say that loneliness would be the number one disease if communities fell apart.

I think of her words now as I go about my rounds today. Already in my time as a postie I've helped an elderly woman who's broken her arm to put on her cardigan and sat in a young mother's kitchen for ten minutes guarding her sleeping baby while she ran down to the corner shop for milk. I've helped wash out cuts, put plasters on elbows, looked through old photo albums with isolated, lonely pensioners. I've rushed ill people to hospital and made cups of tea for semi-invalids. I like this part of the job. I've had so much myself, I feel lucky to be able to give some of it back.

Right now I'm delivering the post in Poldowe. There are a sheaf of cards addressed to Mrs Taylor, whom I know only slightly; she and her husband have always seemed a bit reclusive. I noticed there were batches of greeting cards yesterday too, so today, when Mrs Taylor comes to the door, I say brightly, 'Happy Birthday!'

She looks at me blankly. Her eyes are red; she looks as though she's been crying. 'Oh dear, sorry to intrude,' I say, flustered. 'Uh, these are for you, I thought it must be your birthday. Sorry to disturb you.'

I thrust the cards at her as she says quietly, 'My husband died a few days ago. These are sympathy cards.'

I slink away feeling miserable and embarrassed. There is still so much to learn. *I must never assume,* I mutter to myself as I drive away. After all these months I still make mistakes and often they occur when I'm feeling smug with myself and with the job. *Serves me right,* I say to myself when another one of these incidents takes place.

Yesterday I was feeling wonderfully smug because I'd figured out who a letter was for. It was addressed to 'J-J and Wuffle the Mongrel, St Geraint, Cornwall.'

'Not another one with no proper address,' Margaret sighed a few days ago, handing it to me. 'I haven't a clue who this one's for, nor docs Susie. D'you have anyone called J-J, with a dog called Wuffle?'

I studied the envelope, puzzled, 'Can't think of anyone off hand but I'll take the letter. Maybe it'll come to me.'

As I delivered to my regulars, I asked a few if they knew who J-J was, or a mixed breed dog called Wuffle, but they were as perplexed as I was. It wasn't until I called in at Trescatho, my Brigadoon village, the one with the spooky werewolf (or just an ordinary man with exceptionally large canine teeth) that I remembered. One of the houses, an old stone cottage that had been empty for ages, had been sold. I had been so surprised to see someone walking around the deserted place that I'd stopped, shocked, to stare.

The woman who stared back at me was middle-aged, smartly dressed and obviously from Up Country – a second homer, I thought dismally. Up until now this hamlet had been spared. The people who lived here might be reclusive but they lived here all year round.

I had my baggy, ugly Royal Mail shorts on, my Dr Martens boots and a red polo shirt, my hair pulled up in a tight band on top of my head. I know I looked a sight but that was no reason to look through me, turn her back and go into the house. I made a face at her retreating back.

As she went inside, I heard her call a name which, thinking

back, was definitely Wuffle. And sure enough, following her into the house from the back garden was a funny looking mongrel type dog with big paws, black shaggy fur and floppy ears.

Miss Marple, eat your heart out, I thought as light bulbs went off in my head. *I bet she's the one the letter is addressed to.* And sure enough, there was a bank statement to be delivered to the house and the name was Mrs J Jackson.

I looked at the by now scruffy envelope addressed to J-J and Wuffle the Mongrel. It all fitted. I couldn't wait to tell Margaret and Susie how my sterling detective work had solved the Problem of the Mysterious Letter, how the Royal Mail got through yet again. *All in a day's work,* I said modestly in my head as I was praised by the Postmaster General.

My reverie was broken by J-J, or Mrs J Jackson, or Granite-Face Woman as I was addressing her in my head as she stared coldly at me. I'd followed her into the garden to hand her the post and now she was frowning and saying something to me. She looked cross; I couldn't think why.

Her voice was over-the-top posh. 'What's this?' she demanded, giving me back the grimy envelope addressed to J-J.

'Oh, why, I think it's for you. In fact I'm sure it must be,' I gave her my most endearing (I hoped) smile. 'You're Mrs Jackson and your first initial is J.'

'That might be so, but no one, ever, has called me J-J. They wouldn't dare. And I don't know anyone in Australia,' she thrust the letter back at me again.

I didn't take it. 'But it must be yours,' I blurted out. 'Because it's addressed to your dog too. Wuffle. I'm sure I heard you call him that. And it looks like, well . . .' I began to grope for words. It looks sort of like a . . . wuffle.'

I couldn't say mongrel. Something in this woman's face forbade it. She looked at the envelope again then at me with her scary stare. She had pale skin and pale unsmiling eyes, and looked terrifyingly forbidding. 'My dog is called Truffle.' Her voice was the opposite of pale. Black, actually. 'He is a pedigree Labradoodle. Will you please take this envelope away now? And leave all future correspondence in the letterbox I will have installed at the bottom of my path.'

I took the letter and scarpered.

'Did you ever find out who Wuffle and J-J are?' Margaret had asked when I walked back into the post office that day.

'No, not yet. But I'm working on it.'

I'm back in Trescatho today, hoping the stony looking Mrs J-J (she'll always be that to me) and her scruffy wuffle dog (he'll always be that to me) aren't in the garden. They're not, despite the lovely day. But to my horror, there is scaffolding up on another house with a SOLD sign and painters are already hard at work. This wonderful house, in this idyllic village, is being painted an atrocious bright salmon pink.

I groan out loud. My lovely mysterious Brigadoon is vanishing, taken over by the pink house brigade.

May Bank Holiday, and the emmetts are flocking into Cornwall. The continuing fine weather has brought not only the second homers but the spur of the moment holiday makers, getting into their caravans, taking out their tents or frantically phoning every B&B and guest house in the county to see if they can book a last-minute place.

Glenda phones to say they'd be happy to spend the May Bank Holiday with us. Since I never asked her, and indeed haven't heard from her or Morgan since their last visit a couple of months ago, this is slightly surprising. But I'm on to her now. I say, sweetly, 'I'm so sorry but we've already got visitors, I'm afraid.'

This is true. Seth is coming down again but with a different girlfriend. 'I think Samantha had a bit of an alcohol problem,' he says on the phone when he asks if he can bring his new woman, Philippa, for an overnight stay.

'I hope you've learned your lesson,' I say, a bit briskly I know, but I've known Seth a long time. And I haven't forgotten how wimpy he was over Samantha.

So Seth and Philippa are already here when, despite being told we couldn't see them this weekend, Glenda, Morgan and their children appear unannounced at our kitchen door just as we are sitting down to a lasagne lunch.

'Oh, don't mind us,' Glenda trills. 'A cup of coffee would be fine. I'm sure we can find somewhere to eat in St Geraint.' She says this doubtfully. 'Though I know how crowded all the pubs get on a bank holiday.'

Morgan looks grave. 'We'll have to find somewhere, Glenda. The children are starving.'

All four stare at the lasagne, sitting untouched at the kitchen table. While I get four more plates and hastily throw together more salad and cut more bread, Ben introduces Seth and Philippa, who have only just arrived. Seth asks Glenda where they are staying.

'A holiday home, owned by one of my colleagues in the law firm,' Morgan booms. 'He wasn't using it this weekend.'

'It's very near here,' Glenda gushes. 'We can all get together every day!'

Seth looks shocked. He's taken an instant dislike to them already. Philippa, on the other hand, is leaning over the salad exposing masses of suntanned cleavage to Morgan, asking him about his firm in London. She's looking deeply into his eyes, slightly smiling. She's flirting with him, I think, and then my second thought is: why? Morgan is deeply unattractive.

I soon realize why. Philippa – tall, willowy, bosomy and beautiful – is a flirt. As far as I can make out during the time she is with us, this seems to be her profession: flirting. She doesn't seem to have a job and is vague when we ask her about work. God knows where Seth found her.

But I'm grateful to her, for not long after lunch, Glenda suddenly packs up the family and says they must go, much to Morgan's surprise. 'Why Glenda darling, I thought we'd take all these nice people out to dinner somewhere tonight,' he murmurs, as Philippa stares seductively into his eyes and smiles as if he's just offered her a luxury weekend in Dubai.

Seth looks starry-eyed at her despite the fact that she doesn't seem to mind Morgan's hand on her knee. My old friend is a complete fool about the women in his life, I realize.

Glenda says frostily, 'You already said, Morgan darling, that all the pubs will be packed. I'll cook tonight for the four of us in the cottage. Can't you see Ben and Tessa want to stay home with their friends?'

They make a move to go, Morgan albeit with great reluctance. From outside in the garden come the sounds of their children bickering wth ours.

As they leave, Morgan says, 'Well, what about tomorrow? Shall we all meet in that great pub in Morranport?'

Glenda, watching Philippa smiling sexily at her husband and telling him how much she looks forward to seeing him again, says firmly, 'Morgan, Ben and Tessa have company this weekend. We'll see them another time, when they're on their own.'

I can almost like Philippa after saving us from that dreaded pair, but she ruins it by moving in on Ben as soon as Morgan is gone. Full-beamed headlight eyes on his, sitting far too close to him on the sofa, hanging on his every word – the works. And then doing the same thing when Eddie comes round, to tell me something about the shift I'm working for him next week. Poor Eddie – how is he to know that she can't help it, that she does the same thing to every man who comes into her orbit? He stays for ages, unable to tear himself away.

When Seth and Philippa leave the next day, after Philippa has embarrassed us to death by trying her seductress bit with both the landlord of the local pub and the father of one of Amy's friends, Seth calls out from the open car window as he drives away, 'I'm a lucky man, aren't I?'

We're too speechless to answer.

The holiday weekend, as well as the week before and after, is murder on the roads. Or to be precise, it makes me want to commit murder. It's not so bad first thing in the morning when there are few cars out and about but later, as I'm finishing my rounds, I always come across at least one of the types of drivers that incite me to rage.

It's the man or the woman – and both are equally at fault – who drives down narrow, rural lanes without having learned to reverse. Or, even more maddeningly but occurring more frequently with each holiday, there are the drivers who don't want to get their shiny new cars scratched by a bramble on the side of the road. *Heaven forbid that should happen,* I mutter now as I drive down a steep, narrow hill, round a sharp bend and come face to face with a brand new shiny Saab and a po-faced man in his fifties glaring at me through his windscreen.

Glaring at *me?* What nerve, I think as I glare right back at him. He was the one going like a bat out of hell around that corner, not me. A po-faced woman is sitting next to him, looking as if she has something sour in her mouth. She's glaring at me too. What's with these people?

I try soothing tactics first. It works with animals, doesn't it? I answer the glares with a charming (what hard work it all is sometimes) smile. I make non-aggressive hand gestures indicating that if they'd reverse back a couple of metres, there is a perfectly adequate space at an entrance to a field where not only their car but two Saabs and a tank could wait while I passed by.

The man responds with his own hand gestures. His right hand waves imperiously, telling me to reverse back up this steep, curving hill at once. My smile is wearing thin but I keep it pasted on as I shake my head, shrug my shoulders and do an elaborate pantomime of his car reversing back just a wee tad and finding the passing place. His frown deepens and he does that rude get-out-of-the-way gesture again and what really gets my goat is that the woman does the same thing.

We are at an impasse. I stop smiling, turn my head away from these two sour people and look out the window. I hear a blackbird singing from the beech trees at the side of the road and, above that, the cry of a buzzard. There are primroses and wild violets in the hedgerow. I don't want these two out-of-towners to spoil my day but I seriously don't want to back up.

Usually, I just give in and go into reverse but this time I really don't see why I should have to. I would have to reverse for a mile uphill, around sharp bends just because this idiot won't reverse three metres on a straight stretch of road. I'm not even sure that the clutch on the van will take it either; it's been rather dodgy lately when I've shifted from first to second and I want to have it looked at.

So I take a deep breath of the warm sea-scented, honey-suckle-fragrant air, open the van door and walk over to the driver of the Saab. He recoils as I appear at his open window. I know I don't look my glamorous best – these Bridget Jones big pants shorts, the unflattering short sleeved shirt, and the pencil that I realize later is sticking through the bun at the top of my head – but hey, I'm an official Royal Mail postwoman, not something slimy that's crawled out from behind a damp, mossy stone.

I say sweetly, 'I'm afraid it's a bit difficult for me to back up, sir. It's a good mile uphill on a treacherous road. But if you reverse a very short distance, there is a sizeable passing spot there on your right. You must have passed it.'

The man now looks perplexed, as does the woman. I can hear them thinking: *She speaks properly, not like a Cornish postwoman should speak. What should we make of this? Is she having us on? Is she an impostor?*

I resist an impulse to grin. I love knocking people's prejudices, confusing them about where I fit in, confounding folk who need to slot others into their given places before risking social contact with them.

The man hesitates and then, unfortunately, loses his cool. If he had any to start with. 'I would think,' he says with a sneer, 'that as a postwoman, you'd be able to bloody reverse.' His voice dribbles nastily with rage and sarcasm. The woman is bobbing her head in agreement, her lips pursed as if she would spit at me if I weren't out of reach.

I bite off the retort I'd like to make and say instead, in my most polite postie voice, 'Oh, I can reverse quite well, actually. It's just that I think a gentleman wouldn't mind moving his car a tiny fraction on a straight road so that a woman would not have to go through the trouble of reversing a mile back up a steep hill.'

We stare at each other. Eye-to-eye combat, no holds barred. His are hard and snake-like. Mine have the power of wide-eyed innocence.

The woman breaks the spell, 'Oh Terence, reverse and get this done with. The postwoman isn't going to budge.' She says postwoman like Marie Antoinette must have said the word peasant. She goes on, 'We can write a letter to the local post office when we get back to London, making a complaint.'

It takes him about five seconds. He's a whiz of a driver, obviously in the category that doesn't want to get his car scratched rather than the 'can't reverse' group. I wave a cheery thank you as I drive the van past their car. He and the woman are resolutely looking straight ahead.

I would bet a hundred pounds that they don't bother writing that letter. They're the kind of people who throw threats around like confetti, hoping to bestow a tremor of trepidation into the lower orders or anyone else they think is getting in their way.

As I drive another few miles further along the narrow road, I'm confronted by another obstacle. This time it's a small flock of sheep being driven to pasture by a farming couple and their teenage son. They're going the same way as I am so the farmer flags me down and says, 'We be going a fair way, mebbe 'tis best to reverse and go down the short cut way.'

I know which road he means and nod. His wife comes up and says she'll take their post; she can tuck it into her jacket pocket and save me a trip to the farm. Then she says, 'Tessa, did you pass that emmett in the big black car? He be speedin' like a bull after a heifer on heat.'

'Yeah, I passed him. He refused to back up when we met face to face.'

'We could of killed him. Instead of stopping, or going slowly through the sheep, he starts honkin' his bleedin' horn. Scared the bejezus out of them, scattered them everywhere. Only just got 'em back together again.'

I reverse the short distance back to another road even tinier than the one I was on, with grass growing sparsely in the middle, wondering why people who are impatient with animals, who refused to reverse down narrow lanes, and who obviously look down on local farmers and postwomen, ever bother to come here. It still remains a mystery to me.

* * *

My hens lay their first egg this month and I'm so excited I drop it as I take it from the nesting boxes. But never mind, I'm relieved that they've at least started. We bought them as point of lay and I thought we'd leap up the first morning with six fresh eggs waiting for us though of course they needed to adjust to their new surroundings.

As the days go by, the number of eggs increases until quite soon we are getting our six eggs a day. I love collecting them, love the feel of putting my hand into the warm straw and feathery nest boxes, the thrill of finding an egg tucked away in the dark.

'I hope you're not eating them all,' Annie hoots at me down the phone. 'You'll get egg bound.'

'Wait'll you taste them. You've never tasted eggs like this, believe me.'

'I can't eat eggs, remember?'

I'd forgotten she was allergic to them, but at least the hens won't squawk at her when next she comes to visit. They are quite tame now and in fact they crowd around when I appear, looking for feed. As well as the feed we buy, I've taken to boiling all my vegetable scraps for them: potato peelings, broccoli stalks, carrot heads. With four of us, there is a fair amount and the hens love this addition to their other food of grains.

I get a shock one hot day when the hens, crowding around me as they always do, start pecking at my feet. One or two are quite vicious about it and I yelp and run out of their run in a bit of a tizzy.

'What's the matter with them?' I ask Ben when this happens three days in a row. 'They're usually so sweet and tame, and now they're attacking me like demented seagulls after ice cream cones.'

He doesn't know either. I'm starting to go off my beloved hens.

It takes Amy to say, a few days later, 'Mum, it's only since you painted your toenails bright red that they started pecking you, when you go out in your flip-flops. They probably think your toes are strawberries or yummy raspberries or something.'

Can this be true? As a true scientist and pragmatist, I experiment. I go in with wellies, no pecking. I go in with sandals, they go for me. I get some nail polish remover, rub my toenails pale again, put on flip-flips and stomp into the hen run. The hens crowd around eagerly for a hand out, but they leave my toes alone.

Well, well, well. From now on, I wear shoes or wellies when I go in to feed the hens or collect the eggs. I'm not about to give up my red toenails for even the most tasty eggs in chickendom.

The rest of May passes in a blur of sunshine and those idyllic days we dreamed of when we first decided to move to Cornwall. I'm grateful that my job gives me free afternoons so that when Amy and Will are on their spring break from school, I can pile them, Jake and a few egg salad sandwiches into Minger and drive the couple of miles to the beach where we take long walks, build sandcastles and paddle about in the still icy water. Jake loves these outings and tries to catch seagulls and even little fishes in the rock pools. Most public beaches don't allow dogs on them between Easter and autumn but this is still a relatively unknown cove and Jake is able to go with us at least until the summer months.

Ben joins us too, on some of these picnics, when his work permits. There's something to be said for a number of part-time jobs, he's decided – he has loads of flexibility and can use it to spend more time with the family.

We're already losing our winter paleness, looking lightly tanned and healthy. And it's only May, I think with joy in my heart. Only the beginning of our first summer in our new home. I cross my fingers, wish on stars and scrabble about on the shore for the tiny cowries, the shells that are supposed to bring good luck, the sea's equivalent of a four-leafed clover. When I find one I take it home carefully and keep it in a tiny, special box. I feel so lucky, so fortunate to be here, and I want our luck to last. I want this glorious Cornish summer to go on and on for ever.

June

The glorious Cornish summer has turned into a wet Cornish summer. The days are muffled with a thick fog from the sea, so heavy that I can hardly see the end of the harbour from the St Geraint post office. There are still plenty of perks, not least the stunning, blue agapanthus flowers that grow wild here. They show up starkly in the mist, the colour so dazzling that not even a drizzly rain can subdue them.

Annie arrives for another long weekend and is bowled over by the agapanthus. 'We have them in London, but not anything like this, not the wild ones.' She starts rubbing her eyes. 'Tree pollen now, I guess. I hate the country.'

'You always say that, but you always come back. Anyway, you've got allergies in London.'

'Tessa, they are *babies* compared to the great hulking monsters that attack me every time I come to Cornwall. If you weren't my best friend . . .' she trails off to put some drops in her itching, swollen eyes.

'If I weren't your best friend, you'd still come, now admit it. Cornwall is starting to get to you, I can tell.'

'What do you mean? I can't even *see* Cornwall in this wretched fog. We could be anywhere.'

'Except for your itching eyes.'

'You said it,' she puts on her glasses. The frames are designer, FCUK, and look great on her, but she never wears them except when she comes here as there's no way she can wear contact lenses in Cornwall with all those allergies.

Then she says, 'By the way, are we having lobster tonight? Has your lobster fisherman been around lately?'

I laugh, 'You see? I knew there were other reasons why you come down here.'

Annie and I have a lazy few days. Mostly we walk, and talk, and laze at the edge of old woodlands near a little creek or inlet. I try to show her the delights of the countryside. 'Look, Annie, look at those rooks at the top of those trees!'

'How d'you know they're not ravens, smartie? Or crows?'

I smirk, smugly. 'I've learned a lot since we had this conversation before. Rooks not only have baggy trousers but huge, grey, lumpy bands at the root of their beaks.'

'I'm impressed, despite my better judgement.' She looks up at the rooks, dozens of them, suddenly flying up as one and sweeping away with a great flapping of wings. 'They do look fierce.'

'Maybe, but they're not carnivores. They only eat grain, like the hens.'

She grins, looks sly, 'And red toenails?'

'I haven't put that to the test yet,' I grin back at her.

We stay there for a while longer, listening to the music the stream makes as it saunters along over rocks and stones, sand and water weeds. I point out the great rooks' nests at the top of the trees. 'They're very sociable, y'know. Rooks, that is. They live in those great colonies at the tops of trees.'

'Like us in London living in penthouse apartments or high rises.'

'Yeah, but some of the colonies have been there hundreds of years. Around here, it's considered a bad omen if the rooks suddenly abandon them.'

Soon after this, we get up and start to walk again. After ten minutes or so, Annie stops suddenly. 'Look. Over there. On that fallen tree trunk. That big black bird. Is it a crow, or a rook?'

I giggle, 'There's an old saying around here, Annie, goes something like this. "When tha'se crows, tha'se rooks; when tha'se a rook, tha'se a crow."'

Annie stares at me. She looks seriously worried. 'I'm taking you back with me to London for a good, wholesome dose of city life. Sounds like you're in great need of it, Tessa.'

When I laugh she smiles grudgingly. 'All right. So tell me then, oh wise country one. Is that bloody bird a crow or a rook?'

'Neither, oh idiot city woman. It's a blackbird.'

When Annie goes, I suddenly feel lonely. Despite the many lovely acquaintances I now have, amongst the neighbours, my customers, the people at the post offices, I still feel an outsider somehow, perhaps because I haven't made any really close friends. Having Annie here again makes me realize how much I miss the intimacy that a close friendship can bring.

I'm thinking of Annie as I deliver to the Rowlands. Emma has a mischievous smile very like my friend's; perhaps that's why I warm to her so much. When she sees me, Emma rushes out from their growing garden, where she and Martin have been working. 'You've expanded since I was here last,' I say, noting that part of an adjoining field is now cultivated.

'Yes, Martin's decided to grow potatoes in a big way. All organic, too. Dave's idea; he says he knows loads of people in Bristol who would buy them.'

Dave is Emma and Martin's son. He's a physiotherapist,

lives in Bristol with Marilyn, his partner. I've met Dave before; he's a nice lad and pining for Cornwall. Like so many other young people, he and Marilyn had to leave the county to be able to afford a place to live.

Martin appears holding a load of produce from the garden wrapped in newspaper. 'Take it, Tessa, we've got far too much.' Before I can thank him, a car drives up, and both Martin and Emma's face light up like lanterns.

Dave jumps out of the car, embraces both his mother and father then turns to me. 'Tessa, good to see you.'

'You too, Dave. Marilyn not with you?'

He shakes his head regretfully, 'No, she couldn't get off work. Sent me on my own, to help the old man here for a couple of days.'

Martin pretends to scowl, 'Less of the *old*, lad. Well, get diggin', then, let's see what you be worth.' He thrusts his spade at Dave with a grin.

I leave the family there, laughing and joking, thinking how lucky I am to have such lovely customers on my round.

Nell is now pursuing every newspaper she can get hold of for possible scurrilous references to the post office. 'Look at this,' she says, showing me a page cut from a national tabloid. 'The Royal Mail is scuppering us again, selling stamps online, can you believe it? That's it then, might as well retire right this minute and be done with it. Us little post offices will go right out of business, you'll see.'

I read the article, 'Nell, this is only for people who have businesses, who buy huge amounts of stamps. And they've got to pay a subscription before they can do it.'

Nell isn't pacified. 'If 'tisn't one thing 'tis another. I've had enough. Am giving notice here and now, let 'em find someone else.'

I've heard this before, lots of times, but this time Nell looks more serious than usual. I say, 'You can't retire. The poor owners, off on their travels, entrusting their beloved post office to you. So many people have taken the job then quit, but you've been the staunchest. How can you let them down?'

She harrumphs and snorts and shakes her head but I know my pep talk has hit its mark. Nell is as loyal as she is honest. She won't retire until the owners finally come back and either take over the post office or sell it to someone else. And as everyone in the village knows, that won't happen for a long time.

Before I leave Morranport I go to pick up some cheese at Baxter's, an incredible shop on the outskirts of the village that sells absolutely everything. It's been there for ever and even has its own bakery. As I go in, I'm bowled over as usual by the delicious aroma of freshly baked pasties, bread and croissants.

Baxter greets me as I buy feta cheese and bread. He's a man past retirement age with a lion's mane of thick, white hair covering a broad head on top of a tall, broad body. He's been around for ever too, or so it seems. He's warm, friendly and open to everything, especially if it concerns his shop. I brought Annie here last time she visited and in the course of their conversation Baxter asked her what was new in London, food wise. Annie mentioned some kind of chocolate pots Waitrose were selling that everyone she knew had tried. 'Gorgeous, rich chocolate in delicate tiny pots. Not only to die for but make great hostess gifts. Dreadfully expensive, though.'

Sure enough, next to his racks of books on Cornwall, I see a special shelf in a prominent place filled with elegant chocolate pots. *Didn't take long*, I think with a smile to myself. Baxter is laid back, easy going and superficially shambling but he's also a keen businessman.

On the way out I meet Harry going in. 'Why aren't you at work?' I ask.

'Early closing today, remember?'

'What, for accountants? I didn't know your office closed.'

He looks sheepish. 'All right, I'm taking the afternoon off. I'm on my way home but need to get some provisions. Charlie's parents are coming round for tea.'

'I thought there was a big bust-up last time.'

'There was, but his mum keeps trying to get a reconciliation, so she's managed to talk the old man into popping over for a cup of tea and a chat.'

'Good luck. Hope it goes well.'

Harry looks doubtful. 'Yeah. Me too. But somehow I doubt it. I'll go and see if Baxter has a few freshly baked cakes or pies to thaw the heart of a hardened fisherman.'

On my way back to St Geraint to drop off the van, I take a short cut and once again I'm face to face with a tourist on a narrow lane. This time it's a woman in a Range Rover that looks as if it's never been on anything less than a three lane motorway in its life.

Once again, I know there's a lay-by only a short distance back which she could reverse into easily but the look on her face is the petrified stare of a woman looking into hell itself. She's so terrified about backing up that I don't even wait but immediately begin to reverse around yet another curvy bend.

The story of my life, I think as I manoeuvre the van back along the lane. *Always in reverse*. Then I begin giggling to myself. Maybe it's not such a bad thing, living in reverse. After all, to move here, we had to back down from our stressful life in the fast lane and reverse into something entirely different.

When the woman passes me, tucked neatly against a farmer's gate, she's so intent on keeping her Range Rover in the middle of the lane, not wanting to scratch the sides, that she doesn't bother to give me a thank you wave or nod of the head. Rudeness usually makes me fume, but this time I feel so laid back that I don't bother to get irritated. The van windows are open and some wild flower, I don't know what, is wafting its scent my way. In the field some placid, bovine mooing is going on and there's not another sound except a light swishing of beech and oak leaves in the warm breeze. I close my eyes, let the scents and sounds enclose me in a cocoon of serenity. Above the faraway mooing and the rustle of the trees, I'm sure I hear the cry of a buzzard.

Within minutes I'm asleep and don't wake up for at least twenty minutes. Refreshed, I start the van, pull away from the gate and slowly drive back to St Geraint and the post office car park by the sea, filled with the contentment at having finished another good day's work.

Something happens at the end of June that stirs the whole family and forces us to question again our move to Cornwall, our decision to leave London. Ben has had two small parts in the new television series starring Martin Clunes, called *Doc Martin*, filmed partly in London and partly in Cornwall.

In his first role, in episode two, he played a man on a petrol forecourt. He was then asked to play the role of pub landlord in episode six. Both Martin Clunes and the director, Ben Bolt, liked what he did and said that if a second series were to be made, he'd be on as a regular. This is such wonderful news that we all go out to celebrate. We can't afford dinner at the Roswinnick, not yet, but we go to our favourite pub restaurant in St Geraint.

'Will you be famous, Dad?' Amy wants to know.

Ben laughs, 'Hardly. I don't want to be famous; I just want to act.'

'I'd rather you were famous,' Will says. 'Like Harry Potter.'

Despite the cost, we order champagne, and fizzy apple juice for the children, and before long we're all high on hope and excitement and that amazing tremulous feeling of being on the very brink of a dream-come-true.

'I can't believe our luck,' I say to Ben. 'We've got Cornwall, and now *this*. You don't have to give up acting after all.'

'Hold on, it's not set in stone yet. We don't know for sure if they'll even do a second series.'

'Of course they will. The first one got great audience ratings.'

'That's no guarantee . . .'

I interrupt him, 'It'll happen, Ben. They wouldn't have mentioned a second series if they weren't fairly sure.' I reach across the table to touch his hand. 'I know how hard it's been for you to give up acting, believe me.'

He shrugs, 'I've missed it, yes. I love it here, but . . .'

I take off where he trails off, 'But you love acting too. And soon you'll get a chance at it again.'

He smiles. His face looks young and happy and full of hope. He's had a chance to do the work he was meant to and there is a good chance he can continue doing it.

Despite my positive words, I'm as nervous as Ben is, waiting to hear if a second series of *Doc Martin* is to be made. When news comes that it definitely will be, we are light-headed with relief, joy and mounting excitement. Ben is completely over the moon; he's soaring over the news. At last nearly everything about our life here has come right: I've got time and space for both me and my family and Ben will finally be doing the job he loves best.

This euphoria lasts for some time as we wait for the scripts for the second series to be written, and for Ben to see the ones which entail the pub landlord. But nothing happens. No scripts appear.

Finally, Ben talks to some of the other cast members who

have already got their scripts. Each of these conversations leaves him feeling more and more uneasy, especially as he still hasn't received a script himself. Then, after talking to others and seeing other scripts, it becomes clear. Nothing has been written in about pub landlords. His projected part has been cut.

'Ben, no, I don't believe it,' I say as we sit at the kitchen table to digest the news.

'Nor do I.' He's just got off the phone to his agent, who has confirmed the news. He looks bewildered, like a man who's lost his way. I feel so sorry and angry, so frustrated. But there's nothing I can say or do.

Ben stands, running his fingers through his hair, bemused, stunned. 'Everyone was so positive. The role was going to be expanded, for God's sake, not *cut*.'

He sits down, shaken. I go to him to put my arms around him. We stay like this for a long time, trying to come to terms with this new blow.

And then, a few days later, the agent phones again. Once more Ben hangs up and comes to look for me but this time his face is not drained and forlorn but positively hopeful again.

'Have they changed their minds?' I ask. 'About the landlord?'

'No, nothing like that, but there's good news, Tessa. They've decided to film the entire second series in Cornwall, not use the London set at all. My agent thinks that there's a good chance at getting another role for me, since I'm here anyway.'

Once again we're up in the stars, trying not to hope but unable to stop ourselves. His agent feeds this hope, believing that Ben, having attracted good notice in the first series, will surely get to audition for other decent parts.

'It's only a matter of time,' I tell Ben. 'You'll get that phone call soon, you'll see.'

We try to be patient. Ben stops talking about it, because he wants it so much. He carries on at the Sunflower Café as usual but when I go in there, I can tell by his face that he's miles away. In his head he's not a waiter, or an aromatherapist, or any of the other things he's been since moving to Cornwall. He's what he should be, what he's always wanted to be: an actor.

Nothing happens for over a week. Ben knows they are casting now for the next series, yet the phone remains silent. Finally, on the last day of June, he phones his agent.

They talk for ages but the gist of it is, the only part he's offered is a couple of walk-on one-liners, which Ben quite rightly refuses. He's a professional actor, not an extra. Everything else has been cast in London.

Ben and I talk about it late into the night. We're in the sitting room, the window open not so much for the nesting swallows but for the warm summer's breeze that is wafting in tonight after a hot, humid day.

'I don't understand,' I say, not for the first time. 'You're living here in Cornwall, they're filming in Cornwall, yet all the parts that you could possibly play are going to actors based in London.'

Ben nods. He looks ashen, drawn. 'That's the way it works, Tessa. We've always known it. I just had it all explained to me again by my agent. They go to the London agents first, for all the top roles, and only then, when those parts are filled, do the Cornish agents get a chance. By then, there's nothing left but the walk-ons.'

I take a long deep breath. 'What can we do, Ben?'

He tries to smile but it's not much of one. His unhappiness radiates out of his eyes, his posture, his whole face. 'We can't do anything, can we? That's the way it is, and as I've said before, we knew it when we came here.'

He's right, we did know it, but this episode had given us

hope that Ben would eventually find good acting jobs despite where we lived. Now that's gone and at an especially bad time for Ben, having just had a taste of acting again, having remembered only too clearly what an integral part of his life it has always been. We don't say much after that but as we get into bed, miserable and low, I wonder now if we have done the right thing, moving here. What has it done to Ben?

Much as I love Cornwall, I can't stay here if Ben is unhappy. If he's pining to be back in the theatre or in films, and if it can't be done from here, we'll have to go back. As soon as I think this, I feel such desolation that I have to shut my eyes tightly to prevent sudden tears from falling. Leave here? It will be like losing part of myself, a deep important part that I don't want to let go. But in staying here, the same thing will happen to Ben. Acting has been his life for a long time, much longer than we've lived in Cornwall.

We'll have to go back. I'll tell him soon, when the moment is right, when I've thought it all through and we have time to talk properly. Now I must get to sleep, to be up at four tomorrow. Yet I lie there awake for ages, brain churning. Next to me Ben is awake too, but pretending to sleep so as not to disturb me.

I feel that the decision has already been made. There is no way we can remain in Cornwall. It's far too big a sacrifice for Ben to make.

July

There are hydrangeas everywhere, coloured bright blue to star-tling pink and every shade in between depending on the soil. The summer has settled down into being a normal one weather wise, with sunny days interspersed with the odd days of rain. For now the sun has the edge and everyone is happy, the beaches filling rapidly as the season gears up. Everyone is happy but us, that is.

For the first few days of July, Ben and I have no chance to talk alone for any length of time, as he's had to fill in at the café a few evenings to cover a staff illness. I know he's welcomed the extra work, not just for financial reasons but because it stops him from thinking about what might have been. I've thought of nothing else for days and I'm now deter-mined. Ben must have his chance to get back into acting.

I've got it all figured out. We've done a great deal to the Cornish house since we moved, so hopefully we can sell it for a profit and either buy something much smaller in London or rent until we can afford to buy. We'll then have enough money to tide us over while I find some kind of work during the day while the children are at school. Ben can then devote most of his time to renewing his London contacts, to making a whole-hearted effort to get back into his professional life.

Finally, Ben and I have a chance to talk. Will and Amy are asleep and we're sitting outside on the small terrace, watching a half moon make its way over some willow trees in a neigh-bour's garden. We're drinking chilled white wine, ostensibly enjoying the warm, almost sultry evening. There's no breeze and the moon looks languid, as if it too is going with the flow of summer.

I want this moment to last for ever. I don't want to speak, to talk about moving back to London. But then I see Ben's face, pale in the moonlight. He looks tired, preoccupied. As if it's all, finally, too much for him.

So then I begin to talk. I try to make my voice sound eager, as if this is a great new adventure for both of us, going back to our old life.

'But we left that life,' Ben says, 'because we wanted more, something better.'

'*I* did. I was the one who was stressed and unhappy.'

'We were both unsatisfied, Tessa. In the end, I wanted to move as much as you did. And let's face it, I wasn't doing much acting anyway, up in London.'

I sip my wine, absentmindedly stroking Jake who is lying quietly at our feet. The moon rises higher. 'Ben, you weren't doing much acting because of me, my job at The Body Shop. Someone had to be home for Will and Amy. This time, I'll get a less demanding job, one that doesn't consume me for twelve hours a day. That'll free you to focus on finding an acting job.'

Ben, who has been staring at the moon while I say all this, turns to me with a slight smile. 'So where are you going to find this kind of job? Do you plan on delivering post in London?'

I smile back, 'If necessary. If that's what it takes to get you back on track again.'

He sighs. 'It's a crazy idea. To go back now . . .' He trails off, lost in thought. Then adds, 'How can we even think of moving Will and Amy again?'

I shrug. 'I don't like that part of it, but they're young, resilient. And it's not as if they'll be going to a strange school – we'll make sure they go back to the same one, with all their old friends.'

He doesn't say anything for a long time. Finally he shakes his head, says, 'I don't know, Tessa. Are you really serious about this?'

'I've been thinking about it for days. Yes, I'm quite serious.'

His face changes. The tired look is gone and he looks animated again, for the first time since all this began. He goes to me, takes my face in his hands, 'You'll do this for me? Give all this up?' His hand swings around to indicate the moon, the willow, our house, the village. The sea barely a mile away, our favourite beach. Everything.

'Yes,' I answer without hesitation. 'For you, for all of us.'

I can hardly bear to look at the eagerness in his face, the resurgence of hope. *It is truly what he wants*, I think.

I take another sip of wine to hide my own face, to mask the sadness bubbling up from deep inside me. I don't want him knowing how much this move will grieve me.

Once again, our work and the children prevent us from discussing this further for a few days. Ben seems jauntier though, and happier, so I know he is thinking about it, about having another chance to pick up his career.

I'm just numb. I've deliberately frozen my mind and heart so that I don't have to think. I know that soon we'll have to start making plans but I know we both need these few days to adjust.

Then at the weekend, we take Will and Amy to an annual fête at a nearby village. It's wonderful, traditional stuff: tug-of-war competitions and wellie-throwing contests; brass bands and sing-a-longs; prizes for the biggest vegetables, the tastiest scones. The village green where the fête is held is packed out with families, both locals and visitors.

Daphne and Joe are there, and invite Will and Amy to go home with them to spend the night as their two children are more or less the same age and have become fairly good friends. When the fête ends, they all go off together and Ben and I are left on our own.

It's another fine night and the moon is nearly full. Ben says, 'Let's go to the beach, have a walk. Jake could do with some exercise.'

We go to Penwarren Beach, empty now despite the still warm evening. The moonlight casts a path of light across the dark sea and adds a translucent glow to the stretch of sand on the shore. Jake leaps into the shallows, his splashing the only noise in this still night.

We walk for a bit then sit on the sand, warm from the heat of the day despite the midnight hour. We think about going in for a swim but by now a cool breeze has sprung up and we decide it would be cold when we came out.

'Imagine,' Ben says, his voice soft. 'Not a care in the world at this moment in time except trying to decide whether to have a swim or not. How many people have that good fortune?'

I can't answer him. I'm too choked up.

After a while Ben goes on, 'I've been thinking day and night about what you said, about going back to London. Can you really give up all this?'

I take his hand. 'For you, yes. I can't bear for you to be unhappy. How can I enjoy anything when you're missing out on so much?'

Jake, who has been dashing in and out of the water, bounds up to us and drenches us with a great shake of his wet body. We wave him away, laughing, wiping saltwater from our faces, our clothes.

When we've recovered, Ben says, 'Yes, I miss acting. But I know now that I'd miss this more, much more, if we go back. These moments, nights like tonight. Not just being here at the sea, but all of it: taking Amy and Will to the fête, being involved in village life, getting such pleasure out of the simple things, the way people have been doing for centuries.'

Once again I can't speak.

Ben goes on, 'And even though we're both working hard, we still seem to have more time to do all these things. We wouldn't have this in London.'

'But we'd find something else. Your acting . . .'

He shakes his head. 'Even if things went well, if I was lucky enough to get that break, some decent work, we'd still lose *this*. Time and space, and being together as a family. It would be just as it was before, back to the rat race of fighting to keep a career at the expense of everything else. I don't want that, ever again.'

He stands up, goes to the sea's edge, picks up a stone and skims it across the water. Jake, thinking it's meant for him, madly goes after it and after a few moments of delirious paddling about, admits defeat and swims back to shore.

'So what're you saying, Ben?' I try to keep my voice neutral: I don't want him to hear the joy in it, not yet. It's still his decision, this move. I don't want to go, but I don't want to stay either, if he's unhappy.

He grabs my hand, pulls me up to my feet. 'I'm saying it's time to go home, get some sleep. You might have a day off tomorrow but I've got an early start at the café, remember? C'mon.'

We set off, arms around each other, for the car. Before we get in I say, 'Ben, are you sure? You really do want to stay in Cornwall?'

He nods, 'You know I love it as much as you do.'

I have to say it, 'But even if it means giving up acting?'

'Yes, even that. I'm as sure of it as I am of anything.'

He opens the car door but before we get in we have a last look at the moon, beaming on us like an old friend.

Then Ben says with a grin, 'Anyway, we have to stay in Cornwall. I've signed up for the wellie-throwing competition at the next village fête. Who knows, maybe one day I'll be county champion and Will can have his famous father at last.'

Annie comes down again, for a week this time.

'You can't stay away from here,' I say as she gets off the train.

'No, seems not. Don't know why. I think the county is catching. You know, like chicken pox.'

I hug her. 'You're looking floaty today,' I say as we stand apart and grin at each other, delighted to be together again. She's wearing a loose frock, flowing and colourful. 'D'you like it? Just got it from Whistles. Not bad, is it.'

'Very summery and suitable.'

'They've got loads of great dresses, would look terrific on you. I guess there's not a Whistles in Cornwall though . . .'

'Annie, right now even Whistles is too pricey for me. It's either Matalan or charity shops.'

She looks at me with pity. *Even a high street shop, too dear?* I can hear her thoughts as clearly as if she's speaking out loud.

I give her another hug. 'Annie, I chose this life, right? Remember that. And I don't regret a thing.'

Ben is working but the kids are off school so Annie and I

pile them in Minger and take off to the Royal Cornwall Agricultural show. It's a lovely day and the show is packed; it takes ages to park in the large field allotted for visitors. Putting Jake on a lead, we troop in.

There are acres of white tents, marquees, areas zoned off for animal judging, horse shows and dog competitions. First we pass rows of smart, new farm machinery, state-of-the-art tractors, dung spreaders, combine harvesters and everything necessary to run a sleek and modern farm. You'd have to be a millionaire too, judging by the price of them.

We spend hours wandering around the show, looking at food and craft stalls, buying local honey from the producers as well as cheeses and cream. We peep into the tents and awnings of the traders where farmers banter about prices with agricultural merchants, trying to knock a few pence off fertilizer prices while guzzling gallons of the free beer or wine provided by the merchant.

I deliver to one of the sales people and he sees me, stops to say hello. Pete is a good looking guy in his forties with an open, honest face, a gorgeous, deep, sexy voice and unruly, brown hair going grey around the edges.

And he's openly eyeing Annie who has hardly sneezed once today. 'Maybe I'm getting immune to the countryside,' she whispers hopefully. 'I've only taken one antihistamine today.'

Pete offers us a glass of white wine, a surprisingly decent Chardonnay which has actually been chilled in a vast animal feeder full of melting ice.

'It's wasted on us, Pete,' I say as I take the wine. 'We're not going to buy bailer twine or a couple of tons of straw. Though if you've got an extra bale for the hens?'

'Sure, I'll leave one in my front porch; you can pick it up when you deliver my mail,' he says, offering us some salted peanuts from a big bowl.

Amy and Will take a huge handful and Pete goes to replace the bowl from a big bag of nuts. 'They're hungry,' I say, pointing out the obvious. 'We were going to get some food but all the food stalls have endless queues.'

Pete grimaces. 'Our customers are complaining that we've given up the food on our stall. Years back we'd bring all sorts of sandwiches to give out free to them, and scones too, thick with jam and cream.'

My mouth is watering. So is Annie's. She says, 'Yummy. So why aren't they here? I'd even buy a cow or something to lay my hands on a ham sandwich right now.'

Pete laughs, 'We don't sell livestock. And the reason we can't bring food are the health and safety regulations. No home-made food can be served to the public any more.'

'Really? How ridiculous.'

'I know,' his face takes on a dreamy look. 'I remember those thick ham sandwiches, quality stuff, the ham bought direct from the farmer. And the scones – to die for. The night before each show, the women would sit up all night preparing stuff . . .'

'Hang on,' Annie interrupts him. 'The *women*? What *women*?'

Pete looks bewildered. 'Why – the wives.'

'What wives?'

'Uh, some of the farmers' wives volunteered, the wives of our best customers. But mostly *our* wives.'

'Did *your* wife do this?' She gives him a steely look.

'Uh, yes. Years ago. And, uh, she's not my wife any more. We divorced.'

I cluck sympathetically but Annie does not. Instead, she says in a no-nonsense voice, 'It's a wonder any of your wives stick around, if that's what they have to do, sitting up all night making hundreds of sandwiches for their husbands' work. Why didn't *you* do it?'

Poor Pete has no answer to this. I feel sorry for him and am about to drag Annie away but before I can, he says, 'D'you know, I'm not sure. I mean, we're always busy till late, the night before shows, setting up stalls, bringing in equipment, getting everything ready, but that's no excuse, I know. Maybe I should have.'

He looks so crestfallen that even Annie takes pity on him. 'Well, you could be forgiven, I suppose. In those dragon days no one expected husbands to do anything mundane like baking scones.'

I say, 'Dragon days? Goodness, Annie, Pete is our generation, not your grandfather's.'

'So he is.' She gives him a stunning smile. I can see it enveloping him, like a silvery mist. All of a sudden I'm feeling dowdy and slightly grubby. We've been sweating in the hot sun and I feel sticky, my loose hair getting stringy and limp in the heat. Annie, on the other hand, who has been trudging along with me all day, still looks immaculate, her frothy dress bright and fresh amongst the jeans and cords of the farmers milling about. She's wearing some thin strappy sandals that look like slivers of silver and gold and emphasize her lightly tanned feet, no doubt acquired at great expense at a top London salon.

I'm wearing an ancient pair of Capri pants, an old faded blue shirt and flip-flops. I try not to be envious. I tell myself that Annie has to go back to London to her empty – if stylish – flat while I stay here in my beloved Cornwall.

As Pete and I stare at Annie, he, I notice, with the beginnings of lust and me with my struggle to turn envy into admiration for my dear, whacky, wonderful friend, something odd starts to happen. Tears begin to trickle down Annie's face, under her black sunglasses.

'Annie, what's wrong?' I go to her as Pete's mouth opens in alarm.

She takes off her glasses to rub her eyes furiously. They are getting redder and more swollen by the minute, and watering like crazy.

Pete says, 'What's the matter? What's happened?'

'Must be an allergy,' I say. 'Don't know what it can be now. She thought she was better this time.'

Behind us, we hear a squeal of excitement. Turning to look at what Will and Amy have found, we see that we are almost face to face with a big, furry, brown llama that has just wandered up from the small compound behind Pete's tent.

The llama looks at us with great beautiful eyes while Annie squeezes eye drops between the swollen slits that were once her lovely eyelids. I say to Pete, 'I guess she's allergic to llamas too.'

He gets her another glass of wine to swallow another antihistamine, not a good idea I would have thought but Annie thinks it is. Pete says, 'Why don't you stay here in the back of the tent, in the shade, out of the way of the animals? Give yourself a chance to recover.'

I say, 'It would probably be better if we just left. Anyway, your customers are wondering what's up.'

Sure enough, there are a cluster of farmers around us, peering at Annie who looks as if she's bawling her eyes out, giving a few hostile looks at Pete for ignoring their needs to administer to an obvious city gal.

To my surprise, Annie actually flutters her eyelids at him, which isn't easy given their swollen state, and says, 'Oh thank you, Pete, that's so kind of you,' and lets him lead her away into the cool dark recesses of his agricultural tent.

I start to trot after them but Will and Amy are pulling me to get something to eat. I call to Annie, 'We're going off to battle the food queues. Shall I bring you anything?'

She says she's not hungry. When we get back, nearly an hour

later, fed up with the long wait for our burgers and chips, Annie, still talking to Pete in the back of the tent, says, 'Oh, that was quick.'

'Quick?' Will shouts the word. 'We were ages!'

Annie has the grace to look embarrassed. Amy says, 'Aren't you hungry? I thought you said you were starving.'

'Actually, Pete very kindly found me a pasty somewhere. Lovely homemade Cornish pasty, bliss.' She looks at him through her still swollen eyelids as if he were Apollo bestowing upon her the food of the gods.

Oh dear, I think. *Oh my, oh my, oh my*. He smiles at her as if she were Aphrodite.

My first impulse is to congratulate them both and open a bottle of champagne but I pull myself together and try to act rationally. This is just some crazy flirtation brought on by the heat, an allergy and a wayward llama.

So I say, 'Uh, Pete, business must be slow today.'

He looks sheepish. 'Well, actually we've been pretty busy. I was flat out all morning.'

Annie says, 'Pete's been having a bit of a break. The other sales people have taken over while he has some well-deserved lunch.' She glances at him and their eyes meet and hold for longer than necessary.

He finally, reluctantly, pulls away. 'Guess my time's up now, though. Better get back to the customers.'

On the way home Annie is oddly reticent about the encounter. 'Pete's terrific. I really liked him. But we'll probably never see each other again so what's the point of talking about it.'

This is so unlike Annie, not wanting to dissect every moment, analyze every gesture, that I know she's been smitten.

The day after the show I'm back at work, Ben is busy at the café – he's taken on extra hours during the summer months

– and Will and Amy are back at school for another week, so Annie borrows Minger and decides to do some exploration on her own. 'Just let me borrow a map and a flask as well, and I'll be off. No need to worry about me, I'll be fine. There's so much of Cornwall I haven't seen yet. I'd like to get to know the place better.'

Alarm bells go off in my head. 'This wouldn't be anything to do with meeting Pete, would it? If so, Annie, you've got to be careful. You're worlds apart . . .'

She interrupts me, 'No lecture, please. Don't I know it? This has nothing to do with him. I hardly know him.'

I notice a note of wistfulness in her voice. *We shall see*, I think, glad that Pete is one of my customers and I can sow some seeds there if necessary, forgetting completely my misgivings about their complete incompatibility.

The house feels empty when I get back from work, with everyone gone. I potter around, prepare some veg to stir fry for the evening meal, have a long leisurely bath and put on a skirt, for once. Must be Annie's influence, all those great clothes, her wonderful style. She's reminded me that I had that too, once. 'What do you mean, *had?*' I'd said to her.

'Oh darling, don't get prickly, you still have style, oodles of it. It's just different from your old city style. More . . . more Cornish funky, I'd call it. I like it, I truly do.'

By the time Annie gets back, Ben is home and we've already opened a bottle of wine. We're sitting in the kitchen and though the days have been warm, the evenings are cool and we still have to leave the window in the other room open for the swallows. The three eggs have hatched and are being fed by their parents, much to our delight. We've closed off the sitting room so that the swallows don't get frightened and leave, especially with Jake leaping about the place.

Annie thinks we're mad, of course, as it's the best room in

the house and was newly decorated before the birds nested there. Now swallow guano is covering the walls and they'll have to be repainted once the birds go. But she was as thrilled as we were when she had her first peek of the babies, all huge, open beaks and tiny, fluffy bodies.

Annie rushes into the kitchen now in a state of high excitement. Ben says, 'You've been gone ages, we were getting worried. Are you all right?'

I hand her a glass of wine but she's too fraught to take it. 'Oh, you won't believe what I've found. I can hardly believe it myself. It's in the car, come look – no, don't look, not yet. I'm not sure it's not dangerous, maybe I shouldn't have brought it home.'

'Annie, what are you talking about?'

She slumps down on a kitchen chair. 'I think I'd better have that wine now.' She takes a huge gulp. 'Oh what have I done? Maybe it's contaminated? Maybe I'm full of radiation poison.'

'What, the wine? Annie, what're you talking about?' I give Ben a look that says maybe we shouldn't have let Annie loose in the Cornish countryside. I let the dinner wait while we open another bottle of wine and try to get some sense out of our London friend.

Finally she starts to talk coherently. 'I was on the coastal path then decided to go inland, across a field.'

'A field?' Ben asks. 'With all your allergies?'

'Yeah, well, it was dumb I know, looking back, but I thought I'd get to the car quicker if I went that way rather than going back on the path. I was starting to get itching eyes again so I thought it was time to head for home. Anyway, it was getting late. Up to then, I'd been fine.'

'You seem OK now.'

She nods, 'I must be getting immune to the countryside.'

I don't remind her that she said the same thing before her last bad attack.

'Maybe I'm getting immune to everything. Minger and the rabbits and the chickens. And Jake.' She gives the dog, lying at her feet, a pat. 'Poor Jake, I suppose I could have taken you, but you're just so hairy, and stuck in a car with you on a long trip . . .'

'Annie, stop rambling. What happened in the field?'

'Well, I was very nearly back to where I'd parked when I saw something in the ground, giving off a weird glow. I looked closer and it was some kind of strange stone, sort of glittering and gleaming in the light, in a spooky kind of way.'

Another look goes between Ben and me. Ben says, 'Annie, have you been overdosing on those antihistamines?'

She ignores him. 'The more I stood there looking at it, the more I was sure it wasn't like anything I'd seen, or seen in photos, or even read about. I know what stones and rocks look like, and this wasn't anything like one on earth.'

I look warily at her. 'Annie, are you saying that it was supernatural?'

She gets defensive. 'Look, if you'd seen it, giving off that strange glow, a kind of eerie sparkle, you'd have said it was supernatural too. But I'm not saying it's magic or anything. I think it's something from space — a bit of a star, a meteor, whatever. Things are always falling from the sky, apparently, and I'm sure that's what my rock is.'

She's speaking calmly now and I'm starting to believe her. So too is Ben. Annie is an intelligent woman after all and not given to weird fantasies.

Ben's voice is eager as he says, 'And it's in Minger? You actually brought it home? Let's go have a look.'

'No!' Annie's shout stops us from our rush to the door. 'That's what I've been worried about. What if it's contaminated or radioactive? It's possible, probable even. I've read that those things are, those rocks that drop to earth from space. I could kick myself for picking it up; I should have left it there. I just didn't think and the car was close by, so I prised it up, heaved it back to the car . . .' she stops.

Ben looks grave. I take a step back from Annie, wondering if the glow on her face is radiation or simply too much of the wonderful Chablis she brought us from London. 'You shouldn't have done that, Annie. You shouldn't pick up anything from the fields or moors. It's one of the basic rules of the countryside.'

She looks miserable. 'I was just so excited, I didn't think.'

We are by now hazy with wine, dinner long forgotten. We don't know what to do next, quite. I look out at Minger and imagine I see blue radial lights shining out its windows.

Luckily, at this point the doorbell rings and in comes Susie, carrying a wet paper parcel. 'Some fresh-caught mackerel, thought you'd like some, m'bird. Just given me by a fisherman mate, can't eat it all meself.'

I grab not just the fish but Susie, pull her into the room, push a glass of wine into her hand. She knows Annie; she's been to dinner at our place when Annie was here last time. 'Susie, sit down, so glad you're here. We're in a dilemma, maybe you can help us out? You know everything Cornish, you were born and bred here, you're in the Coast Guard as well – do you think you could identify a strange rock that Annie's found?'

Susie puts down her wine. 'No problem, bird. Where it be then?'

We troop out of the house, warning Susie that it might be radioactive, that we haven't dared to even open the boot of the car yet. Susie says, sensibly, 'If we don't be touchin' it, it be fine. A look won't be harming us.'

Glad to be the recipients of such pragmatic – and sober

– advice, we gather around Minger, half expecting the dear old car to be pulsating and glowing with its out-of-this-world cargo. Ben opens the boot gingerly and we all peer inside.

'*There*,' Annie whispers triumphantly. 'There it is.'

Ben and I don't need Susie to tell us what the so-called rock is. Anyone living in the country can recognize it.

'Annie,' I say after a long pause. 'It's a salt-lick.'

Later, after more wine and food, and a bowlful of fresh strawberries that were given to me by one of my customers, we are still laughing. Susie has stayed for dinner and she can't wait for work tomorrow to tell everyone about the Salt-Lick from Outer Space.

Annie is shamefaced but graceful enough to laugh with us. 'What do I know about the countryside? I'm a London lass, remember? How would I know that farmers put great lumps of salt in the fields for cows and sheep to lick?'

Ben says, 'Maybe for your birthday we can send you a subscription to *Farmers' Weekly* magazine.

When she leaves, Annie says to me, 'Tessa, you won't tell Pete, will you? If you see him? About the salt-lick? He'll think I'm a right city slicker.'

'Well, you *are*. I'm sure he knows it.'

'Anyway, I'll probably never see him again, so I suppose it doesn't really matter.'

'You keep saying that. How do you know you won't?'

She shrugs, 'Just don't tell him, OK?'

I shake my head at her, 'Sorry, Annie. You know I'd keep any secret in the world for you. But remember Susie was there too. By now the story will be all over South Cornwall. It's far too good to keep.'

The next day, I see a note in the front porch of Pete's ramshackle terraced house in one of the villages, in bold red felt tip pen he's written: 'Tessa, here are two bales of straw for your hens. By the way, I liked meeting your friend. When she comes down again, please let me know and maybe we can all meet for a drink.' He's underlined 'Please' three times.

I'm being inundated with gifts from my customers. They all seem to have gardens overflowing with produce and they're generous with sharing it out. I'm grateful, because Ben and I haven't had a chance to try our hand at gardening this year, being too busy struggling to get the house in order and to keep going financially. So I'm grateful for all those courgettes, cucumbers, salad leaves, runner beans, fresh peas and broad beans that are handed to me wrapped in newspaper or in a carrier bag.

The weather is hot but there are fierce thunderstorms nearly every day for a week. I'm forever popping my Royal Mail waterproof off and on over my shorts and shirt when one of these squalls hit, for the rain is always torrential.

The constant gales are proving a bit of a handicap to the boating season. Summer is the time of regattas, for locals and second homers getting out in everything from leaky rowboats to flash luxurious yachts and the noisy electric storms have put a damper on things.

The sea is not always the source of joy and pleasure, though, as every fisherman knows. One sad day everyone is shocked at the news that the evening before, a warm-hearted young man liked by everyone who knew him, had been killed. He was coming home from a nearby harbour town in his small fishing boat when there was a collision with his craft and a speedboat.

The news flies from village to village, hamlet to hamlet, to all the rural isolated farms and the tiny coastal coves. The whole south coast is devastated by the tragedy. Many of my customers talk of the young man with tears in their eyes, even those who only have a slight acquaintance with the family, or who only knew him by sight. I'm aware of the tightening of community bonds, of the gathering of community spirit, as if collectively their grief can be shared, and somehow, in some small way, ease the suffering of the lad's family.

Archie and Jennifer Grenville, like everyone else, are blown away by the tragedy. 'So many people have boats these days. I worry that folk sometimes forget the dangers when they are out in one.' Archie begins talking about other losses through the years, 'The parish records go back centuries and there's one entry after another of people, mostly fishermen, losing their lives.'

We're silent for a moment, paying our respects to all the sea has taken. Then I say, 'No wonder the youngsters don't want to be fishermen. Not only is it a dangerous way to make a living but precarious too, these days.'

Archie and Jennifer agree but then Archie adds, 'Poor lad who died wasn't a fisherman, though. Just an ordinary local lad going out on his boat.'

I leave soon after. From house to house, we talk of nothing else. In the post offices customers shake their heads, buy sympathy cards, wanting to do something but feeling helpless in their anger and sorrow.

The summer has become subdued in our area. The tragedy of a needless death, that of a beloved Cornish son, has affected all of us who live here. Even the thunderstorms have given way to warm, grey, humid days, as if the air itself were grieving for the loss of that one young man.

August

At last the misty sky clears and the sun shines again, much to the joy of all the holidaymakers crammed into Cornwall. They pack out the place, taking all our parking places, getting to the bakeries before we do and clearing the shelves. To sate all the second homers, Baxter has to order the *Guardian* by the truckload, something he never has to do in winter. He gets in another batch of books on Cornwall, everything from well-known novels and histories to obscure self-published pamphlets.

The little wrought iron balconies in front of the Georgian terraced houses along the back streets of Morranport are hung with wet suits and today as I deliver there I pass a couple of men in their Ralph Lauren polo shirts and shorts off to get their early morning croissants at Baxter's. The delightful gardens in front of these wonderful houses are well kept and colourful. It's hard to believe how bleak and lonely these places look in winter with the South Westerly winds lashing the gravelled grassy paths and no one to be seen but the odd local gardener, employed to keep the places tidy over those empty months.

Now, it's packed full. Every house is lived in, cared for, loved. It saddens me that it's not this way all year round.

Still looking for ways to become part of my Cornish community, I take up gig rowing. There's a club at Morranport that seems eager to have me, obviously knowing nothing about my rowing skills which are zilch. Actually, to be truthful they take anyone. On certain days, anyone is allowed to join them, to have a go to see if it suits them.

Having rowed furiously on the rowing machines in the gym at various times in London, I give myself a pep talk and start off feeling jaunty and confident. But that's before I get into the boat. I hadn't realized gig rowing boats were so huge when I watched them zipping across the water from the shore. Close up, they seem not only enormous, but unwieldy, sitting low and large in the water.

The boat wobbles crazily as I get in. I'm trying to do it elegantly, acting cool and poised in front of the onlookers, but I trip over an oar and nearly fall over the side. *Terrific start, Tessa*, I groan inwardly. And the boat hasn't even left the shore.

There are six rowers and six numbered oars, as well as the cox in front giving instructions. I sit where I am told, grab an oar, before I can take a deep breath, or any kind of breath – never mind trying to find my sea legs – we're off and rowing furiously. I have a moment of panic when I realize we're out at sea, way out it seems to me, without even a life jacket. I start rowing faster to get to safety, or rather to the next cove or wherever we're heading, but the cox pulls me back and before long I feel I'm getting the hang of it, getting into the right rhythm.

It feels great! I'm at one with the sea, the sky, my fellow rowers, the world! Well, for a few moments it does. Then my concentration breaks for a nano-second and the oar is nearly ripped out of my hand, almost breaking the two wooden pegs that hold the oar in place.

'That's called "catching a crab,"' one of the rowers says cheerfully after I've got control of the oar, and myself, again. 'When the pegs break.'

For the rest of the time, I concentrate so fiercely that I've got a splitting headache by the time we get back.

'How was it?' Ben asks that evening.

'Oh fantastic.'

'Then why are you rummaging for the pain killers?'

'Headache. Too much sun.'

'And what's wrong with your hands?'

I show him the blisters.

'Hmm. Are you sure you enjoyed it, Tessa?'

'Who said anything about enjoying it? It was hell but still fantastic. Once the blisters heal and I get the hang of it, don't have to concentrate too hard, it'll be better than fantastic.'

Later that night, I try doing some press-ups to build strength. Annie, on the phone from London, laughs hysterically when I tell her, 'You, rowing a boat? Tell me you're kidding.'

'Oh ye of little faith, Annie,' I try to sound stern but her giggles are contagious. Within moments neither of us can speak as we clutch our separate phones, miles apart, but doubled over in helpless laughter.

When we regain some kind of control over ourselves, I say, 'You wait, for my first race. There's a big regatta at the end of the month and I'll be in it, you'll see. I might even invite you down, if you stop laughing.'

This sets her off again. But I don't care, because I'm seeing it all in my head right now: me in the boat rowing powerfully yet gracefully, our gig racing ahead of the other contestants as the crowd on the quayside shout encouragement . . .

'Tessa, are you there?'

'Yeah, Annie, but gotta go now. I need to do more press-ups, strengthen my arm muscles a bit.'

She's still laughing as we hang up.

I doggedly go back, four or five times more. Some days it's good, other days I seem to do everything wrong. One day, I'm out there again and it feels everything is going right. It's a windless perfect day to start with and all we rowers seem to get into a fine rhythm from the start. For the first time I feel really relaxed and confident.

After a time I notice that the cox is ordering constant instructions to oar Number Five. I'm not sure who that is but I'm Number One and that's all I need to know. I glance at my oar to double check: yep, Number One.

I keep rowing, well into my stride, feeling like a dolphin, a mermaid, a sea god, skimming above the water. The cox is still badgering Number Five, 'Pull harder, Number Five; Number Five, you're losing the tempo.' It goes on and on.

Poor Number Five, I am thinking, not without a teeny bit of smugness. Doing everything wrong today. I wonder who it is? Number Five doesn't seem to get any better, because the cox keeps shouting instructions at the same oar for a good half hour. *He's really got it in for this Number Five, glad it's not me*, I think. Suddenly, the cox tells us to stop. Wondering what's up, we put up our oars and the gig comes to a halt, bobbing gently up and down in the calm water.

The cox looks straight at me and says, 'Have you been listening to anything I've been saying? Anything at all?'

I look blankly at him. Why is he pointing at me, not Number Five?

'Well?' he's waiting for an answer, staring at me.

'Excuse me,' I say. 'But you haven't given *me* any instructions. I'm Number One oar. Look.' I wave my oar at him so he can see the number.

He looks bemused. Then everyone looks at their oars and it turns out we've all got the wrong numbers. The cox was calling out Number Five because that's where I am sitting, apparently, in the seat usually rowed by Number Five oar.

We exchange oars, have a bit of a laugh about it, and set off again. Though I only pretend to laugh – deep down, I'm mortified. All the time I was so sure I was rowing perfectly, and all those directions were for me!

Coming back, I concentrate like a demon. I have to, for now the cox has my correct oar number and he's belting me with instructions, do this, do that . . . *Can't I do anything right?* I don't seem to, not today anyway, and I'm working, rowing, as hard as I can . . . When we get back my cheeks are red with exertion, my palms more blistered than ever and the headache I had on the first day is back with a vengeance.

At home, Ben asks how the practice went. 'Oh, it was a gorgeous day. The sea was the calmest I've ever seen it,' I say.

He looks up from preparing some huge crayfish he's brought home. 'That's not what I asked.' How well he knows me.

I tell him about it. In the telling it sounds quite funny and now I'm sincerely laughing, not forcing it as I was doing with the other rowers.

'You'll learn, Tessa. You're tenacious enough to learn anything.'

I'm grateful for his praise but I know my limitations. I'm not going to carry on, not this summer anyway. It's our first one here and there's so much else to do. All that practice time has taken me away from the kids for a start. I want to enjoy Cornwall without any pressure to improve my rowing skills. And besides, I'll need weeks for my blisters to heal.

* * *

The weather this August is not too bad, some rain here and there but not enough to spoil things. As Cornish summers go, so far this is a good one.

I'm inundated with courgettes from my customers, masses of them, now that the peas and broad beans seem to be over. I'm learning the signs of the seasons – courgettes mean summer is slowly coming to an end and the next vegetables will be the squashes of autumn. The trees are heavy with dark leaves nearing the end of their leafy life and all three baby swallows in our nest are taking their first wobbly flights into the wide world of our front garden. I'll miss them when they go, we all will.

Most of the regattas this year have had the blessing of stunning summer days. With my job making me familiar with every nook and corner of South Cornwall, I know the best vantage points. There's nothing more idyllic than sitting in the sun in a meadow overlooking the harbour and watching the boats set off; whether it is gig racing or sailboats or whatever, it's a dazzling sight.

We've been inundated not just with courgettes but with visitors again, though no one has been as troublesome as Glenda and Morgan and Seth's various female friends. Seth has been dumped by the seductress Philippa, and visits us with 'a new hot date' as he put it when he rang.

This one, Becky, does not stop talking for the entire visit, following either me or Ben from room to room as we prepare meals, feed the hens or try to deal with the children. She doesn't stop waffling, mostly about people we don't know, or restaurants in places we've never been to and most likely never will. No one else, not even Seth, can interrupt this monologue. The next time Seth phones to say he's coming down, I'm going to suggest he comes alone.

As for Morgan and Glenda, the problem seems to be solved. Every time Glenda phones to announce their imminent arrival,

I hint that Seth and his woman might be with us that weekend too and so Glenda backtracks, suddenly remembering a previous commitment. I don't tell her that the voluptuous Philippa is long gone and she has no need to worry that Morgan will succumb to her charms.

The joy of visitors is that they finally go and we have our lives back again. On our own once more, I feel even more attuned to the countryside around me, to the cycles of nature that before I only saw through an office window or as I flashed past in a car. At this time of year I'm acutely aware of the heaviness of the foliage, the leaves on the trees and hedgerows turning a darker green, the wild blackberries still red but ripening already in this lush climate.

There is still colour everywhere. Masses of flaming orange montbretia on roadside banks clashing brilliantly with pink hydrangea. One of my customers told me about choosing a Carnival Queen in one of the towns on August Bank Holiday, of how the locals went out the night before and snipped the hydrangea heads to make a magnificent throne of the flowers for the queen.

The fuchsias are still growing wild everywhere, adding to the colour, and the sweet peas in our garden are having a last fling, throwing out their deep purply colours with abandon. Most gardens have sunflowers too, at least a couple, tall and whimsical, nodding their yellow heads and making me smile whenever I see one.

Whatever vegetables and fruit I don't get from my customers, I've been buying at a roadside stand on a narrow lane at the beginning of my route. It's been there for ever, selling onions, carrots, leeks, potatoes and often fresh eggs if the few hens owned by the gardening couple have had some prolific days. Unfortunately the honesty box for the produce is gone now. Several times in the past two months I've seen signs up: 'Will the person who took a dozen eggs and all the potatoes and leeks and forgot to pay please leave the money now.'

The next week there was another sign: 'Will whoever took ten pounds from the honesty box please return it as we are sure it must have been an accident.'

None of the polite requests worked; instead both money and produce were stolen again. Now, there is a secure metal box with a lock, firmly attached to a stake driven into the ground and concreted in.

'A sign of the times,' Martin Rowland sighs when I comment on the metal box with the lock. 'A few years back, even a year or so ago, we all had a stall out near the road to earn a few pence from any produce we couldn't use ourselves. Helped out with the finances that's for sure but hardly anyone bothers now. A box with a key keeps the cash safe but who's to stop someone coming along and nicking the veg?'

Emma agrees. We're standing outside their front door enjoying the morning sun for a few moments and she says now, 'Folk around here can sense the times changing. We all lock our front doors now. No one used to. Sad, isn't it?'

As she finishes speaking a man in khaki shorts and a white tee-shirt comes out, accompanied by a woman dressed exactly the same. They look sour faced and don't answer our 'good mornings'. The man says, 'We've been waiting for our breakfast.'

'We've been in the dining room for ten minutes, waiting.' The woman's voice is as brusque as her husband's.

Emma starts apologizing, says she didn't realize they were downstairs and she'll get it straight away. But Martin says, 'You said last night you wanted breakfast at 9 o'clock. It's not even 8.30.' His voice is dangerously soft.

The couple ignore him but Emma, recognizing his tone, gives him a warning look as she ushers the guests back inside.

'Wouldn't hurt to say please now and again,' Martin says but luckily for his business, they don't hear him. 'Bloody rude bastards. I hate working with people. At least animals have an excuse for bad manners, not being able to talk an' all.' He looks wistfully towards the vegetable garden. I notice that he's culti-vated a bit more of the grassy field next to the one where he's planted potatoes.

I say, 'Martin, are you planning on feeding an army?'

His face brightens. 'Well, would you believe, Baxter in Morranport says he'll buy whatever we grow, in the summer months. We're thinking of expanding even more next year, the garden has done so well so far. It beats dealing with paying guests, that's for sure.'

'Oh come on, they're not all that bad. Are they?'

'No, not all. Most guests are nice enough. But the bad'uns put you off folk for life,' he sighs. 'Better go help Emma get the breakfast but if they be rude to her, don't know what I'll do.'

I brood on this decent, kind couple, once farmers now B&B proprietors. They're so out of their depth in their new job.

Emma had told me they might just sell up and move. 'Not worth the hassle, Tessa. Trouble is, it's a no-win situation. We either run a business so we can keep the family home, or else sell and move to town somewhere, though lord knows what we'd be able to afford.'

I sympathized. She went on, 'Trouble is, we're selfish I guess. We don't want to lose our home, but we also want to do a job we like.'

Isn't that what we all want? I think as I drive away.

My next stop is in Creek to have my lunch. The tide is in, and the few boats moored in this part of the old harbour are bobbing about on the quiet sea. Even now at the height of summer, this spot isn't too crowded, not at this time of the morning anyway. I see a young man fishing from a rowboat and a couple of dog walkers along the lane parallel to the water but that's all.

I'm munching on a homemade pasty I picked up at Baxter's shop and sitting on the sea wall, breathing in the ozone. I feel so much a part of it: the sea, the two cormorants diving into the water, even the tiny molluscs clinging to the rocks at the edge of the water. I feel it more and more as I go on my rounds, noticing ladybirds and stick insects, stopping to watch ducks and moorhens at the edge of rivers.

As I finish eating, my thoughts turn to my morning's customers. After the Rowlands, I saw Mr Hawker, who has a nasty cough. He's had it a few weeks now but won't see a doctor, not even Martin and Emma can persuade him. He's terrified of being admitted to the hospital, feels he'll never come out if he does. I tried to tell him that just seeing a doctor won't necessarily mean being carted off to hospital but he wouldn't listen.

Afterwards I commiserated with a woman whose only daughter had moved permanently to New Zealand, gave her a tissue and tried to comfort her as she shed a few tears. Another woman gave me a recipe for runner bean chutney and still another rushed out to tell me she was pregnant after years of trying and wasn't life absolutely wonderful?

Comparing these conversations with those I used to have at work with my colleagues at The Body Shop, I realize that already I've got to know my postie customers on a much more personal basis than I did in my last few years in the other job. Of course we talked there but it was mostly work-related. We were far too busy to do otherwise.

I finish my pasty and watch the man in the boat pull up a great mass of seaweed on his line. I'm feeling serene and tranquil as the sea is today. I realize I never once felt this way working in London.

My lunch finished, I stand up and get ready to go back to work. It's so still you can hear the whoosh of a bird's wings flying overhead. In the distance I can hear the cry of a pheasant. *Bliss,* I think. *Pure bliss.*

I change my mind about the blissfulness of pheasants an hour or so later. I'm delivering to an old farmhouse at the end of a dirt track when a cock pheasant rushes out from the foliage at the side of the road and flies towards my van. At first I think he's ill and confused but I suddenly realize the bird is actually trying to attack me, for he's coming towards the open window. I shriek and the pheasant retreats, making dreadful, aggressive noises. Then he does it again but this time I get the window shut just in time as he brushes past it.

He must have stunned himself for he doesn't try again. I've stopped the van, trying to calm my beating heart, and roll down the window cautiously when the farmer's wife comes out to get the post. 'I saw 'im, that pesky pheasant, going for you. He don't be likin' red vehicles, y'know.'

'What?'

She nods, 'He don't bother us in they ole blue car, but when we be off in the red pick-up, he be after us just like he did with you.'

'Oh great. Maybe I better tell them in Truro that they'll have to paint my van navy blue.'

She doesn't get irony. 'Best be doin' that, maid,' she says solemnly.

I say goodbye and as I drive away, the blasted pheasant is at it again, following the van, attacking it from behind and squawking like a demon bird until I'm finally on the main road again. Maybe I really should try to talk the Royal Mail powers-that-be to get me a different coloured van, to protect their poor harassed postie.

My next stop is the mysterious hamlet of Trescatho-Brigadoon. Only it's not that any more. Over the last few months the place has been taken over by second homers and there are only the two near-derelict and slightly creepy farmhouses left, whose owners I still haven't seen.

I spot the latest second homers, outside giving orders to the painters and decorators on the scaffold. When the newcomers started encroaching on the village, a few months ago now, I noticed the proliferation of Farrow & Ball colours and now each time I come up I try to identify another one from the colour chart. The house on the end I'm sure is 'Dorset Cream' and last time I was here, I spotted an 'Ointment Pink'.

The Ointment Pink has post today so as I put it into the swish new letterbox outside the new door, I peek inside (the door luckily has a window). *Aha! That's 'Porphyry Pink' in the hallway, or I'll eat my post bag.*

Another of the cottages is being renovated now. This was the old schoolhouse once. Now there's scaffolding up here too and the outside walls are being painted. Thank goodness it's not pink this time or the whole hamlet will look like a giant candy floss. Oh good, it's a stone-y colour. I'm convinced it's 'Elephant's Breath'.

Only my precious red mail box is safe from being sold to second homers and decorated in Farrow & Ball. It's still concreted into the wall with the snail family safely inside. The day I come here to find it painted 'Middleton Pink' is the day I quit my job.

Nell is fuming again when I return to Morranport. She's fuming a lot lately, mostly with good reason because once again the Royal Mail is being threatened.

'Look at this,' she says without a preamble, her indignant bosom thrusting out at the world in a ruby red tee-shirt.

I read the newspaper article. It states that the £2 billion lifeline the government was supposed to hand over to the Royal Mail, to replace aging equipment and reduce a growing pension deficit, might be in jeopardy.

'This isn't conclusive,' I say. 'Doesn't even say why the money might not come through. Just a rumour, Nell, I shouldn't worry.'

She heaves her shoulders and bosom up then down in a massive melodramatic sigh, surprising me by saying, 'You be right, y'know. 'Tis too many other things to be worried about.' Her fury seems to have evaporated completely. Then she catches my eye and I know it's been redirected.

I dread asking but know I must, 'Such as?'

She points out over the harbour, 'Look at all them boats. More every year.'

'Yes, well, it happens. That's why lots of people come to Cornwall, for the boating.'

'Ain't good.'

I'm surprised at this. Nell hasn't minded the pink shirt brigade before, not in general, as they bring business to her shop. They're nice to her too; even the thoughtless ones don't dare to complain in her post office about the pong when the local farmers are muck spreading, or being woken up by cows or lambs mooing or baaing in the middle of the night. Those that tried in the past got short shrift from Nell.

'What's the matter with the boats, Nell?'

'Nothing, if folk can drive 'em. Too many think that driving a boat is a piece of cake. And too many drink and drive too. 'Tis dangerous. Why only last night poor Arnie, out doing some evening fishing, was nearly hit by a speedboat. Could have been another fatality but Arnie was luckier than t'other poor lad last month.'

'Arnie? Charlie's dad?'

'That's the one. Came in this morning, all shook up and raging at the boat that hit 'im. Brand new it was, fancy like, must of cost the earth. Arnie said the bloke couldn't drive the thing, was either drunk or blind. Poor man's still shook up about it.'

The whole community is rightly worried about this. The sea is getting crowded just like everywhere else.

Next day Nell's gloom is gone. I go into the post office and find her in the sorting room, laughing her head off.

'What's up?'

I'm starting to giggle myself without knowing what it is that's so funny. Nell's laugh is infectious, great deep chuckles that shake her chest and echo throughout the shop.

She says, 'Hope that gig rowing back along gave you some arm muscles, my handsome. You sure be gonna need 'em direckly.'

She points to the large canvas sack where the parcels are put before being sorted. I don't see anything unusual. Nell goes on, 'Not in there, too heavy for the bag, maid. Look over next to it, on the floor.'

There, wrapped in brown paper, tied with string, is a huge package. The shape is familiar; in fact you can't mistake it, as bits of the metal ends are poking out between the wrappings. 'It's an anchor!' I exclaim.

'The look on your face. Just like I imagined it. Oh, shouldn't laugh, not funny really. You got to carry the thing.'

I peer at it, trying to see who it's addressed to. To my surprise, it's for Arnie, the fisherman. Charlie's father.

I'm flummoxed. 'Doesn't his boat have an anchor then? I don't get it, Nell.'

But Nell knows everything. ''Tis a special sort of anchor. Fancy like. Arnie's wife got some cousins or nephews up Scarborough way, fisher folk, found the anchor for him.'

219

'Lucky old Arnie,' I say with a sigh, wondering how I'm going to cart the anchor into the van and then to the house.

It's solid metal, heavy and bulky. I can't believe someone has sent an anchor through the Royal Mail. I can't believe I have to deliver an anchor to a fisherman.

Nell has already picked up one end. 'Here, maid, I'll help you toss it in the van.'

I shriek at her to stop. 'Why?' She looks genuinely puzzled.

Because you're old and might injure yourself, I nearly say but manage not to. Nell, reading my mind, says, 'You be thinking I be old, is that it? Do meself some harm, you be thinking?'

She sounds so belligerent that I lie quickly, 'No, of course not, but let's face it, a thing like that could injure anyone trying to pick it up from the floor, no matter how young or fit they are.'

'So we do it together.'

Which we do and manage to get it into the van. I decide to forego my routine and head for Arnie's cottage first to get rid of it. He and his wife live in one of the villages about a dozen miles inland. I don't usually see them as Arnie is either out fishing or sleeping after a night on the sea, and his wife works long hours cleaning houses for the holiday makers. Today, though, instead of putting the post in the box attached to the front gate, I have to knock on the door as someone needs to sign for the parcel.

Arnie, surprisingly, is home and awake. After we make suitable comments about his anchor (a beauty, in'it?), the weather (hot today already), the emmetts (more than last year for sure), I commiserate over the near miss in his boat a couple of nights ago. He's still shaken up about it and tells me, 'The bloke was drinking, no doubt about it. No sober bloke would be driving like he be driving.'

From there we talk about the fishing and the difficulties of his profession: the scarcity of fish and the huge trawlers taking the best pickings; the price of fuel going up and the price of fish (to the fishermen anyway), going down.

When he winds down I say, sincerely, 'I don't know how you lot make a living. It's tough I know.'

'Might have to take on somethin' else, part time mebbe. Hate to, me life's always been on the sea, but might have no choice.'

I nod in sympathy. 'So many people have to do that, down here. Even your son Charlie, he's such a brilliant artist he should be doing it full time but instead he has to cut hair to earn a crust. Luckily he likes doing that, too.'

Arnie frowns. *Whoops*, I think, *I've done it again, spoken without thinking.* I had completely forgotten about his wrath over his son not being a fisherman.

'Charlie's just messin' about, not settling like he should. He could of had me boat all to hisself in a few years, when I retire.'

I risk more wrath by saying, 'But you just said the profession is dicey. Fishing, that is.'

He's about to yell at me, I can tell, his face is getting all red. I hate confrontation and curse myself for getting into this fix, so before he can speak I say, 'Look at me, happy as a lark these days, being a postwoman. I used to have a fancy job, loads of travelling, great salary, but in the end I wasn't happy. So I gave it all up to live in Cornwall. Hasn't been easy, but I love what I'm doing now.'

His anger has cooled but he looks at me as if I'm a weirdo, wondering what this has to do with Charlie and the fishing profession. I go on, 'Isn't that what's important? Doing what makes you happy?'

He doesn't say a word so I plunge on recklessly. *What the hell, you might as well get hung for a sheep as for a lamb, Tessa.*

'You love fishing, you just said so, earlier on. Well, Charlie loves making his wonderful boxes and paintings and installations and sculptures – and all of the sea too, which he loves just as much as you do. How could any father want to take that away from his son?'

I've gone too far, I can tell. Cursing myself for opening my big mouth in the first place, I say, 'Omigod, look at the time, I'd better get on. Bye now, enjoy your anchor!'

I jump in my van and don't look back in case he's throwing something at me.

The August heat wave settles in. The beaches are packed, as are the seas and harbours, full of boats of all kinds, the sailboats colourful with bunting on regatta days, the sky full of fireworks to celebrate a good day's boat racing. On each of my days off I take Minger, rush to the beach with Amy and Will, and Ben if he's not working, and we spend lazy hours swimming, paddling, snorkelling, making elaborate sand castles and in general idling the lovely hot days away. And the beauty is, this is not a holiday. When September comes, we'll still be here. What a delicious thought that is.

September

The summer days of the last week of August linger into September but after the Bank Holiday, Cornwall begins to empty. When school starts again the next army of holiday makers arrive, composed of those not tied down to terms and timetables. This seems to be a favourite month for retired folk, many of whom have been babysitting the grandchildren most of the summer while the parents worked and are now taking a well-earned break for themselves. It also seems to be a month for babies and toddlers not yet school age. The beaches are full of them, the parents fondly holding them in the water for their first experience of the sea.

Annie visits again, only this time it's not just me she's coming to see. She and Pete have been emailing each other and plan to meet again. I invite him to dinner the day she arrives. Pete comes with two bunches of flowers, yellow roses for me and crimson ones for her. These are totally unexpected and it's the first time I have seen Annie flustered. She's touched, embarrassed and speechless, so unlike her that I stare rudely at both of them as she buries her face in the flowers, pretending she's taking in the scent. The look on Pete's face is one of delirious delight.

It looks to me like their emails have already gone far beyond friendship. And then Annie sneezes. And does so about ten times in a row.

'It's the roses,' I say to Pete as I take them away and lead her upstairs to find tissues.

I hear him say to Ben, 'Is she allergic to *everything?*'

Ben says, 'Afraid so. Especially in the country. That's why she hates it, only comes to see Tessa.'

Pete's voice is uncertain. 'She hates the countryside?'

Ben nods. 'Just doesn't understand how we can live here.'

I can't give him a kick under the table or a pinch in the elbow to keep him quiet because the two men are down-stairs in the corridor and I'm in the bedroom with Annie, eavesdropping. I swear at myself for not telling Ben about her and Pete's relationship but then I remember they don't have a relationship; they've only met once briefly and exchanged some emails.

Ben obviously hadn't seen the way they'd looked at each other, though, when Pete arrived. I needn't have worried. By the time we sit down to eat, Annie's hay fever is under control. She's looking ravishing in a skimpy, clinging top, a chunky-knit cardigan thrown over her shoulders and stone-washed jeans that look absolutely made for country living.

Even as I think this she says to all of us, 'Oh, it's so good to be back in Cornwall. You don't know how much I miss it when I'm away.'

Ben looks at her open mouthed and this time I'm close enough to give him a swift soft kick beneath the table before he says anything. Luckily the penny drops. I see sudden real-ization hit him as surely as if a cartoon balloon had appeared over his head saying, 'Aha, so *that's* how it is.'

He smiles at me, a secret, knowing smile that I return. Then I turn guiltily towards my guests, wondering if they've seen our little exchange. No chance. They're too engrossed in each other, with Pete telling Annie all the beautiful places in Cornwall he'd like to show her and Annie radiantly nodding her head as if I've not dragged her around those same places months ago.

I'm thinking of this a few days later, after Annie leaves. She and Pete spent every minute together when he wasn't working and both seem to be wild about each other. She left this morning in tears, wishing she could stay longer, saying she'll be back as soon as she can.

I'm so thrilled at this bit of romance that I'm whistling as I trot into Mrs Pappy Apple's house. Her real name is a nightmare of consonants about five syllables long, compliments of her Bulgarian husband who is in his nineties. I've nicknamed her because every day, rain or shine, she waits for me in the window of her house to give me an apple from the fruit bowl on the deep windowsill. Usually the apple is wrinkled and soft but of course I take it anyway, thank her profusely for her gift. She's a dear sweet old lady, struck with Alzheimer's, being cared for by her loving husband, and I feel quite protective of the two.

Mrs Pappy Apple's front room looks over the garden, where she sits all day watching the birds feed from the dozen or more feeders crammed onto a tiny lawn. There are also gnomes of all shapes and sizes, green ceramic frogs, pottery cats of a ferocious ginger colour, china flower pots and ornamental figures. It's like a child's toy box, so colourful and bright.

As with many of my customers, we have a daily ritual. When she sees me, Mrs Pappy Apple opens the window, hands me – or any other postie delivering to her – an apple and we have a bit of a chat. In fact it's the exact same chat every day – the weather, my health (fine, thank you), hers (not doing too badly, dear), her husband (he's so good but she does so worry about his joints). I have a little game with myself, to see if I can make her smile, for her face is usually solemn and weighed down, understandably, by life. When I succeed, I feel such pleasure that it invariably lifts my mood a notch or two, no matter how high or low it was to start with.

Today, my loud whistling entices out that smile even before we start our conversation. I'm so delighted that it doesn't even register until I'm back in the van, that for the first time ever, she hasn't given me an apple but a banana.

I panic. For months I've had what I think is a brilliant routine, a solution both to the apple disposal and to the harassment I was subjected to from the flip-flop family – a half dozen geese at the next house on my run, whose feet, rushing towards me, sound like flip-flops on tarmac. Discovering quickly that the apples were inedible, yet hating to merely throw them away as they were such a kind gift, I hatched a cunning plan. As the geese came charging at me, honking their blasted heads off, when I ran from the van to the front door I threw the apple as far as I could in the opposite direction. By the time they'd got to it, squabbled over it and demolished it, and were ready to have a go at me again, I was safely back in the van.

Not only did this save me from a nasty peck or two, it also made good use of the apple, ensuring that it didn't go to waste. But today, I have a *banana*. Do geese eat bananas? I have a feeling they won't be thrilled at the idea.

Since I've been at this job, I've handled bad-tempered domestic cats lying in wait to sink claws into my unsuspecting hand, I've dealt with demon dogs – Batman comes to mind – and lived to tell the tale, I've been chased by a cockerel, and by that bad-tempered pheasant, and even once, a turkey.

But the geese are my real nemesis. They are big, can be vicious, attack together, and are seriously scary.

I drive up to the house and sure enough, there they come, honking for postie blood again. Will the banana work? I've got no option but to give it a try. Thinking ahead, I peel it, in case they're dumb geese and don't recognize a treat when they see it with the skin on. As usual, I leap out of the van before they get to me and fling my sacrificial fruit as far away from the house and van as possible.

You can almost hear the screeching of their heels on the tarmac drive as they stop their pursuit of me and turn abruptly, then run as fast as their goosey legs will carry them in the direction of the banana. I don't stop to see their reaction but dash like a demented woman to the door, shove in the letters and race back to the van.

As I drive away, I'm whistling again. Whatever they thought of the change of fruit, they fell for it and I reached the van before they did. Making a triumphantly rude gesture to the honking geese now following my van down the drive, I head for my next drop.

A week later, the weather's changed; it's still warm, but thunderstorms have rolled in again from the sea. One minute I'm engulfed in waterproofs, splashing through puddles in potholed tracks to deliver the post, the next minute I'm in my baggy shorts and polo shirt, my sun visor on to keep the glare out.

I've been issued with an adapted old golf cart by the Royal Mail to lug the post around St Geraint. When I first use it, I feel I could be mistaken for a serious golfer on holiday until I remember the unflattering shorts and my sturdy boots.

The bad weather has driven many of the holiday makers home a few days early. I arrive at the Rowlands' B&B and stop for a drink of cold apple juice in between storms. Dave is down again from Bristol and is in the garden helping Martin pick a load of spinach to freeze. Emma and I sit on the front doorstep sipping our juice, soaking up some sun while we can. Around us there are rumbles of thunder and in the distance streaks of lightning emanating from black clouds fast approaching.

I incline my head towards a couple of nanny goats in an enclosure near the house. They are a new acquisition, as are the dozen hens pecking around the new chicken house Martin built. 'Are those for the guests, to give them that farmyard feel?'

Emma shakes her head. 'We got them for us, to have some animals about. When we had to get rid of the dairy herd, it nearly broke our hearts.'

Dave's girlfriend, Marilyn, who's also here for the weekend, comes out from the house to join us. Grinning, she says, 'Good thing Dave's not like his dad. He'd be a God-awful physio if he couldn't bear the hassle of dealing with people.'

Emma agrees, then says, 'But like Martin, he's not happy in a city.'

'I know how he feels,' I murmur. 'I couldn't bear it now.'

Marilyn nods, 'It was cool at first, leaving Cornwall, the only place I'd ever known. But I'm like Dave now. I'd love to come back but . . .' She shrugs, tailing off.

I leave after another few minutes, despite Marilyn's offer for me to stick around a while. 'I've made some scones, they're in the oven now and ready in a minute. Wait and sample one. Not as good as Dave's mum's but not too bad.'

I get back into the van regretfully, wanting to be around these friendly people longer. Marilyn is the sort of young woman Cornwall shouldn't be letting go. Dave too, belongs here.

Still brooding about the couple, I don't notice at first that Mr Hawker is taking a long time to get to the door. The rain's started again and I'm huddled inside my waterproof, waiting for him to answer. He's normally there at the first knock and opens it eagerly. We do our usual ritual of my handing him the post with one of the tiny KitKats tucked away between the junk mail, and he solemnly thanks me and tells me I shouldn't have done it. Then we stand in his doorway discussing the weather, my family and his health – he always says he's fine – until I make a move to go. He never detains me, rarely asks me in except when it's pouring and then we always stand no more than a foot or two inside the door, but equally he's never, ever, the first to make the move to go.

I'm worried, now. No one in the village and surrounding area can remember when Mr Hawker last left his cottage, not even Emma and Martin. I try to open the door and peer in, but it's locked. Uneasily, I go around to the back but there are so many nettles and brambles covering the concrete path, that I don't even attempt to get through. Besides, it'll be locked too – it probably hasn't been open for years.

I try peering in through the grimy windows but can't see anything through the dust and filth and the driving rain making streaks on the outside. Cracks of thunder and flashes of lightning aren't helping my unease. None of the windows are even slightly open. I try to prise one up but it's solidly embedded into the window frame. Frantic now, I knock on the window again but the only sign of life is a thrush warning me to get off its patch.

I remember Mr Hawker's cough then sigh with relief. *Of course*, Martin and Emma had told me last week that they were going to overrule his protests and get him to a doctor. I'm sure now that's what has happened. The doctor, rightly concerned, must have put him in hospital to make sure the chest infection cleared. Because Mr Hawker gets very little post, I don't see him every day. It's probably been three or four days by now.

The Rowlands didn't mention that Mr Hawker was in

hospital, but I assume that's because they forgot, with Dave and Marilyn there and their guests only leaving today. But I need to make sure, so I drive back up the road to find Emma or Martin.

All four of them are in the garden now, oblivious to the rain which lasted no more than ten minutes then suddenly stopped. They're inspecting the courgettes and having a good-natured argument about whether they should be picked today or allowed to grow a tiny bit more. I refrain from getting involved, saying I'm far too diplomatic a postie for that, and ask about Mr Hawker.

They're horrified when they hear he's not answering the door. 'No, he's not in hospital, Tessa, in fact we even got Neil, our doctor, to come out a few days ago but Mr Hawker wouldn't even let him in the house. Opened the door a fraction to tell us politely to go away, there was nothing wrong with him. We couldn't force him, had to leave him there.'

Martin had seen Mr Hawker the day before, in the morning. 'Looked the same, still coughing, still wouldn't listen when I mentioned the doctor again. I'll go right down now, see what's up.'

I offer him a lift in the van but Martin says, 'I'll cut across the fields. Quicker that way than going along the road.'

I want to go too but I'll only be in the way. The poor man is probably ill, unable to get out of bed. In some ways I'm relieved – this time he'll have to let a doctor look at him and take him to hospital if necessary; at least get some antibiotics into him, to cure his cough once and for all.

I get through the rest of my round with my thoughts still on Mr Hawker. In the doggie hamlet, Great-Grandma notices my concern and is uncommonly cross with Batman for growling and grizzling at me from the other side of the fenced garden. 'Can't be hearing meself think, Batman. Do shush.'

He actually does. He even looks meek. I never thought I'd see the day.

She asks me what's wrong and I tell her about Mr Hawker, how he won't see a doctor and now we're afraid he's really ill. She's not in the same village but she knows him; he's a local after all, and the same generation. 'Stubborn old bugger, that one, but 'twould be hard to find anyone with a kinder heart.' She looks wistful. 'Us'n be sweethearts once.'

'Really?'

'Not for long, mind. He be a bit older'n me, well, a few years mebbe, but such a looker.' Her voice is dreamy. 'But he was that peculiar with folk even back then. A real loner.'

'Do you ever see him? When he's not ill, I mean.'

'You must be joking, maid. Hardly no one gets a look in. Like I say, peculiar. But a good soul for all that. Sorry to hear tell he be ill.'

Back at the Morranport post office a couple of hours later, Nell rushes out from behind the counter in the midst of a transaction, leaving the customer who is trying to post a package, looking at her with annoyance. Obviously a stranger, he raps his knuckles on the wooden counter to let her know he's still there.

She ignores him and pulls me to the side. 'Mr Hawker,' she says bluntly.

'I know, Nell. He's ill. I couldn't get into his house, but I guess the Morranport grapevine has told you that already. Martin and Dave Rowland were going down to see what's up. Have you heard anything else? Is he in hospital or at home?'

She turns her back on the now glaring customer. 'Not one nor t'other.'

'What do you mean?'

'He be gone, maid.'

I still don't understand. 'Where?'

Her look tells me everything. 'Oh Nell, no.' I'm devastated.

She says, 'Martin and Dave found him, already gone, in his bed. Had to break the door open. Happened some time in the night.' She sees my face, pats my shoulders and says, 'There, there,' as if I were a child. 'He'd of wanted to go that way, maid, in his own home, his own bed. A hospital would of killed 'im.'

The logic is a bit off but I know what she means. At least his spirit remained intact, dying where he belonged. But I still feel so sad.

The funeral the next week at the church in Creek, right by the sea, is simple and moving. A vicar who retired ages ago comes back to take the service, as he actually knew Mr Hawker before he became quite so reclusive. A couple of eighty-plus-year-olds stand up and say a few heart-felt words, a couple of well-known hymns are sung, and everyone is out in the September sunshine once again.

Mr Hawker would, I think, have been pleased. Over the months I delivered to him, I'd become convinced that his fear of seeing people, of going out of his house, was not anti-social as much as extreme shyness, aggravated by old age and illness. Not being well enough to keep himself and his small cottage clean and tidy, he would not embarrass himself or others by letting anyone in, not even to help. It was a way of retaining his dignity. But the number of people in the church today, all milling outside now looking at the sea, reluctant to leave this beautiful spot on this serene day, is a testament to Mr Hawker. Though most of them here have not seen him for years, they remember him fondly. I hope fervently he somehow knows this, wherever he is.

Now that the storms have gone back wherever they came from, the air is still and clean, warm but invigorating rather than muggy. Though I love autumn, I'm feeling slightly melancholy when the day comes that the birds' nest on our window sill is empty and the youngsters gone for good. The swallows are gathering together now, getting ready to leave, and I look for my little ones, wish them well on their long flight south, ask them silently not to forget us and to come back home to us next year.

I go out blackberrying as much as possible, bringing the juicy berries home to make pies to freeze and great pots of jam for the winter. Out in the fields the farmers are busy harvesting their maize and the sounds of their tractors and forage harvesters echo through the valleys. I pick elderberries and make refreshing cordial for the family. Next year I'll try making elderberry wine. There are holly berries out too, shiny red amongst the glistening green leaves, a joy to the birds as they forage around the hedgerows.

I'm inundated with apples. We don't have any trees of our own in the garden, not yet – we hope to plant some – but I'm given box loads to take home with me, more than we can keep. I can't give them away as everyone has a surplus this year, so once again I'm baking, stewing, preserving. I've never done anything like this before but soon feel the same as I do about my postie round, as if I've been doing it for years.

Another golden day and I feel in perfect harmony with the world as I drive up to a care estate at the end of my van round. There's a warden on the premises, a quiet but watchful man who greets me politely enough but doesn't say much. I think he's too conscientious, too intent on keeping his eyes and ears on red alert in case trouble breaks out on his patch.

Not that there's been any, as far as I know. Most of the residents in their individual homes are struggling to overcome drug or alcohol addiction, or mental illnesses; they've been rehabilitated, and the project is a kind of halfway house between life in a hospital, prison or care home for the mentally ill and life alone in the real world. Like the warden, the residents are mostly polite but silent, focused on their own recovery as if afraid it will fracture if they lose their concentration even for a moment.

I'd be quite at ease delivering here if it weren't for one of the men, Jamie Newton. I like some of the residents and admire all of them. Some have made a total mess of their lives but are now bravely trying to struggle through. It can't be easy, especially given the background many of them come from.

Jamie is a different case altogether. I'd been told when I first started the job to keep an eye out for him, as he could be unpredictable if he mixed alcohol with his medication. He's a tall, powerful, young man with a shaven head and huge, wild, brown eyes, and though he's never harmed me or anyone I know of, there's something I find threatening and scary about him.

There's a small porch area where Jamie lives, with two front doors: Jamie's and a middle-aged woman who asked me once to call her Poll. Every time I see her she still asks, 'So what's me name, me luvver?' When I say cheerily, 'Poll, of course. Short for Polly,' she beams and pats my shoulder as I give her the post, as if I were her very best friend ever.

Jamie's door has a letterbox, and a few times when I've thrust the letters inside, junk mail mostly, he's grabbed my fingers. I still yelp when he does it, though I know now it's only eagerness to get his pathetic post as he lets go at once. I still can't help getting nervous, though, hoping he doesn't flip one day and break my fingers.

I've learned now to deliver his post first, hoping to divert him while I turn my back on his door to push Poll's letters into her slot. The few times I delivered Poll's first, Jamie crept out of his door and before I realized he was there, stood breathing down my neck, too close, far too close. He's got no idea of personal space, or if he does, ignores it.

Most days he wanders around, weaving crazily along lanes and main roads, tugging obsessively at his shaven skull as if he's trying to pluck nightmare thoughts from his poor head. Whatever the temperature, he always has a thick, dirty yellow scarf around his neck.

I feel sorry for him. Known as the local nutter, he's constantly being picked on and made fun of by the local kids. I've heard their parents telling them off for it, thank goodness, but when do kids listen to their folks when they're with their peers? Still, I was glad when I heard Jamie being defended. It's another thing I've discovered about closely knit communities; they'll protect one of their own and Jamie was born and grew up around here. He's a misfit now, the resident crazy, but he's still one of them.

Even as I think how admirable this is, I feel my usual vulnerability as I step into the tiny porch. I'm a fairly tall woman, and strong from all my months outdoors delivering the post, but Jamie towers over me, makes me feel fragile and weak. I've heard him talking jibberish behind his front door, seen his agitation as he roams the streets. I might feel compassion for him, but he still frightens me.

Poll had picked up her mail outside as I'd parked my van. After our exchange over her name she grinned and waved, walking away towards the shop on the corner. I'm a bit edgy knowing that hefty Poll isn't behind the other thin front door in case Jamie grabs my fingers a bit too hard this once. If he ever does, naturally I'll report it and won't have to deliver to him again, but by then I'd have a few broken fingers, so it's a scenario I hope never happens.

My imagination begins running riot. There are only a few circulars and a white envelope which contains a form letter from the local council about rubbish collections. I'm tempted to bring them back to the post office and let the relief postman deliver them tomorrow as it's my day off.

I'm tempted like this every time I have to deliver to Jamie but talk myself out of it each time. *You wimp, Tessa,* I scold myself. *All you have to do is shove the letters in the slot but keep your fingers well back.* I'd learned that trick ages ago but sometimes you can't quite get the post through without a finger or two pushing it in.

Wondering if he's home, I put my ear to the door to hear if there are any sounds. I nearly fall on my face as the door opens suddenly and Jamie is standing right there. He looks manic, his pupils abnormally large, dark circles underneath wild eyes. He's wearing a black tee-shirt, black jeans, and as usual his yellow wool scarf is wound around his neck, wrapped so tight you wonder he's able to speak properly.

I stand upright, tall as I can, and start to bluster. 'Oh, hello, I wondered if anyone is at home. I've got your post here.'

Instead of giving it to him, I'm so flustered – and scared – that I clutch it tightly to my chest. He doesn't say a word but takes a step closer. I take a step backwards and he takes another step forward. This goes on for a couple more steps until I'm backed against Poll's door and Jamie's only a fraction away from me, breathing fire down at me.

Well, alcohol fumes anyway. Oh God, he's mixing the booze with the drugs again, I think, frozen with terror. I want to scream but I know there's no one around to hear me. The warden is way down at the other end of the housing estate and there are only Jamie's and Poll's places here.

Jamie lunges at me and then I scream. He jumps, more terrified than I am it seems. I try to run but he grabs my hand. I scream again. I'm going to be killed, I think, feeling the blood run cold, just as they say in the cheap thrillers. But it truly does. I never knew that blood actually does turn cold with fear. I feel as if ice is coursing through my veins.

I'm trying to push Jamie away as he tries to grab me. Or so it seems. Then he suddenly lets go. He retreats, some scruffed up paper in his hand, and bolts back into his house. He gives me a fearful look, frightened and pathetic, before the door slams. I can hear locks clicking as he barricades himself inside against the weirdo postie.

I feel like a fool as I realize what's just happened. Jamie had come out for the post, like any of my regulars, and after telling him I had some for him, I clutched it to my bosom like some ridiculous Victorian maiden. He wasn't trying to attack me, just trying to get his mail, since it looked like I was keeping it from him.

Driving back to St Geraint, I'm still brooding over the incident. Though it was my stupidity that triggered it, technically I should probably report it. He had grabbed my hand after all as he tried to get his pitiful bits of mail from me.

I park the van, trying to stop thinking about it, focusing on the sea – calm and azure and as serene as summer, despite the late September day – and then looking out at the shop fronts. Harry, in front of his office, waves at me and I wave back. Passing the sad old-fashioned shop, the closed sign still on the door, I commiserate with the dejected looking mannequins, arms missing, faces dusty, fifties-style nylon wigs sitting awry on their heads. I feel sorry for myself too. I'd acted without thinking at the care estate, letting my fear run away with me. If I'd handed the post to Jamie, he'd have taken it, walked away like he'd done dozens of times before when I'd met him in that porch, when he wasn't behind the door waiting.

I'd have to report it. The frustrating part was, whatever I said, it would still be Jamie who got into trouble. Whatever fear made me do, the authorities would say he still shouldn't have touched me.

I walk glumly into the post office. Margaret picks up my mood, asks what's up. I shake my head. 'Nothing.'

'You sure? Has anything happened?'

I take a breath and look her in the eye. 'No, honestly, I'm fine. Just tired, that's all. Late night last night.'

Without thinking, I've made up my mind. No one, not even the village crazy, is going to suffer for my over-reactions. Feeling much better, I make my way to the Sunflower Café. Ben's on today and if it's not busy maybe he can grab a coffee with me.

Passing the grocery shop, I see Lulu standing in the doorway, gazing out towards a yacht setting out from the harbour. 'Ah, Mrs Posh Post Lady, how are you?'

I assure her I'm just fine. 'And how are you, Lulu? How's the English going?'

I know it's practically flawless now, clever girl that she is, but I also know she likes being asked, takes an understandable pride in her new knowledge. 'Oh good I think.' She frowns, worried that this is immodesty on her part. 'But of course I know improvement can always be made.'

'Your English doesn't need any improvement,' I say and her whole face dimples in smiles.

'Yes and now I can go back home. Soon.'

'For a holiday? To see your parents?'

'Oh no. For good.'

Surprised, I say, 'But all that serious study you've been doing, learning the language and the culture. And now you're leaving? What made you change your mind?'

'Oh, I always am planning to go back.' She frowns again. 'Or I should say: I always did plan to go back. Or should it be, I always planned to go back?'

'Either one, Lulu. Did you?'

'Yes, to teach English to the village children so they have something for the future. Your language, Mrs Posh Postie, is world language now. Children in my country need to learn English, even poor children like those in my village. Only then can they help make a future for themselves.'

I wish her luck, impressed at her intelligence, her dedication. I can't help comparing Lulu to Jamie. They must be about the same age, but how different life is for the two of them. Not only a world of difference in backgrounds but in their futures too. There is one similarity, and it's the one of community solidarity. Jamie, in a loose sort of way is protected by his community, and Lulu is going back home to do all she can to help hers. This thought cheers me immensely. I skip once or twice as I say goodbye to Lulu and head towards the café and Ben.

'Mrs Posh Postie,' Lulu calls after me, laughter in her voice. 'Be careful. Remember how you fell that time, before Christmas, when you hopped too close to the edge of the path.'

Hopped? I have a fleeting vision of how she sees me, how she'll describe the local post deliverers in England to her charges back in her tiny Asian village. *Like jumping rabbits,* she'll say, making the little kids laugh as she gives a demonstration. *Little bunnies. Or like kangaroos, children. Now, do you remember where kangaroos live?*

I skip into the café, which is thankfully empty. Ben kisses me, and I'm pleased to see how well he looks, and how content. He's realized, since we talked about moving back to London, how very much he too loves our lives here. Making the decision to stay has somehow liberated him, and his face, his body language, reflects this.

He says now, 'I see you've had a good day.'

'Oh I have. An amazing day.'

We sit down and I tell him all about it. Predictably,

he's worried about me, about Jamie. I say, 'Ben, if he'd wanted to hurt me, he could have done it easily. He grabbed my arm but was aiming at his post. Even in his wild state, even with the booze in him he still wasn't violent. In fact, I'm kind of glad it happened. I don't think I'll ever feel so frightened of him again.'

Ben is still worried, but he accepts my judgement, after warning me that if anything like that ever happens again, I'd have to report it, or *he* would.

I agree, and we spend the next half hour talking about the things that have become important to us: the rhythms of the sea, the seasons, our new life. Though we don't yet feel fully integrated into our Cornish community, and sometimes wonder if it'll ever happen, we're going with the flow, taking on the tempo of life here and trying not to rush things. We've learned you can't force anything in the countryside and it hasn't been easy at times adjusting to a rural life. As we lapse finally into silence, looking out through the glass front of the café onto the harbour, our minds still and hearts at rest, I know. For this moment anyway, we're part of it all.

October

The first week of the month is perfect. The temperature is a steady 70 degrees with no wind or clouds, just a gentle sun. It's a glorious perk before the winter months looming ahead. Bookings are suddenly up in the guest houses and B&Bs for the autumn school break and I marvel at the optimism of the English. Just because it's perfect weather now doesn't mean it'll be like it tomorrow, let alone in another few weeks.

The fine weather brings many of the second homers down for an unplanned weekend but during the week Cornwall is fairly quiet, the visitors sparser. The locals are settling down to think of autumn carnivals, Hallowe'en, school fund-raising fêtes and all the activities leading up to Christmas.

The leaves are slowly beginning to change colours, the beeches glowing yellow in the sunlight, adding to the golden haze that seems to be caressing the countryside. The oak, ash and birch trees start to add their tinge too and every shade of bronze, orange, yellow and red appears.

One midweek day the peace in St Geraint, dozy after the frenzy of summer, is shattered by the boom and roar of four

Harley motorbikes, their guttural engines revving through the little place like the Hell's Angels everyone thinks they are.

It takes about five minutes for every shopkeeper, postie, fisherman, baker and local resident to hear about the newcomers, as they park their bikes in the car park at the end of the village. St Geraint doesn't do bikers, or rather bikers don't do St Geraint, so everyone is askance and in a tizzy. Eyes peer behind shop windows as the bikers strut through the town in their black leather jackets and heavy boots.

When they go into the Sunflower Café and order basil and mozzarella salads with olive ciabatta, the locals there realize they can't be Hell's Angels, not with those accents. The waitress, a local woman (Ben's not on duty) spreads the word around. 'Talked posh,' she whispers. 'Asked if there be sun-dried tomatoes in the salads.'

This intrigues the locals so one of them begins a conversation. It turns out that the Harley tearaways are middle-aged men having a mid-life crisis, though of course they don't admit to that. They've rented the bikes and are roaring through England on them. 'If we don't do it now, never will,' one of them says.

'Trip of a lifetime,' adds another.

They nod solemnly. The locals wish them luck, then chuckle behind their backs. I listen to it all and remember a trip I took across the States on the back of a Harley, from Miami to San Francisco, courtesy of an old boyfriend. How he'd laugh if he saw me now, driving about in clapped-out Minger and a postal van that's seen far better days.

Coming out of the café I see Harry going to the bakery. I haven't seen him to chat for a while, so I run to catch him up. We both have time, so we sit at the rickety table for two outside the bakery on the harbour and order tea and Millie's delicious scones.

After we've chatted to both Millie and Geoff about the bikers, and Geoff brings us tea and Millie the scones, Harry and I settle down to talk.

I find myself telling him about Jamie, and his reaction is the same as Ben's, worried for me and warning me to be careful. But Harry knows Jamie; he and Charlie live in the same village as the care estate. I tell him about my feelings about the local community, how I think they keep an eye on their own, even if their own is a bit odd.

Harry agrees with me, 'When I first moved down here with Charlie and we set up house together in the village, I know there was talk. We're the first gays openly living together there, so it caused a stir. But because it was Charlie, whom everyone knew from a kid, it was OK. I feel more or less accepted now, probably more than you do, only because Charlie's a local. I think they're proud that even after going off to the big city, becoming a successful stylist with a top salon, he still wanted to settle back home.'

'Except his dad,' I say, biting into my jam and cream layered scone. 'Ironic isn't it, that his own father is still fuming at him.'

Harry puts down his own scone without taking a bite, 'Oh Tessa, I forgot, we've not talked properly for ages. I think Arnie is coming round at last.'

'What?'

Harry nods, 'He stopped by Charlie's workshop a while back, said he wanted to have a look at what his son was up to.'

I've stopped eating too, so surprised by this news, 'What brought that on? He's never done that before.'

'No, never. Refused to even talk about Charlie's work. Charlie did a double take, he told me later, seeing Arnie standing there, watching him for a few minutes without him realizing.'

'Did Charlie find out what caused the change of heart?'

'Not sure what did it. Arnie said something about thinking

things over, about being lucky enough to do what he's loved all his life and maybe he shouldn't be so pig-headed about Charlie only wanting to do the same.'

I'm stunned. I think of my conversation with Arnie a month or so ago. It never occurred to me that it might influence his own thoughts in any way.

A few days later I'm delivering in Morranport. Though the weather has held until now, I feel it's changing. Just as birds and animals seem to know when a storm front is on its way, I do too, after nearly a year in this job. I don't exactly start to ache in the joints, as some of the older folk do, but my body feels different. It feels tenser, almost electric. It felt like that when I left the house this morning, so though it was still warm and the sky cloudless, I grabbed my waterproofs.

Good thing too, for by the time I reach the Grenvilles' house at the end of the village, I see a black mass looming on the horizon. The wind has whipped up and is blowing the storm this way fast, driving the rain with it. When Jennifer Grenville opens the door and asks me in for a cup of tea, I nip inside gratefully.

As usual, Archie is sitting at the kitchen table with his books but he leaves them to watch the storm with me as Jennifer brings out the brown teapot and some Rich Tea biscuits.

'It's come up so fast,' I say, still awed at the power and speed of these flash storms that lash and flood the village, then disappear without a trace leaving the sky a clear rinsed blue.

'Typical autumn storm,' Jennifer says, pouring out the tea and handing it around.

'I'd hate to be a fisherman,' I muse, thanking her as she offers me a biscuit. 'Can you imagine being caught in that?'

Archie says, 'I can remember my grandfather and uncles out in storms like these, the women at home praying. Then the worry getting stronger as the weather got worse and they'd all set off out of the house to stand on the shore in the driving rain, us kids huddled alongside not larking around for once, looking out and waiting for our fathers, older brothers and granddads to get home safe.'

I munch on a biscuit, 'What kind of fishing did they do?'

'Oh, anything. Years ago, just about anyone, no matter how poor, could manage to own an old boat, find a hidden cove, catch some fish. Not all fished full time; they did it for extra cash, to feed the family whenever they had spare time. Even the farmers hereabouts often had a little boat to get about in, then.'

'And your grandfather?'

'He was full time all right. Did all sorts, in all weather. But of course the big catch in Cornwall used to be for the pilchards. The sea was rife with them, years ago.' He goes quiet, remembering.

Jennifer and I sip our tea, listening to the rain hurling against the big window, watching the sea froth and foam.

Archie goes on. 'My granddad often spoke of the great days of the pilchards, the ones he recalled from his own childhood, in the 19th century that would be. They used nets, the seine nets. You'll have heard of them, no?'

I have but didn't know much about how they were used. Archie explains. 'They used huge nets that were kept down with weights at the bottom. It took several large boats and many men; it wasn't easy, believe me. When a shoal was spotted the boats set out with the seine nets and circled the pilchards, tried to herd them into the shallows. They had to be really skilful, each man knowing his stuff, working together . . .'

He pauses again, for so long that I think his reminiscences are over and I make a move to go, but he goes on, barely noticing me. 'Pilchards provided the livelihood for years, for my family way back, and for nearly all the fishermen in Cornwall. All the houses had fish cellars where they stored the pilchards and cured them. Matter of fact, our spare bedroom downstairs used to be the fish cellar.'

'I've seen some of the pilchard lookouts,' I say, as he seems to have stopped again. 'Old sheltered places with wooden or stone slabs to sit on, high up on cliffs and ledges.'

He nods. 'A few of them were left, saved from dereliction and preserved as a tiny reminder of the past. I remember Grandfather talking about being sent on pilchard duty in the summer months, he and the other kids sitting at the lookouts, staring out to sea until they spotted a shoal. They'd race like maniacs to be the first into the village to cry out the news. The men would dash for the boats and the women and children, the old men, all ran down to see them off, to wish them luck with the catch.'

And now I see that Archie really has finished talking. Along with his memories of the fishing, the tales heard at his grand-father's side, are his own stories and those of his long-dead parents and siblings. I know Archie is the last one of his family still alive.

Jennifer and I exchange looks as I get up to go. At the door she says, 'You've got to forgive us old dears, Tessa. We get a bit nostalgic now and again.'

I tell her truthfully that I love to hear Archie's stories. Thanking her for the tea, I set off again, amazed to see that the storm is already dying out, the rain stopping, the sun shining and a brilliant rainbow arching across the sea.

It is Hallowe'en and there's a party on the village green. It's a cold but clear night, happily for all of us, especially for Will and Amy, dressed as pirates which is apparently all the rage this season.

But ghosts and spirits, the proper kind, are even more prevalent in the days leading up to Hallowe'en, or so I'm told by some of my customers. These are the spirits of all those poor souls shipwrecked over the centuries, their bodies never found, their souls unable to rest. They call out over the sea at this time of year, even venturing inland to sigh and moan and scare poor, innocent folk nearly to their death.

There's many a vicar too, I'm told, still haunting old rectories, churches and graveyards. Some were as odd in life as they seem to be in death. One apparently hated his parishioners so much that he chose never to see them, except in church where he had no choice. Ordering his food and other provisions to be left in a box at the end of the rectory path, he managed never to see anyone at all except at the church services.

He soon stopped seeing his parishioners there too, for naturally folk got fed up and refused to go to church. As they tailed off, the vicar made life-size figures out of wood or cardboard and placed them in the pews, to replace his vanishing congregation.

It's said that when the bishop finally got round to visiting that isolated village, he found his vicar preaching to rows and rows of life-sized effigies, without a real human being in sight. Even the organist was made of cardboard, her stick fingers stuck for ever on the organ keyboard.

'That ole vicar, he still come out every Hallowe'en, I heard tell from my ma, not just in his own church but in every church in Cornwall. He wanders around from one t'other all night long, looking for his lost congregation.'

This was Nell, adding to the story that morning in the post office. The Grenvilles had heard it, of course, and Archie added a story of the supernatural of his own. Or rather one handed down by his family, he told me.

It was about a smuggler, one of his great-uncles – or maybe

it was a great-great one – who did a spot of harmless carting of illicit tobacco and brandy to earn a little spare cash. There was some kind of a tussle with another smuggler, this one part of a larger ring that thought great-uncle was muscling in on their business. There was a quarrel, knives were drawn and great-uncle's body was washed ashore the next morning, his chest still harbouring the knife that killed him.

'He's supposed to come out and roam the coast this time of year, on the first of November, with all the other unhappy spirits,' Archie had said. 'Even my grandfather claimed to have seen him. Scared the bejesus out of him, he said. Threw him a cider apple to placate his spirit.'

'That sounds so pagan.'

'Oh it is, it is.' Archie quite relished the thought. 'Up until the fifth century, we were all great worshippers of fire, the sea and the sun. You can't kill off the old faiths in just a couple of thousand years or so.'

Now, at the party in the village, a great full moon beaming down on the green, I can believe it. There are spooks and skeletons, black cats and witches, wandering around eating toffee apples, along with gypsies, pirates, spider ladies and firemen. As Amy and Will run off to find their friends, I crunch a piece of toffee and wonder why no one wants to dress as a postwoman. Maybe I'll bribe Amy to do it next year.

Ben has wandered off to find more substantial food than a toffee apple and is talking to one of the neighbours who is selling hot pasties at the food stall. Daphne and Joe come over to talk, asking me about the kids, how the job is going. We still haven't got to know them any better, though. Our relationship with all the locals has gone so far, then no further. It's as if an invisible wall stops us from going that extra pace, that step that changes acquaintances into friends.

Daphne and Joe finally see some other farmers and excuse themselves to catch up with them. For a short time I wander around alone, looking for Ben. Before I can find him, I see Emma and Martin watching with amusement a pumpkin competition going on at a table set up on the edge of the green.

I go up to them eagerly, wanting to thank them again for the huge pumpkin they gave me for Amy and Will to carve into a lantern. They wave away my thanks and the three of us stroll about together. Ben comes along and I introduce him to the Rowlands but Amy calls him away for some urgent advice on the best way to bob for apples without getting her eye patch wet. Taking it off is definitely not a solution, so Ben laughs and lets her pull him away, apologizing to the Rowlands as he leaves us.

I say to them, 'You must be glad the autumn half term is over.' I know their B&B was full up that week.

Martin nods. 'And it looks like we made enough to close up shop till after Christmas, anyway. That last sudden splurge of guests was a godsend.'

'Great.' I'm pleased for them, though I'm not sure what these energetic, hard-working people will do with themselves during the next few months. They're not the type to rush off and holiday in the sun or sit around at home all winter.

As if reading my mind, Emma says, 'We've got loads to do in the next few months, if we're going to get the market garden going. And then there's the goats – we're building up the herd.'

'Herd? Last time I counted, you had two nannies.'

'Ah, things have progressed since then. We're going to buy quite a few more, eventually sell the milk and make yogurt from it. And eggs – we're getting more hens.'

Martin looks happier than I've seen him for ages. 'We been thinking it all out, Tessa. The B&B business 'tisn't us, not by a long shot. The garden, though, has been booming – even sold loads of pumpkins for Hallowe'en.'

'So we're expanding it, going into market gardening, see if we can scratch a living that way.'

I'm amazed. 'Can you really?' The doubt must have sounded in my voice, for Martin smiles ruefully.

"'Twill be hard at first, touch'n'go, but mebbe one day. Marilyn and Dave have found some good outlets for the produce, some shops in Bristol actually and we got some good orders already. Organic stuff, see? All the rage.'

Emma says, 'Of course it'll take time to get organic certification, but bit by bit . . .'

They both look so hopeful with their new plans. I wish them luck. 'That's great. So no more B&B at Trelak Farm?'

'Goodness, not so fast, Tessa,' this is Emma. 'We need the B&B to finance the other stuff. But that'll be Dave and Marilyn's job.'

I'm getting confused here. 'But – they live in Bristol.'

Emma and Martin look at each other with such a sparkling look that I say, 'Don't tell me, they're coming back to Cornwall.'

Martin grins, 'Renting old Mr Hawker's cottage. He had some great-nephew living in Scotland, some fellow he never knew who inherited the house. This bloke don't care about selling, got several houses Up Country apparently, so we made a deal – a low rent and in return Dave and Marilyn do up the place. After that . . . well, we'll see. One thing at a time.'

We talk some more. I learn that Dave and Marilyn, who is also a physiotherapist, hope to get part-time work at the hospital in Truro, work it in with the B&B business while Martin and Emma crack on with the livestock and garden. 'And of course Martin or I can do the B&B if it overlaps sometime with their other work.'

I'm distracted for a few moments as Will goes by with a

mate, leaping about in a pretend sword fight and nearly knocking me over. He's gone as fast as he arrived and I turn back to Emma.

'You've got it all planned,' I tell her, admiration in my voice.

'You've got to plan, Tessa, if you want to stay in Cornwall. We're all of us scheming and doing all we can to stay put here, where we were born and bred.'

She doesn't mean anything by it, and maybe it's the strange mood I seem to be in tonight, but those words make me feel excluded. Will I never forget that I wasn't born and bred here? More important, will anyone else ever forget and treat me like one of them?

I'd had a sudden impulse, when I ran into the Rowlands, to ask them over to our house to see the lantern the kids made with Ben's help, out of their pumpkin. Perhaps we could have a drink, get to know each other, give Ben a chance to get to know this kind couple. But her words unintentionally stop me. They probably wouldn't come anyway; after all, I remind myself, they're not friends, they're my customers. I only see them on my rounds, except for rare nights like tonight.

So I let it go, drift away from them, and wander to the other side of the green, past the crowds of over-excited children, indulgent parents and watchful villagers, until I'm standing in front of the old church, its stone gleaming in the moonlight, the tombstones in front lit up now and again by a wayward torch beaming from the green.

It's chilly now. A sudden wind, sharp and autumnal, has sprung up, ruffling the drying leaves of the trees, sending a few scattering down over the graveyard. I shudder in the sudden cold and button up my jacket.

Maybe I'll see the people-hating vicar, I think as my eyes roam across the stones, wandering about looking for his wayward parishioners. A figure stepping out of the shadows makes me leap a foot into the air. My heart doesn't start beating again until I see it's one of our neighbours, taking a short cut through the churchyard to the Hallowe'en party.

He waves at me and I wave back. Then I make my way slowly back to the house to put on a sweater under my jacket and to bring warm clothes for the children. There are still fireworks to come and a barbecue. It will be a long evening.

The leering face of our carved pumpkin lantern on the front step seems as eerie as any spirit out roaming tonight and the wind now whipping around the bushes of the front garden makes a ghostly moan as it gathers strength. My body is telling me there'll be another storm but not yet, not until the party is over.

This early autumn storm will be different from the summer ones. There'll be a chill of winter, a foretaste of what's in store over the next few months. But the house itself looks warm and welcoming, a few lights still burning to guide the family back inside after the revelries end.

Tomorrow is November, the month I began this job. The year is drawing to an end and I have a sense of other endings too. Mr Hawker, for one. A death and a funeral. I think of him for a moment, hoping his spirit is at peace, this night when the dead are said to walk the earth. But this month has brought some good endings too. The feud between Arnie and Charlie, the father and son. And perhaps, with luck, the end of an unsuitable occupation for Martin and Emma, an end of exile for their son and his partner.

With luck. So much depends on that, I think. No matter how hard we work, strive to achieve, plan and scheme, we still all need a little luck. Tapping the round pumpkin head grinning on my front doorstep, I let myself into the house, find some sweaters and jackets, and rush on out back to the party.

November

I am tiptoeing out of the bedroom the next day, the day after Hallowe'en, as usual trying not to wake Ben at this ungodly hour. But before I can leave the room he sits up and runs to the bathroom where I can hear him being sick. I go to him but he motions me away, indicates he'll be all right.

When he comes back into the bedroom he's not all right. He's shivering with a severe chill, yet when I touch his forehead, it's blazing hot.

'Don't know what's brought this on,' he says as I get him water and some paracetamol for the fever.

'Probably the flu. It's getting towards that time of year again, and I heard last night that one or two others in the village are in bed with it.'

He groans, 'I'm on at the café for the lunch hour.' He's been leaning back on the pillows and now tries to sit up then flops back down, the movement having exhausted him.

'Not today,' I say.

I know he's really ill when he agrees to stay home in bed and miss a day's work. I stay hovering until he tells me I'd better get going, that I'll be late, and that he'll be fine, the kids will be fine. 'Just go, and don't worry about us. Amy and Will can get themselves dressed and breakfasted and I'll surface long enough to get them to school.' His face is drenched in sweat.

'Ben, are you in pain?'

He nods, 'My gut. Probably some wretched stomach bug.'

That would explain it, with the vomiting and everything. He seems prone to stomach viruses; the last year or so he's had a few minor attacks of pain and nausea but nothing as agonizing as this one seems to be.

Ben says again, 'Tessa, you'd better get moving.' His eyes close. 'I'll try to get a couple more hours sleep before the kids get up. Don't worry, I'll be fine.'

I try to hurry my round, to get back home as soon as possible. Ben phones me when he wakes again, saying he's feeling a bit better but still has the bouts of shivering followed by bouts of feverish sweating. Definitely the flu, so I make him promise to get straight back to bed when he's taken Will and Amy to school. I've already phoned the café owners, told them he won't be in.

Of course today, when I'm in a hurry to return to Ben, is the day when everything seems to hold me up. First is the weather. As I'd thought the night before, there was a sharp change during the night and though it's only the first of November, we're having a cold blast of early winter with icy rain and a Siberian wind that gets under my waterproof and turns the skin under my fleece goosebumpy.

At Morranport post office, Nell looks like a cuddly toy in a chocolate-coloured mohair jumper which frizzes up from her shoulders, arms and bosom like the fur of a teddy bear. ''Tis too early for this sort of weather,' she mutters, clapping her hands together for a bit of warmth. As she speaks, a frenzy of hailstones batters the window that faces the sea.

I agree, 'Flu season's already begun. Ben's down with it.'

She picks up a newspaper she'd been reading when I walked in. 'Slanging season started too, m'lover. Look here at this slanderous stuff.'

I take the paper reluctantly. 'Nell, you ought to stop reading the newspapers. You take it all too seriously.'

'There be a conspiracy, maid, you better believe it.'

'By *whom*? About *whom*? And *why*?'

'You be saying I don't have a clue what I'm talking about?'

'Never, Nell, believe me, but I'm not sure who's behind this so-called conspiracy.'

'The government, that's who, against us small post offices, because they want to be ridding themselves of the lot of us.'

I sigh loudly and impatiently but I know I'll never get away before I read yet another article about the Royal Mail. This time, someone has uncovered the fact that huge amounts of letters and parcels are lost every year, some by accident and some by deliberate fraud.

'Nell, everyone knows that postal workers are like everyone else, totally human. There're thousands of us, and maybe a few are careless, and even a tiny few are corrupt. Happens everywhere. But everyone also knows that the overwhelming majority of us are honest and hard working.'

She won't have it. Straightening up to her full height of five foot, her ship's prow bosom trembling with indignation, she says, 'It be scurrilous scandal. You wait and see, maid, 'twon't be long before every small post office in rural England is being threatened with closure.'

I know better than to argue with her. Besides, she's probably right about the post offices. It all comes down to money, like everything else.

'Nell, can we finish this conversation another day? I've got to get going.'

She's reading the article again, probably for about the fifth time, not looking up as she waves me off.

The hailstorm has stopped but the road up the hill out of Morranport is treacherous and slippery. My mood plummets as I hear a strange noise coming from the van. It sounds rattley and tinny as I edge up out of town. I put on the radio to drown the sound but it seems to be getting louder and more frantic, so when I get to the first lay-by, I pull over to see if I can spot what's wrong.

One glance tells me the problem: I left the back doors open when I zoomed away in such a rush. *Great start,* I think. *Really, Tessa, you're such an idiot sometimes. Every ounce of Royal Mail deliveries could have flown out of those back doors.*

My cheeks burn when I think of the article Nell just gave me to read. I'm glad I defended poor, human, accident-prone postal workers. It can happen to anyone. But luckily, the mail is intact with nothing missing and I can go on, now that I'm soaked again by another lashing of hail.

The morning doesn't get much better. A flock of sheep on the road keeps me idling behind them for ages and for some reason the van is stalling every time it idles. I'll have to report that. My door isn't shutting properly again either and there's a leakage of icy water on my seat as I hop back into the van after another delivery in the wet.

And oh no, oh dear lord, there's a letter for my worst delivery place, a run-down farm at the end of the long track with three five-bar gates to open and shut before reaching the house. That means getting in and out of the van *twelve times* just for one piece of mail.

I sit in the van in front of the first gate wrestling with my conscience. The hailstones have changed to a slushy, cold, steady rain drenching the windscreen, the wipers not able to keep up with the deluge. How tempting it would be not to deliver it but sneak it back to the post office and let the relief postie take it tomorrow, my day off.

I've never done anything like that before but oh, how I am tempted now. I'm still worried about Ben, despite his phone call to say he's feeling better; I want to get home and see for myself. But the vision of Nell, always loyal to the Royal Mail, always trying to defend it from accusations of incompetence, floats before me in all her bosomy righteousness. How can I even be thinking of letting her – or the Royal Mail – down?

Resolutely, or more accurately, resigned, I open the first gate, get back in the van, drive through it. Another moral quandary now – do I risk leaving the gate open for the time it'll take to deliver the post? I glance at the fields. The sheep are way on the far side, huddled near a copse of scrub oak, trying to shelter. They're not going to move from that spot for quite some time. But if they do? I know sheep can spot an open gate a mile away and then they'd be down the road and away as fast as you can say *that bloody postwoman*.

I get out of the van, shut the gate behind it. This whole routine is repeated twice more as I make my way up the track. I'm cold and wet and know, just *know*, I'll be joining Ben in bed with the flu before long.

After the last gate is past, there's another hurdle. Part of this farm track is actually a small stream, making it muddy at the best of times. During rainy bouts the water and mud can be quite deep, and sure enough, today it happens again. I've only been stuck here once before, last winter, but that was enough. I was hoping it would never happen again but today's not my lucky day.

I trudge up to the farmhouse for help after a great deal of revving back and forth to try to get the van unstuck with no success. Mr Barker, the farmer, comes out in the rain with tractor and rope and finally pulls the van out. 'Will you be wantin' a cuppa, maid? Wife'll be glad to brew one up. She be in kitchen.'

Tempted as I am, I decline and give him the letter. He takes a cursory glance at it and crumples it into a ball, stuffs it into his jacket pocket. 'Another of them circulars. Shouldn't of bothered, maid.'

I finally get home, wet and cold, longing for a hot bath. Ben is up but doesn't look great. He's pale, and there's a thin ridge of sweat on his forehead though his hands and face feel cold. He says he's better, though, 'Just these stomach pains. Quite bad at times. Must be a bug, or something I ate at the fête last night. I feel as if my whole body has been poisoned.'

That night, Ben hardly sleeps. Nor do I, worrying about him. He's feeling nauseous and the pains are getting worse but he's convinced by now it must be a stomach virus. In the morning I try to get him to the doctor's but he says, 'Give it time to get better, Tessa, it only started yesterday. If the pains are still bad tomorrow, I'll see the doctor.'

But he is getting worse, I can tell by his white face and the way he clutches his abdomen when the spasms of pain hit. By midday he's doubled up in agony and I call the doctor who immediately calls an ambulance. Ben is shaking uncontrollably despite layers of clothes and a hot-water bottle. I insist on going with him in the ambulance but he whispers, 'Amy and Will. You've got to stay home.'

I'm frantic. I can't leave Ben and I can't let the kids come home to an empty house. There's Jake too, growling at the ambulance men, nervous at all the strange activity. I feel trapped, not knowing what to do, only knowing that I can't be in two places at once. I feel helpless, bereft. Annie would help, or any of my old friends, but they're all in London. I've never felt so lonely, and so alone, in my life.

Desperate, I grab the phone, punch in the first local number

I can think of, one of the first I was given after moving here. Susie answers on the third ring, 'Just got in, bird. What's up?'

When I tell her she says only, 'Go with Ben. I be there in half hour, leave the key under a plant or something.'

The hospital in Truro is large and impersonal as all huge institutions are. Everyone seems to know what they're doing and after what seems like days, but can only have been hours, Ben is in a clean ward, pain under control, with an intravenous tube feeding antibiotics into his system. A scan has confirmed the diagnosis of diverticulitis.

My heart stops when I hear this. One of my older relatives had this when I was a child, and died of it, so I'd been told. It had been undiagnosed, and that was many years ago, but still . . .

When Ben drifts off to sleep I find a helpful nurse and ask her exactly what diverticulitis is. She takes me to a tiny office, gives me tea and explains that it's an inflammation, or swelling, of an abdominal pouch in the intestine wall. These pouches are usually found in the colon and if they do get inflamed, as Ben's are, the pain can be excruciating.

'We're treating your husband with a high dosage of antibiotics, which should bring down the inflammation,' she says. She notes my stricken face and smiles reassuringly. 'Don't worry, he'll be home in no time, I'm sure. We just need to keep an eye on him as he's had an acute attack.'

I don't mean to, but I tell her about my relative. 'He couldn't really have died from diverticulitis, could he? I mean, Ben's not in danger, is he?'

She shakes her head. 'Your relative must have developed peritonitis, which can happen when the intense swelling causes a rupture in the colon. But Ben's not in danger of that, not now. The diverticulitis is under control; the antibiotics go to work at once.'

I can't ask anything more as she's called away, but now I understand why the doctor called an ambulance to take him to hospital so quickly. To prevent the rupture that very nearly happened.

It's nearly nine when I get home, but the children are still up. I've talked to them – and Susie – on the phone several times in the past hour but they wanted to wait up to hear the latest about their father. Susie very sensibly made no protest.

Stopping to fuss over Jake who is frenziedly wagging his tail and trying to get himself noticed, I go in to see the kids. They are in pyjamas and dressing gowns and look clean, wonderful, and practically asleep in front of a DVD of *One Hundred and One Dalmatians*. I tell them that their dad is on the mend, get them to bed gently, while Susie makes rich hot chocolate drinks for the two of us before she leaves for home.

I see that the hens have been shut in the hen house for the night, and the rabbits taken care of, and that there's the remains of a homemade cottage pie in the fridge, all thanks to Susie.

I try to thank her but she brushes me off and says, 'I been on phone to Daphne up the road, had a long chat.'

'You know her?'

'Bird, you forget I be knowing most folk in these parts, I was born here, remember? Now I reckon you be wanting to go straight onto hospital after you get the kids to school tomorrow, stay with Ben, so she's bringing 'em home to her place when she collects her own kids. Amy and Will are thrilled to bits, especially as they be getting a chance to see the new calf just born today. Oh, and Daphne'll be popping by here as well, see t'hens and rabbits.'

I'm stunned by all this, and mightily relieved. Then I groan, 'Work. God, Susie, I'm on tomorrow.'

'No you're not, bird. Eddie and me'll split your round, no problem. Already asked 'im.'

I burst into tears. Despite my terror as Ben was rushed to hospital, my fears for him all day, my exhaustion, lack of sleep and lack of food, I had managed, only by a thread, to hold myself together. Now I'm undone by all this kindness, this thoughtfulness, this generosity of time and compassion.

Susie lets me cry and cry, pats my shoulder and says, 'There, there, my bird, all's gonna be just fine now,' as she hands me tissues, gets me another hot drink. 'Oh, and by the way, I'm taking Jake home with me until Ben's home and you be back to normal.'

'But your cat . . . !'

'No problem. She practically hibernates in me bedroom from October to March. Jake'll not get a whiff of her nor she of him.'

I'm feeling much better for the good weep but still don't go to bed after Susie leaves despite hardly sleeping the night before. It's nearly eleven o'clock but I'm both exhausted and agitated, a poisonous combination where sleep is concerned.

So I'm still sitting in the living room when there's a ring of the doorbell. I go to the front door and open it without a qualm. I haven't a clue who's here at this hour but I don't think to ask before I open up.

Another thing I'd never do in London, that's for sure.

Daphne is standing there, apologizing for arriving out of the blue at that hour. 'I was coming back from a film club get-together just down the road and saw the light, saw you were still up. I'm so sorry about Ben. What can we do to help?'

I ask her in and to my surprise she accepts, first making a quick phone call to Joe saying she'll be later than usual. She sits at the kitchen table while I open a bottle of white wine, a sudden impulse that Daphne seems to approve.

'I suspect you need this,' she says, as we drink the wine. 'What an awful day.'

She repeats what Susie has told me, that she wants to take Amy and Will out to her place tomorrow after school. 'They get on like a house on fire with my kids, Tessa, as you know. They may as well be spending the night and I'll get the lot of them off to school.'

Like Susie, she won't hear of any thanks, simply changes the subject. She stays an hour, and we drink the whole bottle, talking without a pause about everything under the sun. When I ask her about the film club she'd mentioned, she says, 'Oh, it's just an informal thing, taking turns watching new films and old classics on DVD at each other's homes and chatting about them afterwards. And I nearly forgot. Everyone there sends warm wishes, hopes Ben is better soon. And Clara said to ask if you want to join us. When Ben's home and better, that is, no need to be thinking about it now.'

Clara is another neighbour, a sparky Cornish woman around my age who lives a few houses away in the village. I hardly know her, though I've spoken to her in the shop and at various village functions. Like so many of the others, she was friendly but distant, too distant for me to make any overtures towards friendship.

I say uncertainly, '*Clara* said to ask me? Are you sure?' I've never been asked before to anything in the village, except for the big fêtes and parties that everyone goes to.

'Of course we're sure, all of us. Anyway, think about it. There's only about eight of us, a good-sized group. Some you'll know from around the village and the others you'll get to know.'

When she realizes the time, Daphne giggles and says, 'I'd better call Joe, I can't really drive like this. Good thing my mum's staying with us, to be there with our kids.'

So Joe comes out in his battered old farm truck, stays about ten minutes to ask about Ben and send his regards. When they finally leave, I fall into bed and have no trouble falling asleep at once, not stirring until its time to get the kids ready for school. A quick phone call to the hospital assures me that Ben is still sleeping and has had a pain free night.

When I see him later, I begin to worry again. He looks pale and wan, his skin clammy. Though with this neon lighting I suppose I look just as bad. During the morning we learn that there is still concern about a possible rupture, so Ben is being monitored carefully. He's going to have another scan and some blood tests. There's talk now of a possible operation.

The day drifts, as hospital days do. I'm getting used to that pervasive hospital smell of milky drinks, bitter medicines, disinfectants and occasional cigarette smoke as visitors from outside walk in. When Ben dozes, I leaf through magazines or listen unashamedly to the Ozzie surfer in the bed opposite, talking on his mobile phone. 'Alright, mate, good, good! . . . Well actually tell a lie, buddy, not so good 'cos I'm in hospital, got hit by m'board in the old fella!'

He's been surfing in *this?* I look out of the hospital window at the rain still drizzling against it. It's November, for goodness sake, but of course the surfers are out all year now, thanks to wet suits. *Far better you than me, mate,* I think with a shiver.

Ben is being fed intravenously. He'll have to be on low fibre liquids for a time, to reduce the amount of material going through the colon until it heals. Later, we'll have to take special care of his diet, adding the fibre he'll be needing to keep his colon healthy and hopefully prevent this happening again.

He's more concerned about me. 'When did you last eat, Tessa? Go down to the cafeteria and get something, please. You don't want me to start worrying about you.'

It's the last thing I want so I finally go down, grab a ham and cheese baguette and a weak coffee. At first the food is hard to swallow, but once I start to eat my stomach tells me how hungry it is and I fill it rapidly.

When I go back up it's visiting time and to my surprise, Ben has a visitor. It's Susie, still in uniform having just finished her round and part of mine. She's brought a pile of magazines for Ben: a selection of news magazines, a science monthly and a men's health magazine. She doesn't stay long but before she goes, says she and Eddie can do my round again tomorrow, no problem.

I've talked this over already with Ben, so now I say, 'Thanks, Susie, but since Amy and Will are staying overnight at Daphne's and she's bringing them to school, I may as well work. I'll come to the hospital straight after. I'll have a couple of hours with Ben anyway before getting the children.'

'Well, if you be sure, bird, but don't be worrying pickin' up Amy and Will. At least a half dozen of the mums of their friends have phoned Daphne, offering to have them after school and overnight. Clara wants to do it next. Oh, and there be a rota going to feed the rabbits and hens. So you can stay with your man as long as you like.'

I'm so overwhelmed I can't think straight. Susie says, 'You not be needing to think, bird. Your friends be doing the straight thinking for you. Just you two concentrate on Ben here getting better.'

That afternoon Ben has several visitors. Joe comes, with homemade get well cards Amy and Will have made at school, signed by all the children and their teacher.

'They're over to our place now,' Joe says. 'Daphne's got them baking cakes with the eggs they just collected from your hens. You're not to worry about them.'

Harry visits next, with sandalwood scented soap, hand lotion and men's face cream. 'Why should you females get all the pampering?' he tells me as I smell the products and threaten to confiscate them for myself. 'You leave them alone, woman.'

Because Harry usually has lunch at the Sunflower Café, Ben knows him quite well. They talk easily, but like the other visitors, Harry sees Ben tiring and leaves before overstaying.

As soon as he's gone, one of the waitresses from the café, who shared shifts with Ben in summer, arrives with a bunch of carnations. 'Everyone in St Geraint sends piles and piles of love, Ben,' she tells him, planting a kiss on his forehead as she leaves. 'Don't you be doing this again, scaring us to hell being rushed to hospital like that.'

Later, as Ben is getting ready for sleep and I'm preparing to go, he murmurs, 'I didn't think we had so many friends in Cornwall.'

'I didn't think we had *any*. Oh, lots of people we liked, but I didn't know they were friends. Didn't know they'd come to our rescue like this, take care of us like . . . like . . . like *family*,' I shake my head in wonder. 'I'm completely bowled over.'

'And I'm completely whacked,' Ben says, his eyes closing. 'It's been a long day.'

We say goodbye, kiss, and I leave the hospital, go straight to Daphne and Joe's farm. I've never been there but when I talked to her earlier, to see how the kids were, she asked me to stop by, have a bite to eat. They've got a comfortable old beamed farmhouse, two golden Labradors and a casserole waiting for me in the Aga.

Will and Amy are in bed but Daphne takes me to see them so that I can kiss them goodnight. Amy stirs, wakes up for a moment and asks, 'How's Dad?'

'Doing really well. I'll take you and Will to see him tomorrow.' She's back asleep in seconds.

Daphne and Joe have eaten, but they open a bottle of red wine, have a glass with me as I tuck into a succulent lamb stew, thick with gravy and vegetables. We talk about everything and nothing whilst I have two helpings. It's incredible how I feel at home here, in this house I've never even set foot in before.

The night nurse on Ben's ward doesn't mind my phoning her in the early hours, before I start work the next day. Ben's had a good night, he's sound asleep, and yes she'll give him my love, tell him I'll be in later. She sounds calm, unharassed, unlike some of the day nurses yesterday. And who can blame them? They're overstretched, overworked.

I ran into one of them, Rachel, coming out of the ward yesterday. She's a sweet young woman in her late twenties and I know her slightly as she is still, out of necessity, living with her parents who are on my postal route.

At the post office in Morranport, Nell accosts me at the door. 'You be asking me, why did I not be coming out to see you, come out to see what's to be done?' she scowls at me accusingly.

Before I can answer she tells me, 'Because no one had the sense to tell me, that's why. Not till late last night, too late to go over and give some comfort or mebbe make a pot of tea, some supper, give a hand doin' summat or other.'

I'm slightly bewildered. 'Give a hand doing what, Nell?'

'Why anything that need be doing,' she says in the tone of voice one uses for stating the obvious. 'Looking after your kiddies, cookin' a meal – whatever.' She shakes her head at the missed opportunity but brightens as she adds, 'But now you be here, you can let me know what I can do.'

'Nell, thanks, you're a star. But Susie, and the neighbours, everyone has been great. Not anything to do.'

She's not sure of this but decides to leave it for a minute. 'Poor Ben, but at least he be having a good sleep now, so don't you go worrying, me handsome.'

I start to nod then wonder how she knows this. It turns out

that Rachel had a last peep at him when her shift finished, found him sleeping peacefully. She told her folks who rang Nell to give her the news, if she hadn't heard already, that the postie's hubby was in hospital but doing just fine, according to Rachel.

When I've finally got the mail sorted and am on my way out of the door, Nell blocks it. She won't let me go unless I promise to let her know if there's anything, anything at *all*, that she can do.

That day is surreal. The news of Ben in hospital seems to have spread through all my customers and I'm inundated with fruit and chocolates, cards, good wishes, prayers, a couple of loaves of homemade bread, books and magazines for Ben to read, and offers of help.

By the time I get to the Rowlands I'm all talked out and ready for a break, and accept gladly when Emma asks me if I want a coffee. They, like everyone else, are full of commiseration and offers of help; in fact, they'd already left messages on our answerphone.

'We'd have Jake but he seems to be happy driving about with Susie,' Emma says. 'We saw them both when Susie did your round yesterday.'

'Strange to be seeing Jake and not her cat,' Martin adds.

I nod, remembering that of course Susie's cat often goes out with her in the van. Poor thing, brought into early hibernation because of Jake. Typical Susie not to mention it but to sort it out smoothly.

The Rowlands press me to come back to lunch, or dinner, but I explain I'll be at the hospital till late. Emma runs inside and comes back with a brown ceramic ovenproof dish. 'A lasagne. Just heat it up,' she says as she hands it to me.

As I try to thank her she interrupts me, 'Soon as Ben's out of hospital and recovered, you two come over for a meal.

We were going to mention it at Hallowe'en, after we'd met Ben, but then we somehow got sidetracked.'

I smile at her, 'You know, I was thinking the same thing that night.'

'Well, let's hope it's soon. We've been wanting to meet Ben for ages, thinking he must be a great guy, if you chose him. I can't tell you how often you've cheered us up, coming up the drive with a smile whatever the weather. Especially when we'd had a bad day with the paying guests.'

The unforeseen compliment unnerves me and I get out of there quickly before I start to cry again.

Ben is in the hospital for nearly a week and during that time, our neighbours and new friends take over my life, helping to keep it running smoothly. Amy and Will, once they've seen Ben and know he's going to be all right, are thrilled to be spending each night at different friends' houses so that I can do my round in the morning. I could take compassionate leave but I'd like to save it until Ben is home, as he'll need rest and recuperation for some time. He had a very nasty acute attack of diverticulitis, the consultants told us, and though they don't think now that an operation is necessary, he'll still have to take care, keep an eye on his health, on what he eats.

Annie is on the phone every day, gutted that she can't get down to help. It's not just her job that is keeping her away, but the fact that she's ill too with a nasty bout of flu and can hardly get out of bed herself she's so weak. Her Cornishman, Pete, now the love of her life, is actually in London looking after her, having taken off a few days work to spend a long weekend making her tasty soups to get her eating again.

'Pete's wonderful,' Annie sighs on the phone after we've talked about Ben. 'I'm crazy about him, Tessa.'

'But . . . look, Annie, I hate to be the one to burst your

balloon, but don't get too involved, OK? He'll never leave Cornwall and you're a Londoner through and through. I don't want to see you hurt.'

'Oh, we'll cross that bridge when we come to it. Right now it's bliss, and oh Tessa, it must be love, if I can feel blissful with a raging temperature and aching joints.'

'Maybe the fever is making you hallucinate.'

She ignores my last remark, 'Isn't love terrific, Tessa? Pete has seen me sweaty, smelly, feverish and disgusting, and he still cares. Amazing, isn't it.'

Her words come back to me when Ben gets home, thinner but less pale and definitely on the mend now. Yes, love *is* amazing, I think, for nothing in the world could make me happier than having him home safe with me again.

I take a week's holiday to stay home with Ben. The weather blesses us with autumnal sun and a splendid showing of autumn leaves. We take slow ambles along the beach and the sea fronts, sit over long lunches at home, talking and talking.

Some days it's even warm enough to have a picnic, so we pack sandwiches and a flask and go down to the church on the estuary at Creek. As usual, we grin when we pass the sign on the road that leads to the sea. BAR, it says. I've lost count of the times I've met hikers wandering around down the track, asking where the pub is. I have to explain to them that BAR here means sand bar and if they want something to eat or drink they'll have to go back up the steep hill to the village centre. The look on their faces is always one of such dismay that I feel sorry for them sometimes and offer them a lift when I go back up.

When we visit, there's no one around, not even a local dog walker. Only a few ducks are waddling about on the wet sand, and a grey heron standing in the stream leading to the water's edge. The sea is still and so are the trees around the old church.

It's rare that there's no wind at all this time of year. The sky is as blue and cloudless as a perfect summer's day.

Wrapped in warm jackets, we sit on the sea wall, eat our sandwiches, drink tea from the flask. When it gets too cold to stay still, we walk along the sand bar, giving our leftovers to the ducks.

Mostly we're silent, but when we talk, it's about the kindness of our neighbours, the kindness of this whole Cornish community to us when Ben got ill. 'I still can't get over it,' I say, throwing a last bit of crust to a tiny duck who seems to have been left out of the scrum for food. 'I know I've said this a dozen times, but I'm still so overwhelmed.'

We walk silently for a time, thinking of all the visitors we're still having, bringing warm wishes, get well cards, sometimes a cake or scones, often with an invitation to come and have tea, or a drink, or even a meal with them when Ben is well.

'I feel like I should cross my fingers and my toes, saying this, but it seems like we've been accepted at last,' I say after a time.

Ben nods, 'I suppose it sometimes takes an accident or illness to pull people together. The kindness is there but maybe doesn't have a chance to come out, unless something drastic happens.'

It is Susie who explains things to me, the way things happen in Cornwall.

We're sitting in the Sunflower Café after work, having a coffee and a gab, and I'm talking to her about how our lives seem to have been turned around by Ben's illness. I finish by saying, 'I was despairing, y'know, of ever being accepted here. You Cornish are hard to get to know sometimes.'

I grin as I say it, but I'm serious. I can talk to Susie like this now. That invisible boundary that I felt I couldn't step over is gone. And not just with Susie but also with Daphne and Joe, and Emma and Martin, and others like Clara in the village.

Susie ponders my last remark. 'I suppose we are, bird, but we got a reason for it. Cornwall be changing fast, *has* been changing fast these last ten years. So many folk like you movin' in, wanting the good life here, then not stickin' it and going back Up Country for good.'

She stops, remembering, before she goes on, 'We be wary, now, of befriending strangers too soon, for some of us got burnt, bringin' people to our homes, sharing our lives, only to have them suddenly leaving with no word from 'em again.'

She looks away from me, out at the harbour. Millie and Geoff at the bakery are sitting outside at their tiny table, basking in the precarious November sun while waiting for customers. They're wearing identical heavy navy fleeces and their faces, turned upwards, have an identical small smile.

We watch for a few minutes: the ferry about to leave, the gulls eyeing an old man eating a pasty, a lone lad fishing on the end of the harbour. The sea is a deep green, the rolling waves as undulating as a Cornish hillside.

Turning back to Susie I say, 'So I guess people believe now that Ben, the kids and I are going to stay put.'

She grins at me. 'Well, you've stuck it over a year now. I'd say the odds are pretty good that you be settled here.'

A year. 'Susie, do you know it's a year almost to the day that I've been in this job?'

'I do, my bird, and that's why I be buying you a slap-up dinner soon. You name the date.'

'Because I'm such a great addition to the South Cornwall postal service?' I say jokingly.

'Because I won fifty quid off Eddie. He said you wouldn't be stickin' six months and I bet 'im fifty quid you'd stick it a year.'

Laughing, I tell her that she has more faith in me than I did, a year ago. Then I get serious, try to thank her for all she's done for me. Brushing me off in her usual brusque way, she says, 'Look, my bird, I only did it to get my fifty quid off Eddie.'

I let her have the last word. That's another trait I've found more than once in the Cornish, they hate to admit that under all that tough, rugged individualism, there's a rich seam of kindness and compassion.

December

'I can't believe it's only three weeks till Christmas,' I say to Archie and Jennifer Grenville as I sit in their kitchen again overlooking the sea. It's the first time I've stopped at their place for a proper chat since before Ben was ill.

After they've asked about him, and I tell them he's fine now and has had no recurrence of the illness, we talk about Christmas in Morranport. The town council has decided it's time to buy new lights for the village but the problem is, the old ones will have to be taken down. No one, it seems, got around to it last year, and January turned into February and February into March and so on, until someone said, Why bother? So all that's needed is for the lights to be turned on.

'It's only the second homers in the town that think we need new lights,' Archie says.

'I thought it was the village council.'

He taps the side of his nose knowingly, 'The second homers infiltrate everything, maid. Remember that.' He nods sagely, solemnly, but at the same time, his left eye drops in an exaggerated wink.

The talk turns to the weather. A fierce wind has been blowing for two days now and the seas are treacherous. As we crunch biscuits and drink tea, watching the foamy sea and the horizontal rain, Archie says, 'There was a horrendous shipwreck here one December, in a southeast gale just like this one. In the early 1800s – a French brig, loaded with sugar from the West Indies. If 'tweren't for the bravery of a young fellow from a nearby village, all the crew would've drowned for sure.'

'What happened?'

'He swam out through the rough sea to the boat where the crew threw him a line, then managed to swim back to the shore with the rope. The onlookers were fearful he'd drown in that horrendous sea, but he made it, and one by one the Frenchmen were pulled along the rope to safety.'

'He must have been a strong swimmer,' I say.

Jennifer says, 'Amen,' as the three of us look out of the window at the wild sea, the breakers pounding the shoreline not that far from the Grenville's house though it's built high above the water.

'And a brave man,' Archie adds. 'Even if I were fifty years younger, I wouldn't have a hope in that sea.'

We sit peacefully silent for some time, watching the furious sea and thinking of all the brave men and women who risked their lives, and sometimes lost them, in that foaming, turbulent water.

I can't help comparing this run-up to Christmas to last year's. The weather might be just as bad, with westerly storms now thrashing the coastline, but my spirits are way up above the dark skies and the bruised clouds.

Ben and I have a social life as lively as any we've had in London, going out to dinner at Emma and Martin's place, or to the cinema with Susie and Eddie and some of their friends, or meeting Daphne and Joe, and Clara and her husband at the pub, or having them to our house for a meal. One of the best things about it is that I can enjoy it, not being stressed and agitated over work problems. When my day's work is over, that's it, it's finished. No bringing it home, no brooding over it. I love this new peace of mind I've found here.

Amy and Will have helped me make dozens of little Christmas cards to give to my customers. I'm grateful to so many of them, for all the gifts of fresh produce throughout the year, for the hot drinks in winter and the cold ones in summer, and especially for all the support when Ben was ill. What's so amazing and heart warming, are all the cards I'm getting back from them as I deliver mine. Many of them have notes inside thanking me for the year of 'smiling' postal deliveries, as more than one has put it. Gifts are pouring in too, wine and chocolates, and cash tips tucked into cards, but it's the written notes that please me most.

On the last day of postal deliveries before Christmas, I'm dragged inside nearly every other house, offered coffee and mince pies, brandy and even cider though it's still only morning. I decline the alcohol but accept so much coffee that I'm zizzing as I drive.

The morning goes by in a whirl. The only place where I'm not invited in is Trescatho, my hidden village that's no longer a secret. The made-over cottages are shiny and new looking, with their tasteful Farrow & Ball coatings of paint, their smart new doors, windows and roofs. But every one is closed up and dark. The second homers will be here for New Year, no doubt, but now it looks desolate.

When I first delivered here, the isolated village seemed abandoned too, but the emptiness today is different. Then, it was mysterious, with the filmy lights in the windows, the dark, morning starlight touching old stone walls and ancient slate roofs. The atmosphere was eerie but vibrant, as if the whole village was merely waiting for me, the intruder, to go before coming alive again. Now, the emptiness feels sad and lonely. Even the ghosts have gone.

I can't wait to put the few cards into the letterboxes of the two farms and get back into my van.

There's another emptiness too. Though I don't need to, for there's no post to deliver, I go to Mr Hawker's old house for the first time since he died. As I go up the lane and park the van next to the front garden gate, I get a strong feeling of déjà vu. It doesn't look any different. The house and garden were a shambles when Mr Hawker lived here and though Martin, Dave and Marilyn when they've got some time off, are starting to clear the overgrown foliage, there's a long way to go before they make a visible difference to the property.

It's going to be a huge job, not just the garden but the house as well. It's practically a shell and will take years to do up. Though that will content Dave and Marilyn. The longer it takes, the longer they can live there for minimum rent. And because the cottage has an agricultural tie, second homers can't buy it. Perhaps there will one day be a chance for Marilyn and Dave. I hope so.

As I stand looking at the house, I feel a soft drizzle of rain on my hair and face. My waterproof is in the van but I don't bother to get it. I'll be off soon, homeward bound. Ben's waiting for me, and Amy and Will too.

Tonight we're having a Christmas party at our house, inviting all our new friends and some old ones too. Annie will be arriving in an hour or so from London, to spend Christmas with us, and Pete will be around most of the time, no doubt. But that's not for hours. First I want to pay my respects to the gentle, dignified man who gave me my first Christmas gift in my new job, that day when I was ill, distraught and ready to give it all up, admit defeat and abandon our Cornish dream.

A fifty pence piece wrapped in a sheet of lined paper. Better than any gold, frankincense or myrrh. I whisper to the dark house, *Thank you, Mr Hawker. May you rest in peace.*

Getting into the van and starting it up, I look back at the house one more time. And there, standing in the doorway, as I used to see him so many times, stands Mr Hawker. Call it a trick of the light, an illusion conveyed by the misty rain in the trees, or my over-active imagination, but there he is, just as I remember him.

'Merry Christmas, Mr Hawker,' I whisper through the window and then drive away slowly over the potholed track.

I don't look back. I've got goose bumps on my skin but I'm not afraid. I don't look back because I don't want him not to be there. I want to remember him always like this, standing in the doorway, hand raised in greeting, a half smile on his old wrinkled face as he waves me goodbye for the last time.

On my way home I pass the same church I'd driven by last year on my way back from Mr Hawker's house. Once again, the tree outside has been decorated by the locals. I don't see them this time as I did last year, stringing up the lights in a rough wind, but the tree is lit and gleaming this Christmas Eve morning. The fairy lights strangely reflect in the now heavy drizzle, glistening on every surface so that it looks as if everything – the grass of the churchyard, the few tombstones in front, the slate path – is a kaleidoscope of light and colour.

Dazzled, I stop the van, enjoy the sight for a few moments then rev up again and drive back to St Geraint to park the van in the boat yard where it will stay with the other Royal Mail vehicles till after Boxing Day.

The sea, like the Christmas lights, also sparkles in this misty rain despite the greyness of the day. But there's a wonderful, yellowish light across the horizon, cutting through the dark and lightening the whole sky. It's both dramatic and mysterious, and quite beautiful.

Not yet completely able to read the signs, I'm not sure if this strange amber light means another storm, or fair weather, or something in between, but it doesn't matter. The enormity of the sea, the vastness of the sky, makes speculation somehow pointless.

I take a last look at the seascape, a deep breath of the salty air, and jump into Minger. The old car starts at first go, for a change.

'Time to get going, Minger,' I say out loud, not caring how daft it is to talk to a car. 'Everyone's waiting.'

We roar up the hill towards Treverny, Minger chugging and puffing, and me singing Christmas carols at the top of my lungs, all the way home.